SEASON OF '42

Also by Jack Cavanaugh:

Damn the Disabilities

Tunney

Giants Among Men

The Gipper

SEASON OF '42

*Joe D, Teddy Ballgame, and Baseball's Fight
to Survive a Turbulent First Year of War*

JACK CAVANAUGH

Skyhorse Publishing

For my two favorite ballplayers, Rogan and Tanner Wells, and for their younger brother and an up-and-coming prospect, Rylan Wells.

Skyhorse Publishing books may be purchased in bulk at special discounts for sales promotion, corporate gifts, fund-raising, or educational purposes. Special editions can also be created to specifications. For details, contact the Special Sales Department, Skyhorse Publishing, 307 West 36th Street, 11th Floor, New York, NY 10018 or info@skyhorsepublishing.com.

Skyhorse® and Skyhorse Publishing® are registered trademarks of Skyhorse Publishing, Inc.®, a Delaware corporation.

Visit our website at www.skyhorsepublishing.com.

10 9 8 7 6 5 4 3 2

Library of Congress Cataloging-in-Publication Data is available on file.
ISBN: 978-1-61608-740-1

Printed in the United States of America

CONTENTS

"I honestly feel that it would be best for the country to keep baseball going."

> —President Franklin Delano Roosevelt in his "green-light" letter to Baseball Commissioner Kenesaw Mountain Landis, who had asked the president in January 1942 whether he thought major league baseball should continue during World War II.

INTRODUCTION

BIG LEAGUE BASEBALL would seem to have been a hard sell in 1942. World War II was not going well for the United States in the Pacific, the Atlantic, North Africa, or Europe. Close to home, unescorted ships were being sunk at an alarming rate after being torpedoed and in some cases blown up by German submarines, some of them within sight of East Coast beachgoers, with the loss of thousands of lives. Even though it had seemed inevitable that the United States eventually would be drawn into the war, the country's armed forces were woefully and inexplicably ill-equipped with insufficient planes, ships, submarines, tanks, torpedoes, bombs, and almost every aspect of weaponry and ammunition.

Since early 1941, the country had been sending ships, planes, tanks, and other materials to England, Russia, China, and France under a so-called "lend-lease" program, which had been authorized by Congress and eventually would cost $50 billion. During the previous year, the United States had loaned about fifty World War

I-era destroyers to Britain, which was already at war, and to Canada after President Franklin Delano Roosevelt had proclaimed that the United States was prepared to be an "arsenal of democracy" to countries that eventually would become its allies. Roosevelt, along with many of his closest advisers, felt that the more the United States helped its friends who were already at war, the more it could both act as a deterrent to Germany and make it less likely that America would be drawn into the war, although deep down he felt that involvement was virtually inevitable, Roosevelt also felt that the longer the United States stayed out of the war, the more time it would have to prepare for war. Meanwhile, by 1941, the United States had quadrupled its defense budget even before the attack on Pearl Harbor despite considerable isolationist opposition, both in Congress and to a lesser extent by an "America First" movement determined to keep the United States out of war, which Roosevelt and other realists knew was quixotic. Warships, many of them from World War I, were in short supply in early 1942 after much of the Pacific fleet had been destroyed at Pearl Harbor, and many more would be sunk in naval engagements between May and December. Moreover, it wouldn't be until late 1943 before some of the aircraft carriers, battleships, cruisers, destroyers, and other ships that had been sunk on December 7 and in 1942 would be replaced. But even granting the devastation at Pearl Harbor, the question arises as to why the United States was not better prepared on December 7, 1941. Most of the blame for the carnage and devastation at Pearl Harbor was pinned on Admiral Husband Kimmel, commander in chief of the Pacific Fleet, and General Walter Short, his army counterpart, who like Kimmel was headquartered on Hawaii. Both were accused of dereliction of duty and fired. Kimmel and Short were certainly at least partially to blame for logistical and training failures—Kimmel in part for having most of the Pacific Fleet anchored or docked in port, where the ships were virtually sitting ducks for Japanese torpedo bombers, and Short for ordering that all aircraft be moved out of hangars onto air strips at Hickam, Wheeler, and Bellows Army air fields in Honolulu, ostensibly to protect them from sabotage, but leaving them out in the open and easy targets for Japanese attack planes. In Kimmel's defense, he had pleaded for more aircraft—long-range B-17 bombers and PBYs, "flying boats" used both as patrol planes and bombers—for defensive and patrol purposes, but almost all the B-17s built were being sent to Britain, and the PBYs were in short supply. It's also very likely that miscommunication was at least partially responsible for the inadequate defense and late response to the Japanese attack at Pearl Harbor. Apparently at least some of the intelligence about Japanese intentions to launch air strikes in the Pacific that was being picked up by American code breakers in Washington was never relayed to Kimmel and Short, the eventual scapegoats for the December 7 attack who, unfairly or not, took the fall for the disaster at Pearl Harbor. That the Japanese attacked was not surprising. It was expected after President Franklin D. Roosevelt ordered an embargo on shipments of oil—Japan produced very little oil—aircraft parts, and scrap metal to Japan and had all Japanese assets in the United States frozen after Japan refused to get out of China, which it had invaded in 1937, and Indochina (Laos, Cambodia, and Thailand, which were French possessions) and to renounce its pact with Germany and Italy. But if indeed the Japanese were to attack—even while Japanese emissaries were meeting with U.S. officials in Washington—the targets were expected to be in the central Pacific, most likely in the Philippines, and not at much more distant Pearl

Harbor. While American cryptographers had broken the Japanese diplomatic code, it had not been able to break Japan's naval code. Thus the United States could not determine the Japanese Navy's intentions in the Pacific.

☍❧ ☍❧

Even months after the Japanese attack on Pearl Harbor, manpower was in very short supply, and Uncle Sam needed men, millions of them, including those from twenty-one through thirty-five years of age who had been ordered to register for the draft, the age range of most big-league baseball players. As 1942 progressed, the United States also needed women in the newly formed women's military services, as civilian pilots, and to work in shipyards and defense plants. During the winter of '42, fears of a Japanese invasion of the West Coast rose after the shelling in January of an oil field in Santa Barbara, California, by a Japanese submarine. Then in June, German saboteurs landed on beaches on Long Island and the east coast of Florida, demonstrating that submarines could come undetected within a few hundred feet of American shores. To say the least, the United States was in a crisis mode, and the coming baseball season not only seemed unimportant but appeared to be in jeopardy.

But after what would come to be called a "green-light" letter from President Roosevelt, major league baseball played on in 1942, as it would throughout World War II. In addition to some critical voices of that decision, the game would be played in the aftermath of perhaps its greatest season, which had been highlighted by Joe DiMaggio hitting safely in fifty-six consecutive games and Ted Williams becoming the first batter since 1930 to reach baseball's most exalted batting status—a .400 average (in Williams's case, .406). Indeed, it was almost as if it had been preordained that 1941 would be a momentous base-ball season because of what was to follow on December 7 and over the next four years. Although it was almost impossible to surpass that magical baseball year, the first wartime season of 1942 turned out to be extraordinary, too, and also the last one for DiMaggio and Williams before they and scores of other major league players went into military service—DiMaggio as a reluctant member of the Army Air Corps, who sulked and complained even though he was to spend all three years of his service time playing baseball in California and Hawaii, and Williams as a Marine fighter pilot, who, though he never saw action during World War II, was so skilled as a novice flyer that he spent most of his service tour teaching other pilots how to fly and later, after being called back to duty, flew thirty-nine combat mis-sions during the Korean War.

It was also a season unlike any other, except perhaps the one in 1917 when the United States became involved in what was then called the Great War. (No one called it World War I, presumably because no one knew there would be another world war, and so soon at that.) As in 1917 and 1918, the 1942 season was overshad-owed by war, with many people wondering whether it was really appropriate for four hundred seemingly healthy and athletic men to play baseball, or even to sit on the bench, and earn far more money than the thousands of young Americans whose lives were at risk as they fought the Germans, Italians, and Japanese. How, many people wondered, could this be justified? The legitimacy of major league baseball during the darkest days of the war would become even more problematic when as many as a thousand American sailors would die in less than an hour during a naval battle off the Solomon Islands in August. Thus if a player dared to hold out for more money than he was offered to play in 1942, as DiMaggio did while spending the first few weeks of spring training living in a beach house not far from the Yankees training camp in St. Petersburg, Florida, he drew scorn from his own fans, even if in DiMaggio's case he was offered $2,500 less than the $37,500 (about $500,000 by 2012 monetary standards) that he had received in 1941 when he thrilled much of the country with his supernatural hitting streak and beat out Williams to win the Most Valuable Player Award in the American League, even though the Boston Red Sox superstar had had forty-nine more hits, hit seven more home runs, and drove in ten more runs while earning $20,000 (the equivalent of about $245,000 in 2012). DiMaggio said that Yankee general manager Ed Barrow, in asking him to take a pay cut, pointed out that there was a war going on, which rankled the Yankee center fielder. "While I was battling for more money, the Yankee front office [meaning Barrow] put out a lot of propaganda about guys being in the Army for $21 a month, the insinuation being that I was lucky to be playing ball," DiMaggio said years later.

Of course DiMaggio *was* lucky to be able to play baseball in 1942, although that should not have figured in his salary discussions with Barrow. Possibly because of his highly publicized holdout, the *Sporting News*, the so-called baseball bible that covered both the major and minor leagues extensively, said in a February editorial that baseball club owners "have calculated what they can afford to pay the players, and they have not given the club treasuries all the best of it," and then added, "Let's have no more of this nonsense." Taking the owners' stance was not surprising, since the weekly paper had a vested interest in baseball and tended to lean toward the club owners' points of view.

Even after DiMaggio had signed for $43,750, making him the highest-paid major league player and netting him $6,250 more than he had earned in 1941, many Yankee fans booed and taunted the Yankee Clipper, as he was called. The booing intensified when DiMaggio got off to a bad start, as did derogatory ethnic chants of "dirty dago," "guinea," and "wop," and even hate-mail letters ridiculing his Italian ancestry, which was an easy target since Italian dictator Benito Mussolini had aligned himself and Italy with Adolf Hitler and Nazi Germany in 1939, shortly before Germany invaded Poland. Williams, who signed for $35,000 in 1942, also was booed and heckled occasionally during the first two months of the 1942 season, because he had sought and received an enlistment deferment on the grounds that he was the sole support of his mother and because he had reacted angrily to the verbal and written criticism that ensued.

Despite the war, DiMaggio and Williams along with such outstanding hitters as Ernie Lombardi, Mel Ott, Johnny Mize, Joe Medwick, Dolph Camilli, Pete Reiser, Enos Slaughter, and rookie sensations Stan Musial and Johnny Pesky found themselves confronted with such pitchers like Johnny Vander Meer, who had thrown two consecutive no-hit games in 1938; Mort Cooper; Ernie Bonham; Carl Hubbell; Kirby Higbe; Lon Warneke; Whitlow Wyatt; and Rip Sewell.

Wartime? Fans would never know it from the looks of the lineups during the first full wartime year in the United States, since they were pretty much the same as they were during the previous season. Indeed, only four All-Star players from the 1941 season were missing—Bob Feller, the Cleveland Indians pitching ace; Detroit Tigers slugger Hank Greenberg, Washington Senators shortstop Cecil Travis, and Philadelphia Athletics outfielder Sam Chapman. Only one other first-line pitcher, Hugh Mulcahy, the first major leaguer to be drafted in 1941, was in the service. Greenberg had been drafted into the army in April 1941, the year after he had been voted the Most Valuable Player in the American League, but then had been discharged December 5 under a new provision under which men over twenty-eight—Greenberg was thirty—could be discharged if they had served at least 180 days, which Greenberg had. Two days after he was discharged, the Japanese attacked Pearl Harbor, and Greenberg immediately reenlisted. Feller, by 1941 the most dominant pitcher in baseball, also did not wait long, joining the navy on December 10. Travis, who had finished second in the American League to Williams with a .359 batting average in 1941 and had batted over .300 in eight of his nine big-league seasons, was drafted three weeks after the attack on Pearl Harbor and entered the army in January of 1942. He would not be the same player when he returned. That only four All-Star players were in the service when the 1942 season began seemed strange and even unfair, since by then almost ten million American men had been drafted or had enlisted in the army, navy, marines, air corps, and coast guard since the war broke out. It would also hold true during the Korean and Vietnam wars when, inexplicably, few major-league players were drafted or enlisted, and during the wars in Iraq and Afghanistan when no major-league players served in the military at a time when there was no draft. However, with a few exceptions, the same could be said for many men from the other major sports, although the country's, and probably the world's, most famous athlete, heavyweight champion Joe Louis, joined the army in 1942. Hollywood did its part in 1942, with a number of "leading men" going into the service, most of them by enlisting, even though the head of the Selective Service System, which operated the draft, had decreed that at least some star actors and other movie-industry personnel were considered essential to the war effort, both because of the entertainment they generated and through appearances in training films and other movies produced expressly for the military. Baseball, of course, also provided entertainment, but you had to be at the ballpark to see the games, while movies could even be viewed aboard warships and at other military facilities in war zones. Indeed, far more Hollywood stars saw action during the war than baseball stars. Among them were Jimmy Stewart, who became a bomber pilot in the air corps; Clark Gable, who joined the air corps at the age of forty-one and flew several bombing missions as an aerial gunner aboard B-17s; Henry Fonda, who saw action aboard a destroyer in the South Pacific while rising from a third-class quartermaster to a lieutenant in the navy; Mickey Rooney, who earned a bronze star while an army sergeant serving under the legendary general George C. Patton in the Third Army in Europe; Robert Montgomery, who rose to the rank of lieutenant commander in the navy and served as operations officer aboard a destroyer during the D-Day invasion in June 1944 and later commanded a PT boat in the South Pacific, where he saw action at Guadalcanal and in other war zones; and Dale Robertson, a first lieutenant and commander of a tank unit who was wounded twice while attached to the Third Army. Gable, perhaps Hollywood's biggest star at the time, enlisted shortly after his wife, Carole Lombard, one of filmdom's biggest stars, was killed along with her mother on January 17, 1942, in a plane crash near Las Vegas while returning to California after helping sell around $2 million in war bonds during appearances in her native Indiana.

Meanwhile, a skinny young man from Hoboken, New Jersey, named Frank Sinatra was emerging during the war as one of the country's most popular singers, especially among teenagers, who came to be known as bobby-soxers. By 1942, Sinatra, who had been rejected for military service because of a perforated ear drum, was singing with the Tommy Dorsey Orchestra, one of the country's leading bands. Sinatra was a singing waiter at a nightclub in Englewood Cliffs, New Jersey, in 1939 when he was heard and then signed by another well-known bandleader, Harry James, to sing with his orchestra before switching over to the Dorsey band. By the early forties, Sinatra was rivaling Bing Crosby as the country's most popular crooner with such hits as "All or Nothing at All" and "I'll Never Smile Again." By then the thin boyish-looking Sinatra's appeal had encompassed almost every age demographic in the United States, including many GIs, because some of his songs evoked thoughts of girlfriends at home, although, inevitably, there was some resentment over his having been deferred from military service. As for Sinatra's older singing rival, Crosby, his recording of a new song by Irving Berlin called "White Christmas," which had been introduced during the summer of 1942 in the movie *Holiday Inn*, turned out to be a sensation during the following Christmas season. It also eventually became the most popular and biggest-selling Christmas recording of all time and a staple of every Christmas season. A year later, Crosby recorded "I'll Be Home for Christmas," which also became a Christmas standard. Like "White Christmas," it was a melancholy song, written from the perspective of GIs overseas, with lyrics that expressed a longing for home while at the same time making a heartfelt connection with loved ones with the last lyric of "I'll be home for Christmas, if only in my dreams." *Yank*, the GI magazine during

World War II, said that Crosby, who made frequent trips abroad to entertain U.S. troops with Bob Hope during the war, "accomplished more for military morale than anyone else of that era." No one complained about the thirty-nine-year-old Crosby not serving in the military in light of his songs, which managed to link GIs abroad with home, along with his frequent appearances not far from the front lines.

❧ ❧

Largely because of his concern that there might be widespread opposition from the public and some GIs to a continuation of major league baseball during the first wartime year, Baseball Commissioner Kenesaw Mountain Landis wrote a letter to President Roosevelt in January 1942 asking whether the president thought play should continue. In reply, Roosevelt, who might have been influenced by his friend, Clark Griffith, the owner of the Washington Senators and an occasional visitor to the White House, told Landis he thought "it would be best for the country to keep baseball going." While citing baseball's recreational value, Roosevelt added, however, that he thought "individual players who are of active military or naval age should go, without question, into the service." That was a strange phrase, because the navy was part of the military. As it developed, hardly any players of the age group Roosevelt was referring to, which included practically all of them, did enter the service during 1942. At any rate, Roosevelt's letter was baseball's "green light," as far as Landis and baseball's sixteen club owners were concerned. If the largely beloved president, who had just begun his unprecedented third term and was totally enmeshed in the war, thought it was okay to play, then maybe most people felt it was okay, too. This seemed, as time went on, to be the case. So, it seemed, did most service-men feel this way, including those who had seen battle, and not only because GIs were admitted without charge to all sixteen major league ballparks. If there was any opposition, it was subdued.

Though overall attendance decreased in 1942, fans still turned out much like in most recent prewar years, but often at different times, with more night and "twilight" games played to accommodate the millions of daytime defense-plant workers. Lights were still a novelty at this time, though—the first major league night game was played in Cincinnati in 1935—and five ballparks still were not equipped with them—Yankee Stadium in New York, Fenway Park and Braves Field in Boston, Wrigley Field in Chicago, and Briggs Stadium in Detroit. However, with German submarines coming closer and closer to the U.S. mainland and with fears of possible air raids, the War Department, after initially ordering curfews regarding which night games were played at the Polo Grounds in Manhattan and at Ebbets Field in Brooklyn, completely banned them, because the glare of floodlights from the ballparks could silhouette ships off the New York coastline. That put an end to Roosevelt's hope, expressed in his "green-light" letter to Baseball Commissioner Landis, that more night games would be played so that dayshift defense workers would be able to see more games.

Before the navy ordered a total blackout along the East Coast in early April, some resort areas in New Jersey and Florida refused repeated requests to douse or to at least dim their signature neon lights, which in some cases silhouetted merchant ships for German U-boats. That, of course, was an egregiously outrageous and insensitive reaction and may well have cost the lives of many merchant seamen and U.S. Navy sailors. As it was, there were news accounts almost every day of American cargo ships and tankers being sunk by German submarines close to the East Coast. In some cases, huge fireballs from blazing tankers could be seen on shore from Long Island to the Florida coast. Even some navy ships were U-boat targets. Among them was the World War I–era destroyer *Jacob Jones*, which was torpedoed by a U-boat while on submarine patrol off Cape May, New Jersey, on February 28, killing 131 crew members, including all 7 officers. The *Jacob Jones*, the second of seventy-one U.S. destroyers that would be sunk during World War II, was the namesake of a destroyer that also was sunk by a German U-boat in December 1917.

Actually there had been two harbingers of war before Pearl Harbor, both off Iceland. On October 17, 1941, the American destroyer *Kearney,* which had been commissioned only the year before, was torpedoed by a German submarine, killing eleven men and injuring twenty-two. However, the ship, which had gone to the aid of an American and British convoy that was being attacked by a German wolf pack, managed to remain afloat. Fourteen days later, 115 men were killed, including all 10 officers, and the other 45 men aboard were rescued after another American destroyer, the *Reuben James*, also was hit by a torpedo and sank within minutes while escorting merchant ships from Canada to Iceland, from where British escort ships would take over for the rest of the voyage across the North Atlantic.

By the middle of the year, shortages of some foods, especially sugar and coffee, had developed, along with gasoline, rubber, aluminum, and even some clothes, which led to rationing of many goods and other items that would last until the end of the war. Automobile production ceased midway through the year, because auto plants, at the government's request, had agreed, somewhat reluctantly, to convert to the manufacture of bombers, fighter planes, and transport carriers, while other factories switched to the production of necessary war materials or increased the manufacture of items needed by the military. By the middle of the year, "dimouts" left the Statue of Liberty, some Manhattan skyscrapers, and the "Great White Way" in Times Square all or at least partially dark. Similar dimouts were put in place on the West Coast, in particular, where, right after Pearl Harbor, several thousand Japanese aliens living there and in Hawaii were rounded up and placed in internment camps, where most of them would be detained until the end of the war. Then on January 19, 1942, President Roosevelt signed an executive order mandating that Japanese residents in California, Alaska, much of Oregon, and the state of Washington leave those areas voluntarily or be confined to internment camps in ten western states. About ten thousand left voluntarily, but most of the remaining approximately one hundred thousand, for financial or other reasons, were relocated to the internment camps. The government's action would later become regarded as a flagrant abuse of civil rights and a dark chapter in American history, especially since Americans of Japanese descent could leave the camps to fight, and in many cases die, an irony that was not lost on many Americans. Similar roundups occurred, but on a smaller scale, on the East Coast, where several thousand Germans and Italians, most of them non-citizens who were suspected of being spies or potential saboteurs, also were placed in internment camps. One of the few beneficial aspects of the nascent war was that tens of thousands of American men who had been left out of work during the Depression and were not drafted or enlisted found it easy to get jobs in defense plants. As more and more men were called to active military duty, a serious manpower shortage developed, which was alleviated by millions of women who went to work in defense plants as welders and by handling other tasks normally held by men, thus giving rise to the term "Rosie the Riveter."

Meanwhile, from 1942 until the war's end in late summer of 1945, about five hundred major league players would go into the service, but only a small number, including Feller, would see action. Most of the rest would spend their time in the military playing baseball and serving as physical training instructors. Only two men who had played major league baseball would be killed: Elmer Gedeon, an outfielder who had played in five games for the Washington Senators in 1939, and catcher Harry O'Neill, who had appeared in only one game for the Philadelphia Athletics the same year. Meanwhile, 137 of the slightly more than 4,000 minor league players who had served were killed in action.

Though the war would permeate baseball, as it would almost every aspect of American life in 1942, and major league teams tried their best to link baseball to the war effort, the level of play remained equal in 1942 to recent years. Perhaps the most notable change in ballparks was the playing before games of the national anthem, "The Star Spangled Banner," which up until 1942 had only been played at World Series games and on such holidays as Independence Day and Memorial Day, still commonly referred to in the 1940s as "Decoration Day." Another innovation was for spectators to be requested before each game to throw balls that had been hit into the stands back on the field so that they could be shipped to military posts for GIs to use. Blood donations and the purchase of war bonds also enabled spectators to gain free admission to big league games on special days, as did contributions of scrap metal, aluminum, and even grease, which was recycled to make soap and glycerin. Meanwhile, millions of Americans, particularly on the East and West coasts and including players from the Boston Red Sox and Boston Braves, volunteered to do tours of duty as "air-raid wardens," who scanned the sky in search of enemy planes, none of which, so far as is known, was ever spotted. Civilian pilots who were not drafted or who did not enlist volunteered to serve in the Civil Air Patrol, whose planes primarily patrolled both coasts in search of enemy submarines. For many of those volunteers and millions of other Americans, a big league baseball game could divert them from what would become the deadliest worldwide conflict in history, as would listening to radio broadcasts of games or reading about them in newspapers. The televising of games on a regular basis was still almost a decade away, although a game between the Brooklyn Dodgers and Cincinnati Reds became the first one to be televised on August 26, 1939, with the legendary Red Barber doing the commentary from Ebbets Field. Still, when the baseball season began in 1942 and with the Germans and Japanese continuing to make advances in Europe and the Pacific, the United States was pervaded with a deep sense of anxiety and apprehension. Millions of men were concerned about their draft status, families were worried about loved ones already engaged in service, and there were fears on both coasts of possible air attacks. By then, too, the Japanese had occupied Hong Kong, Malaya, Singapore, all of Indochina, and the American possessions of the Philippines, Guam, and Wake Island. Meanwhile, the Germans had swept across Europe; were on the outskirts of Stalingrad, Russia's second largest city; had the British Army on the run in North Africa; and continued their almost daily "blitz bombing" of London.

Maybe not everyone thought it was right, but a Gallup Poll released shortly before opening day on April 14 showed that 65 percent of those polled felt that professional sports should be continued during the war. At the time, the most popular sports in the country were baseball, which was far and away the most popular; football (primarily the college game); college basketball; horse racing; and boxing. (The National Basketball Association would not be launched until after the war, and the National Hockey League still had only six teams made up almost entirely of Canadian players.)

The poll seemed to reflect the mood of the country. And as more and more major league players got drafted or enlisted in the military, support for the continuation of major league baseball grew as the war went on, even though the quality of play deteriorated year by year until the first postwar year in 1946, when most of the big league players who had gone into the service had returned. Like those players, baseball had survived the war.

1

OPENING DAY AND MORE BAD
WAR NEWS

AMERICANS AWOKE ON Tuesday, April 14, 1942, to newspaper headlines reporting that Japanese planes were continuing
to bomb what the *New York Times* called the "last stranglehold" of
U.S. forces on the island of Corregidor in the Philippines and that an
unescorted French passenger liner had been sunk off the East Coast
by a German submarine, but that all 290 people aboard had been
rescued and brought to Charleston, South Carolina. It was the kind
of news that most people in the United States, then a country of
135 million people—compared to more than 300 million by early
in the second decade of the 21st century—had become accustomed
to almost every morning, though even bleaker news had begun to
reach relatives of American servicemen who had been killed in action
or lost at sea as the result of submarine attacks against unarmed and
unescorted freighters and tankers. It would be months before the

well-known radio commentator Gabriel Heatter would often begin his popular evening network newscast with what would become his signature opening, "There's good news tonight." Certainly there was nothing to cheer about in early 1942. Nevertheless, many Americans were being inspired by a song written shortly after the attack on Pearl Harbor and recorded by the popular band leader Sammy Kaye entitled "Let's Remember Pearl Harbor":[1]

Let's remember Pearl Harbor
As we go to meet the foe,
Let's remember Pearl Harbor
As we did the Alamo,
We shall always remember
How they died for liberty,
Let's remember Pearl Harbor
And go on to victory.

The rousing song, sung by a chorale backed by the Kaye orchestra and played often on the radio and on jukeboxes, resonated and served as a rallying cry for Americans. During 1942, another patriotic song, "Praise the Lord and Pass the Ammunition," which had stemmed from the encouraging words of a navy chaplain to crew members of the cruiser *New Orleans* during the Japanese attack on December 7, 1941, became both popular and inspirational. Subsequently, most wartime songs related to the painful separation of GIs and their wives or girlfriends, such as "I Walk Alone," popularized mainly by Dinah Shore; the equally tender "I'll Be Seeing You," made popular by Bing Crosby; and the lighthearted ditty, "Don't Sit under the Apple Tree with Anyone Else but Me," whose lyrics depicted a GI's

---

[1] 1941, Republic Music Corp., New York, N.Y.

request to a girl back home not to transfer her affections to someone else while he was away.

❧ ❧

One of the few semblances of normality during America's first wartime year was big league baseball, thanks largely to President Roosevelt, who was in the second year of his unprecedented third term in office. To many it was incongruous that so many people were fixating so much attention on men of draft age lucky enough to be playing America's so-called national pastime. But they were unsure as to whether there would be future seasons if the war dragged on, which it gave every sign of doing so in early 1942. Even some people with a vested interest in baseball had misgivings about healthy young men playing the game for a living while thousands of others their ages were risking their lives at war. Among them was the general manager of the Cincinnati Reds, Warren Giles, an army artillery captain during World War I, who, in a letter to the team's players in January 1942, said he'd rather have the team finish last than have any players shirk military service:

> I urge every player on the Cincinnati club to take personal stock of his personal situation, analyze it carefully, and ask himself this question: can I stand at the bar of public opinion in wartime and conscientiously justify good and sufficient reasons for not being in government service. If you cannot answer that question in the affirmative, look me straight in the eye and justify in your own heart and mind that you have justifiable reasons that you should not be playing on a professional baseball team during wartime.

Whether any of the Reds took Giles's advice and were able to justify not being in the service in 1942 was never determined. At any rate, the Reds, like almost every major league team, did not lose any starting players from its 1941 team, although several players, including Johnny Vander Meer and infielder Bert Haas, would eventually be drafted or enlist in the armed forces in 1943. Meanwhile, spring training for the sixteen major league teams in advance of the first wartime baseball season was uneventful but tinged with an undercurrent of anxiety and apprehension. No one knew what to expect from the fans, nor did anyone know that the spring of 1942 would be the last time the teams would train in warm-weather climates until 1946.

Major league baseball in 1942, as in the immediate years before, was a far cry from what it is today. Most significantly, perhaps, it was still an all-white game played mostly in the afternoon by players wearing flannel uniforms, with pants that ended at the knees and not at the shoe tops. Batting helmets were still more than a decade away, while batting gloves and arm and leg shields for hitters were even more distant. Most games ended in fewer than two hours, about an hour faster than games in the 21st century, mainly because most pitchers went the distance, batters rarely stepped out of the batter's box to adjust nonexistent batting gloves or to kick dirt from their spikes, and there were no commercial delays during innings, because television broadcasts of games were almost ten years in the future. Adoption of the designated hitter by the American League in 1973, wherein a batter who did not play in the field batted for the pitcher, also prolonged games, because it tended to produce more hits.

While every team had several "relief" pitchers, none of them were called "middle relievers" or "closers," terms and specializations that didn't exist until the 1970s. Neither did the "slider," a pitch that veers sharply away from a batter but did not become popular until about two decades later. It also was a time when infielders and outfielders tossed their gloves on the outfield grass when their teams changed sides to go to bat rather than carry them into dugouts. Occasionally, gloves lying on the field proved to be hindrances or helpmates. That was the case in a game at Yankee Stadium in 1943, when a batted ball seemingly destined for a single hit the glove of Yankee first baseman Nick Etten on the grass in short right field and rebounded to the second baseman, who threw the Yankee hitter out. That led Joe Trimble, a sportswriter for the New York *Daily News*, to write that Etten's glove could be more productive when his right hand (Etten was left handed) wasn't in it. Etten did not see the humor in Trimble's prose and let him know it in uncertain terms the next day when the story appeared in the newspaper. Another difference: Broken bats, so common today, were a rarity, with some players using the same bats—which tended to be bigger and heavier—for weeks at a time, if not longer. And of course all games were played outdoors on natural grass.

If major league baseball had hardly changed at all, neither had seventy-eight-year-old Connie Mack, a big league catcher from 1886 until 1896, who was in his forty-second year as manager of the Philadelphia Athletics after having been the playing manager of the Pittsburgh Pirates from 1894 to 1896. By the time Mack, whose real name was Cornelius McGillicuddy, retired in 1950, he had won nine pennants and five World Series and managed 7,775 games, a record that most likely will never be broken. How did Mack manage to last so long as the A's manager? Simple: He was a co-owner of the team from its founding in 1901 until 1936, when he became its sole owner. Thus the only one who could have fired him earlier, particularly during its perennially bad years in the 1930s and 1940s, was Mack himself, and he chose not to do so until 1954, when he was eighty-seven years old and relying heavily on his coaches to help run the team.

Besides being baseball's only owner-manager in 1942, Mack was the only manager at the time who always wore a suit, tie, and usually a straw hat during games while waving his trademark scorecard. The only other manager in modern times who managed in street clothes was Burt Shotton, a former big league outfielder. In 1947, Shotton, then sixty-two and who had not managed since 1934, was persuaded by Branch Rickey, then the Dodgers president and general manager, to manage the Brooklyn Dodgers on an interim basis after Leo Durocher was suspended for one year for associating with what Baseball Commissioner Albert (Happy) Chandler considered undesirables. Shotton proceeded to lead the Dodgers to their first pennant since 1941 and stayed on as the Dodger manager for three more years after Durocher became manager of the New York Giants when he was reinstated in 1948. As it developed, both Mack and Shotton ended their managerial careers on the same day—October 1, 1950. From then until the second decade of the 21st century, no other manager has worn street clothes during a game.

❧ ❧

Because big league baseball was restricted to white players, not much attention was paid to the appearance of two young black players at the Chicago White Sox training site in Pasadena, California, on March 18, 1942. At their requests, the players, Jack Roosevelt Robinson, a recent graduate of UCLA, where he had been a star four-sport athlete best known for his exploits as a football halfback, and Nate Moreland, a pitcher in baseball's Negro Leagues, were given a tryout by the White Sox. Even though he had been slowed by a charley horse, Robinson, in particular, was highly impressive. "I'd hate to see him on two good legs," said White Sox manager Jimmy Dykes, who had spent twenty-two years as a big league shortstop. "He's worth $50,000 of anybody's money." Impressive as both Robinson and Moreland were, the White Sox passed on them, and shortly thereafter Robinson joined the army, where he became a lieutenant, and then five years later the first black major league player. (Some baseball historians point out that Fleet Walker, a black catcher, spent the 1884 season with the Toledo Blue Stockings of the old American Association, which was then regarded as a major league. A number of dark-skinned Cuban players also had played in the major leagues during the 1930s and would during the 1940s, an exception that many people found odd.) Before signing with the Dodgers in 1946 and being assigned to their Triple-A Montreal farm team, Robinson also would get short shrift during a tryout in April 1945 with two other outstanding Negro Leagues players, Sam Jethroe of the Cleveland Buckeyes and Marvin Williams of the Philadelphia Stars, at Fenway Park in Boston. That tryout was arranged by Wendell Smith, the well-known sports editor of the *Pittsburgh Courier*, a prominent African-American newspaper, and H. Y. Muchnick, a white member of the Boston City Council, who had threatened to oppose the issuance of licenses for Sunday base-ball in Boston unless black players were given an opportunity to play with the Red Sox. Robinson, Williams, and Jethroe all did very well during the tryouts, which were run by Red Sox manager Joe Cronin and his coaches. After the workout, Cronin said he was impressed by all of them but did not say whether he was inter-ested in signing Robinson, Jethroe, or Williams, which of course the Red Sox did not and obviously had no intention of doing no matter how well they did. As it developed, the Red Sox would be the last major league team to integrate when they signed twenty-five-year-old infielder Pumpsie Green in 1959, twelve years after Robinson broke the "color barrier" with Brooklyn and nine years after the Boston Celtics of the National Basketball Association had signed Chuck Cooper as their first black player, followed by the great center, Bill Russell, in 1956. (Earl Lloyd actually became the first black player to appear in an NBA game with the Washington Capitols during the 1950–51 season.) By the time Green joined the Red Sox, Robinson had already retired. So had Jethroe, who was the National League Rookie of the Year in 1950 with the Boston Braves, with whom he played through 1952 and led the league in stolen bases his first two seasons. Green would spend four seasons with the Red Sox and then seventeen games with the New York Yankees and finish with a .246 career batting average. By contrast, Jackie Robinson wound up with a .307 average during his ten-year major league career, and, of course, was later inducted into the National Baseball Hall of Fame. In August 1942, Bill Benswanger, president of the Pittsburgh Pirates, said he had authorized Wendell Smith to pick some Negro League players whom the Pirates might consider. Smith did, selecting the great catcher Josh Gibson, often called "the black Babe Ruth," and outfielder Sammy Bankhead of the Homestead Grays, which played in Homestead, Pennsylvania, as well as shortstop Willie Wells and pitcher Leon Day of the Newark Eagles. The Pirates said the tryouts probably would take place at the end of the 1942 season, but apparently they never did happen. Day, one of the best Negro League pitchers of all time, never did make it to the major leagues but did make it to Omaha Beach in France during the Allies' D-Day invasion, when he was a member of the 818th U.S. Army Battalion.

☙ ❧

On a mild sixty-degree spring afternoon in New York, either to enjoy a respite from depressing war news or, more likely, just eager to see the first baseball game of the 1942 season in New York, a crowd of 42,653 plus about 1,500 servicemen turned out at the oval-shaped Polo Grounds in upper Manhattan to see the New York Giants host the defending National League champion Dodgers on Tuesday, April 14. Both lineups were virtually intact from the 1941 season except for the absence of Dodger third baseman Cookie Lavagetto, who had joined the navy in February as an aviation machinist mate but would spend practically all his four years in service playing baseball, as would most big leaguers who would serve in the military. Also missing from the Dodger roster was backup catcher Don Padgett, whom the Dodgers had acquired from the Cardinals in December 1941, but who had joined the navy on April 1.

As would be the case at almost every major league park on April 18, there would be military pageantry blended with a strong patriotic spirit at the oddly shaped Polo Grounds, whose dimensions were 257 feet to right field, 287 feet to left field, and almost 500 feet to dead center field. Before the game, both teams, along with New York's short, rotund, and colorful mayor, Fiorello La Guardia, marched to the flagpole in center field, where the army's 17th regiment band played the national anthem and a wreath was laid at the memorial to Eddie Grant, a former Giants infielder who was the only major leaguer to be killed during World War I while he was in the army and for whom a "liberty" ship (cargo ships built during the war) would be named in June 1943. Continuing the patriotic theme, Dodgers manager Leo Durocher and Mel Ott, the Giants star outfielder, who was making his debut as the team's playing manager, presented war bonds amounting to 10 percent of their first paychecks of the season to La Guardia, after which the five-foot two-inch mayor threw out the first pitch—a strike right over the plate.

During the game, which the Dodgers won, 7–6, twelve balls were hit into the stands, and, following an announced request before the game that would become a standard practice before every big league game during the war years, eleven were thrown back for shipment to military bases. The twelfth was not, whereupon the man who caught the ball was booed vociferously but still declined to return the ball, incurring the wrath of fans around him.

Four days later at Brooklyn's Ebbets Field, whose forty-foot-high right-field fence and close proximity of the grandstand to the playing field were its trademarks, a fan described by the *New York Times* as a "pugnacious patriot" threatened to punch a man who refused to return a ball hit into the upper deck behind third base. Relenting under the threat and a barrage of boos, the fan finally tossed the ball onto the field. The third New York team, the World Series champion Yankees, opened in Washington, where, following an opening ceremony during which Vice President Henry Wallace threw out the first pitch and an army band played the national anthem, thirty-eight-year-old Red Ruffing pitched a three-hit shutout and singled twice as the Yankees beat the Senators, 7–0, before a crowd of 30,000 along with almost 2,000 servicemen. In Boston, Ted Williams picked up where he left off in 1941, when he batted .406, by hitting a three-run homer in the first inning and adding two more hits as he went three-for-four as the Boston Red Sox beat the Philadelphia Athletics, 8–1, before a crowd of only 11,000, including 1,200 servicemen, at Fenway Park. Because Williams had had four hits in six times at bat in his final game the previous September, his three-hit opening day gave him a remarkable seven hits in his last ten times at bat. During his long career, Williams always hit particularly well on opening day and would end his nineteen-year career in 1960 with an opening-day average of .449.

In one of the day's most notable games, twenty-four-year-old shortstop Lou Boudreau made his debut as the youngest manager in major league baseball history by getting two hits in three times at bat to lead the Cleveland Indians to a 5–2 victory over the Detroit Tigers in Detroit before 39,627 fans, the second-largest crowd of the day. Boudreau would continue to manage the Indians throughout the war, since he had been rejected for military service because of chronically bad ankles, a condition he incurred as a star basketball player at the University of Illinois. To say the least, Boudreau, whom sportswriters would call the "boy manager," often led by example, such as in a one-game playoff in 1948 at Fenway Park, when he had four hits in four times at bat, including two home runs, as the Indians beat the Red Sox to win the American League pennant, which would be the team's last until 1993.

What made Boudreau particularly remarkable, apart from becoming a big-league manager so young, was his ability to make contact at bat. During Boudreau's fifteen major league seasons, he never struck out more than 59 times, which he did during his third season in 1940; during his other fourteen seasons, he never fanned more than 30 times, and in 1948, when he was voted the

Most Valuable Player in the American League, he struck out only 9 times in 560 at bats while hitting .355. That was six more times than another Hall of Fame infielder, Joe Sewell of the New York Yankees, who struck out only three times in 353 at bats in 1930, and, as he was prone to point out, all three of those times he was called out on strikes, the last of which, in each instance according to Sewell, was out of the strike zone. By contrast, many players in the 21st century strike out that many times in one week and more than 100 times during a season, and some, like Mark Reynolds, as many as a major league record 223 times in 2009. Reynolds partially atoned for all those whiffs by hitting forty-four home runs that year for the Arizona Diamondbacks of the National League, second to Albert Pujols, who was then playing for the St. Louis Cardinals.

Besides rarely striking out, Lou Boudreau also rarely ever made an error in the field. For example, in 150 games during the 1947 season, he made only 14 errors while handling 778 chances. During his fifteen-year big league career, Boudreau never made more than twenty-six errors in a season, a remarkable fielding accomplishment. Boudreau may be best remembered, though, for what would come to be known as the "Boudreau shift." In an effort to better defense Ted Williams, a left-handed hitter who mainly hit to right field, Boudreau devised a defensive scheme wherein the third baseman moved into short right field behind the second baseman, where Williams often hit line-drive singles. That, of course, left the extreme left side of the infield open, but Boudreau knew that Williams's ego was such that he was not about to alter his swing and try to stroke what would almost certainly be easy base hits in the area vacated by the third baseman. The system was at least partially successful, and, seeing that it was, a number of other teams soon followed suit, without, it must be noted, much success.

⁊⁌ ⁊⁌

Overall, paid attendance for the eight opening-day games was 190,775, just under 7,000 less than the number that attended seven games on opening day in 1941. That was a good omen for baseball club owners, many of whom feared that fans might stay away, and, in some big league ballparks, that was the case at the start of the season of '42.

Perhaps the biggest military parade of opening day—and the smallest crowd—was at Comiskey Park in Chicago, where Bob Moncrief of the St. Louis Browns duplicated Red Ruffing's feat as he blanked the White Sox with three hits before a gathering of 9,879 in a game that lasted only one hour and twenty-seven minutes. (On September 26, 1926, the St. Louis Browns swept a doubleheader from the New York Yankees, 6–1, 6–2, that lasted two hours and seven minutes, with the first game taking only fifty-five minutes.)

Before the opening game in Chicago, several hundred soldiers and sailors from nearby bases paraded across the field while a military band played and participated in a flag-raising ceremony. It had been a day of military pageantry, and similar events would be held at major league stadiums throughout the 1942 season as major league baseball would continue to try to link the game to the war effort on the home front. That effort seemed to succeed, while also taking baseball fans' minds off the war, at least briefly. Once games were over, that would be hard to do, though, as news, at least in the Pacific, continued to get worse. Indeed, April would become the most disastrous month of the war for the United States. Five days before opening day on April 14, Bataan, a peninsula in the Philippines, fell to the Japanese, and the infamous sixty-five-mile Death March of around seventy-five thousand exhausted American and Filipino troops began, during which about ten thousand died from beatings by their Japanese captors or from starvation, thirst, or various medical problems. That same day, Japanese submarines sank two British heavy cruisers in the Bay of Bengal. Shortly thereafter, in early May, the remaining battered and beleaguered fifteen thousand American troops on the Philippine island of Corregidor were overwhelmed by a constant Japanese aerial and artillery bombardment and a huge invasion leading to a surrender in early May not only of Corregidor but, at Japanese insistence, of all the Philippines. By then, General Douglas MacArthur had long since left Corregidor, which had been the Allied headquarters in the Pacific, for Australia, where, referring to the Philippines, he famously said, "I shall return."

At sea, the news was as bad, if not worse. It has been said that the first casualty of a war is usually the truth, and that certainly applied to war news in the United States. In late March, American admiral Thomas Hart had his small Asiatic fleet linked up with ships of the Australian, British, and Dutch navies to attack a far superior Japanese armada in what became known as the Battle of the Java Sea in the southwest Pacific. The naval strike turned out to be a disaster, as practically all the nine cruisers and eleven destroyers of the combined allied fleet were sunk, including the American cruiser *Houston*, which after being hit by about six torpedoes and a dozen shells went down with the loss of all 632 men. It would turn out to be one of the most ill-advised blunders of the war, even though the U.S. War Department proclaimed a victory in the one-sided battle. One reason for the Allied defeat was that the Japanese had developed far superior torpedoes, which rocketed through the water at up to fifty miles an hour and were accurate at up to a mile. Not only did they go farther, faster, and with greater accuracy, they also were longer—about twelve feet—and with an explosive charge a thousand times more powerful.

Even good news was late in being disclosed on the American home front. In early 1942, the only good news to emerge—and it was sensational news when it was disclosed by the War Department a month after the event—was a surprise bombing raid on Tokyo by sixteen B-25s on April 18—eight days after the fall of Bataan—which was led by a forty-seven-year-old, five-foot four-inch veteran of World War I, Lieutenant Colonel Jimmy Doolittle, who had retired from the Army Air Corps in 1930 to become a highly successful executive in the aviation unit of the Shell Oil Company but was persuaded to return to active duty after Pearl Harbor by his friend, General Henry "Hap" Arnold, the head of the army air corps. Between the two world wars, Doolittle became nationally famous with his exploits as an aerial daredevil and a record-breaking pilot who was the first person to make a transcontinental crossing in less than twenty-four hours.

President Roosevelt had let it be known shortly after Pearl Harbor that he wanted the United States to retaliate against the Japanese mainland as soon as possible. Because no American plane could reach Japan by land, it was decided to have a carrier get as close to the mainland as it safely could and then launch U.S. bombers. The attack by the Doolittle-led squadron, which caught the Japanese completely by surprise, as it did the mechanics who worked on the B-25s before the attack, actually did only slight damage but gave the United States, starving for some good news, a huge morale boost, both in war zones and on the home front, albeit weeks after the attack, and dealt a blow to Japan, which felt it was invulnerable to bombing attacks. But the overall plan did not end as intended. The plan called for the planes to take off from the aircraft carrier *Hornet* once it got to within five hundred miles off the Japanese coast and to attack during the early hours of the morning while it was still dark. But the carrier *Enterprise*, which was part of a task force that included the *Hornet*, picked up two Japanese ships nearby on radar while the American ships were about 650 miles from Japan, and crew members on the *Hornet* spotted a radio-equipped fishing boat, which was quickly destroyed by shells fired from one of the cruisers accompanying the two carriers. Planes from the *Enterprise* then spotted several more enemy ships that were certain to become aware of the task force, if they hadn't already. That left Doolittle with a tough decision: Call off the mission or have the planes take off early and run the risk of running out of gasoline before they could land in China as planned. Despite thirty-five-foot-high seas, gale-force winds, and the danger of arriving over their targets in daylight rather than under dark as planned and of not having adequate gas for the bombers to make it to China after the raid, Doolittle decided to go, and the sixteen B-25s took off shortly before dawn.

Slightly more than six hours later, undetected as American planes though they were flying very low, the bombers began dropping their bomb loads in broad daylight, the War Department was to say almost a month later, on port facilities, oil refineries, airline factories, and railroad yards in Tokyo, Yokohama, and Osaka. Japanese fighters eventually took off in pursuit of the bombers, but it was too late. Despite poor visibility and heavy rain, most of the bombers reached a prearranged destination in China still occupied by the

Nationalists, but some ran out of gas, with four crash landing and the crews of eleven other B-25s parachuting out. The sixteenth bomber, even shorter on fuel, was unable to reach China and landed in Khabarovak, Russia, north of Manchuria, where at first the five crew members were greeted warmly by Soviet soldiers and given vodka and borscht but then, supposedly on orders from Prime Minister Josef Stalin, were interred for more than a year, even though by then Russia had become an American ally. Eight of the crewmen were captured by Japanese troops in Japanese-occupied China, and three were eventually beheaded following what appeared to be a sham trial. One of the others died in captivity after being tortured, while the remaining four spent the rest of the war in prison. Two others died after their plane crashed off the China coast, and another was killed after parachuting from his bomber. The remaining sixty-nine, including Doolittle, who was among those who bailed out when his bomber ran out of fuel, survived after landing among friendly Chinese farmers and peasants, who had been startled and frightened by the crashing B-25s. Chinese forces then took them on a hazardous thousand-mile journey through mountainous terrain, some of it in Japanese-occupied territory, to Chungking, where they met Nationalist leader Chiang Kai-shek and his wife and then were flown back to the United States.

The day after the raid, American newspapers carried front-page stories about the surprise attack based on reports on Tokyo Radio, which claimed that sixty "enemy" bombers, not sixteen, had dropped bombs on Tokyo and the industrial cities of Yokohama, Kobe, and Nagoya. The reports, which did not mention the United States, said bombs had hit hospitals and schools but no military targets and had caused only slight damage. Furthermore, the radio reports claimed that nine "enemy" planes had been shot down in "an inhuman attack" that had caused "widespread indignation among the Japanese populace." In light of the Japanese sneak attack on Pearl Harbor only four months earlier, that seemed like an outlandish comment, to say the least. Meanwhile, the U.S. War Department and the army refused to confirm or to deny the attack, which the Japanese reports said had killed about three thousand people. However, the next day the Japanese Imperial Command said the planes that conducted the attack "bore the insignia of the United States Air Force," confirming for the first time that the bombers were American, which surprised no one. When the War Department finally confirmed the attack in mid-May, it denied that schools and hospitals had been hit and that any American planes had been shot down. Confirmation of the attack immediately made Doolittle a national hero. President Roosevelt promoted him to brigadier general and awarded him the Congressional Medal of Honor. At his age, the bald five-foot four-inch once-retired World War I flier became an unlikely hero and gave heart to men approaching middle age who wanted to fight the Germans or the Japanese but had been discouraged, if indeed not turned down, when they tried to enlist. All the crew members on the mission were awarded the Distinguished Flying Cross, while two received the Silver Star. Sadly, thirteen of those who survived the first bombing attack on Japan—there would not be another one for twenty-six months—would be killed during other missions, while four were captured by the Germans and held as prisoners of war. Doolittle, whose knowledge and skills were considered invaluable, later served in Europe as a major general while commanding the 12th and 15th Air Forces and then as a lieutenant general in command of the 8th Air Force in Europe and the Pacific until the war's end in August 1945.

Furious over the raid and the humanitarian actions of the Chinese, Japanese Emperor Hirohito, it was later reported, ordered about seventy-five thousand troops into the area where the American bombers had crashed and unleashed a month-long and deadly vendetta, killing an estimated two hundred thousand Chinese, almost all of them farmers and peasants, for having given succor to the American fliers. For the Americans who had taken part in the attack on Japan, it was a deadly price for the Chinese to pay and heartbreaking news.

When news of the attack first reached the United States, it gave a huge boost to most Americans, who felt that it might have marked a turning point in a war effort that was not going well. It was to a degree, but only a slight one. On a more somber note, more and more gold stars were appearing in the windows of American homes, signifying the deaths of family members. Baseball might be a good outlet for defense-plant workers and other Americans, but it could hardly make Americans forget about a war, which President Roosevelt estimated in mid-April could last up to three more years.

Two days before the first bombing of Japan—there would not be another one for more than two years—the Office of Price Administration (OPA), a wartime agency, announced that starting May 6, a rationing program would take effect, wherein families or individuals would be restricted to a half-pound of sugar a week. Then six days later the OPA announced that rationing of gasoline would begin in seventeen East Coast states and in Washington, D.C. Under the rationing plan, most drivers would be restricted to as little as five gallons of gas a week, barely enough for a long Sunday drive. However, defense-plant workers and others doing what the government considered essential war work would be allowed more, depending on how far and how often they had to drive to work.

That same day, New York Governor Herbert Lehman signed a bill into law that would lower the speed limit in the state to forty miles an hour in an effort to lengthen the life of automobile and truck tires. No less a citizen than Eleanor Roosevelt announced that she would apply for an A card, which entitled an automobile owner to the lowest amount of gasoline, and to conserve gasoline would ride around the Roosevelt's Hyde Park estate on an English bicycle that had been given to her by a friend. Whether Mrs. Roosevelt's announcement convinced any other Americans to ride bicycles as a gas conservation measure was difficult to determine.

Meanwhile, the government continued its crackdown on Japanese, German, and Italian aliens who it thought might have become, or were thinking of becoming, saboteurs or were providing information by short-wave radio to the German government. One such crackdown, on the night of April 21, occurred in New Jersey, when FBI agents and local police raided a number of what they said were, of all things, birthday parties for Adolf Hitler, who had been born in Austria on April 20, 1889. In all, the FBI said, eleven "enemy aliens" were arrested, and more than one hundred people were questioned. In addition, the FBI reported, contraband seized included three hundred rounds of ammunition, eleven firearms, radios, cameras, binoculars, a storm trooper's uniform, German propaganda literature, and photos of Hitler. Among those questioned was August Klapprott, one of the leaders of the former German-American Bund, an organization of German immigrants who were sympathetic to the Nazis but which was disbanded shortly after Pearl Harbor. In the meantime, FBI agents in Lancaster County in Pennsylvania arrested thirty people who the agency said also were attending Hitler birthday parties at the homes of German aliens. Honoring Der Fuehrer on his fifty-third birthday was not a very good idea in the United States and many other countries in 1942.

∞ ∞

Meanwhile, attendance at major league baseball games, which had been far lower than usual at the beginning of the season, began to pick up gradually. In the American League, both the Yankees and Red Sox got off to fast starts, winning their first three games. In their second game, the Yanks beat Washington, 9–3, before a crowd of 7,500 that included 2,500 servicemen. Rookie shortstop Phil Rizzuto and Joe DiMaggio, in his seventh season, both had three hits. One of DiMaggio's was a tremendous clout into the center-field bleachers that was estimated to have carried more than five hundred feet. In their home opener the next day, the Yankees raised their American League pennant flag, after which Ernie Bonham out-pitched thirty-two-year-old rookie Tom Judd as the Yankees won their fourth straight game, edging the Red Sox, 1–0, before 30,308, including 1,243 servicemen. Ted Williams had one of Boston's three hits, while DiMaggio went hitless in three times at bat in a game that lasted just under two hours. By then, the Yankees had asked fans before games to give balls hit into the stands to ushers rather than throwing them back onto the field. That system had proven to be dangerous to players, coaches, and umpires, because none of them knew exactly when balls would be tossed back. On the same day as Bonham's shutout, in nearby Brooklyn, the Dodgers also raised their 1941 pennant-winning flag but drew only 15,430 spectators, of whom just over 2,000 were GIs, to their home opener, in which they beat the Philadelphia Phillies, 7–1, behind pitcher Johnny Allen, who helped his own cause by delivering three singles.

Two days later at Yankee Stadium, one would never have guessed a war was on as a crowd of 51,523, 1,700 of them servicemen, turned out on a Sunday afternoon to see the Red Sox beat their arch-rivals, 5–2. Despite their good start, the Red Sox found themselves playing before crowds of less than five thousand at Fenway Park. That changed dramatically, though, on Sunday, April 26, when more than forty thousand fans, the biggest crowd in memory, turned out to see the Yankees beat the home team for the second day in a row, 7–2. The day before, the New Yorkers had scored seven runs in the seventh inning to trim the Red Sox, 8–5. Both Joe DiMaggio and Ted Williams had rough days at bat that Saturday, with DiMaggio going hitless in five times at bat and Williams making out all four times he was up. To make his day even worse, Joe, very uncharacteristically, dropped a fly ball in the eighth inning, which was followed by a home run by his younger brother, Dominic, who had two hits in the game and was out-hitting his brother with a .349 average to Joe's .325. During Joe D's fifty-six game hitting streak in 1941, Dommy, as his Red Sox teammates called him, had robbed his brother of a hit late in a game by making a great catch in left-center field at Fenway Park. As Dom DiMaggio recalled years later, as they passed each other while changing positions, Joe glared at Dom without saying a word. "He looked at me like he wanted to kill me," Dom was to say. As it turned out, to Dom's delight, Joe's streak was extended when, in his last time at bat, he singled. "I couldn't have been happier," Dom DiMaggio said. "Otherwise, because of me robbing him of a hit, Joe probably wouldn't have talked to me for the rest of the year and maybe even longer." Dom DiMaggio knew that his brother was inclined to hold a grudge, quite often for a long time.

With matters for the Allies going worse, especially in the Pacific, the government widened the draft. During the weekend of the Yankee–Red Sox series in Boston, all men between the ages of forty-five and sixty-four were ordered to register, starting Saturday, April 24. In all, more than thirteen million men registered, including President Roosevelt, who was sixty but certainly in no danger of being drafted.

By then, a Cardinals rookie named Stan Musial, who had been converted from a pitcher to an outfielder after he injured his arm in the Class-A Florida State League in 1939, was off to a blazing start and leading the National League with a .379 batting average. What made Musial stand out particularly was his so-called "peek-a-boo" batting stance, whereby he stood with both legs close together while in a slight crouch and with his right shoulder seemingly blocking his view of the pitcher. "He looks like a kid peeking around a corner looking to see if there's a cop around," Ted Lyons, a Hall of Fame pitcher, once said. For the Cardinals, it was also good to know that, though Musial was only twenty-one, he already was married and the father of a year-old son and thus was unlikely to be called up for military service, at least during the 1942 season. As it was, draft boards seemingly were being generous to big league ballplayers, and through the first few weeks of play, apart from occasional patriotic pageantry and the playing of the national anthem before games, one could hardly tell that there was a war going on.

2

THE WAR GETS CLOSER TO HOME

NOWHERE WAS THE impact of the war being felt more in the United States than in the western Atlantic. By baseball's opening day, the situation along the eastern American coastline had become dire indeed, and it would get even worse. About two weeks after the Japanese attack on Pearl Harbor, top U.S. military intelligence became aware of a German plan to launch submarine attacks on merchant ships off the East Coast as early as January 1942. That was alarming news, especially since the navy and coast guard had fewer than twenty-five ships, and none larger than 165 feet, and only about one hundred old and slow aircrafts to cover the U.S. coastline. They also knew that no additional ships or planes would be available until late summer of 1942. That meant that almost all the cargo ships and tankers plying the western Atlantic and the Gulf of Mexico were unescorted, and, until the navy began putting gun crews aboard merchant vessels by the middle of the year, unarmed and therefore defenseless against German U-boat attacks.

But even the navy and coast guard did not anticipate how successful the German plan would be. The initial phase of the plan, nicknamed "Drumbeat," involved five submarines, which were to leave Germany in late December 1941, only three weeks after Pearl Harbor. The ease with which the U-boats were able to sink merchant vessels would be illustrated by one of the submarines, commanded by twenty-nine-year-old Lieutenant Reinhard Hardegen, a former pilot in the German Naval Air Force. Hardegen had transferred to the submarine service in 1939 after he was seriously injured in a plane crash and left with a shortened left leg and chronic stomach bleeding that required him to eat only easily digested foods. The young lieutenant commander obviously was a quick study, because by 1940 he already had been given command of a submarine, and in December that year, during his first patrol as a commander, his U-boat sank a Norwegian tanker. He then took command of U-boat 123, which sank five ships in West Africa during the summer of 1941 and torpedoed and heavily damaged a British cruiser in October that year. Those accomplishments elevated him to star status in Germany's submarine service, far and away the best in the world during the early years of World War II. After being picked to take part in the elite "Drumbeat" operation, Hardegen, a slender, good-looking, and highly intelligent naval officer, was determined to show that, as a submarine commander, he was no one-year wonder.

Hardegen wasted no time in elevating his status in the eyes of the German Admiralty. While en route to the East Coast, U-123 spotted the British freighter *Cyclops* in Canadian waters near Halifax on January 12, and, although that was not Hardegen's target area, he ordered his crew to fire a torpedo that sank the ship on January 13, killing ninety-eight men. That unscheduled mission turned out to be a warm-up for what was to follow. Less than twelve hours later, during the early-morning hours of January 14, Hardegen's submarine was about 60 miles southeast of Montauk on Long Island and around 150 miles from New York City when it struck in American waters for the first time, firing three torpedoes into the Norwegian tanker *Norness*. Thirty-eight crew members managed to get into a lifeboat and eventually be rescued, while two others died after they were thrown into the frigid Atlantic when the ship keeled over on its port side while they were getting into a lifeboat. Less than an hour after the first two torpedoes had hit the tanker, it sank with its bow thrust upward in the shallow water. The *Norness* had become the first of more than three hundred ships that would be sunk by Nazi submarines in the Atlantic, most of them along the East Coast, during the first six months of 1942.

Following a prescribed plan, U-123 headed toward the entrance to New York Harbor, where Hardegen hoped to find both U.S. Navy and merchant ships at anchor. After cruising along the coast of Long Island while guided by lights on the nearby shore, the U-boat reached lower New York Bay at about 10:00 p.m., where Hardegen was surprised to find the harbor devoid of any ships. Around midnight, the submarine surfaced, and, with the captain's permission, the crew of fifty-five men went on the sub's deck for a look at the Manhattan skyline, ecstatic to know that they were the first German military personnel to get so close to American shores. The sub then headed back east in search of more potential prey in the western Atlantic not far from the U.S. mainland. It did not have to go very far, spotting the British tanker *Coimbra* about five miles from the tiny Long Island summer resort town of Quogue. The ship, carrying around seventy-five thousand barrels of oil and thirty-five crew members, was hit with one torpedo and exploded into flames that could be seen vividly on shore. There were no survivors.

Continuing to attack unmolested along the East Coast for the next two weeks, U-123 sank six more ships as far south as Cape Hatteras in North Carolina in a manner that to Hardegen was akin to knocking off ducks in a shooting gallery. After running out of torpedoes in late January, U-123 set course for home after having sunk more than fifty-thousand gross tons of shipping. Arriving back in Germany on February 9 to a hero's welcome, Hardegen was awarded the Knight's Cross, his third medal and one of Germany's most prestigious military honors. During Hardegen's assault on ships plying the waters of the Western Atlantic, not once, Hardegen told his navy superior, was the U.S. Navy or U.S. Coast Guard able to confront his submarine and drop depth charges, indicating how unprepared the United States was for U-boat attacks right off American shores.

By now an ace of the German U-boat fleet, Hardegen and his U-123 crew headed back to the western Atlantic, where, from March 22 through April 17, they would wreak more havoc, sinking eleven tankers and cargo ships, with the loss of about three hundred lives. But for the first time in his two patrols, Hardegen and his crew encountered opposition after firing a torpedo that hit the Navy Q ship *Atik* about three hundred miles east of Norfolk on March 27. As U-123 pulled closer to launch another torpedo, gunners aboard the *Atik* opened fire, killing one of the submarine's crew members on deck. The U-boat then applied a *coup de grâce*, firing a torpedo into the *Atik*'s engine room and sinking the ship, with the loss of all 141 men aboard.

Continuing on to the Florida coast, U-123 sank eight more ships over a fifteen-day period. But once again, the much sought-after Nazi U-boat had close calls. On April 2, after sinking the tanker *Liebre*, U-123 had to submerge quickly while being pursued by a navy patrol boat. Nine days later, after torpedoing the tanker *GulfAmerica*, which was on its maiden voyage with ninety thousand barrels of oil, off Jacksonville, U-123 had to flee and submerge while pursued by a navy destroyer, a patrol craft, and overhead aircraft in full view of hundreds of people on nearby beaches. The destroyer *Dahlgren* eventually dropped six depth charges, damaging the submarine and prompting Hardegen to consider having the crew abandon ship. However, when the *Dahlgren* failed to follow up with more depth charges, U-123 managed to get away. Even though it was damaged, two days later the German sub proceeded to sink the American freighter *Leslie* with its fiftieth and last torpedo off Cape Canaveral and then shelled and sank a Swedish motor ship. Even though it was out of torpedoes and headed for home, U-123 made what would be its final attack when it shelled and sank the American freighter *Alcoa Guide* on April 16. By the time the U-boat headed back to Germany, it had sunk nine ships during its first patrol and eleven ships during its second, amounting to approximately 115,000 tons and taking almost one thousand lives.

More of a hero than ever, Hardegen received his fifth decoration for meritorious service and, along with another German military hero, was invited to dine with Hitler. As brazen as he was as a submarine commander, Hardegen incurred Hitler's wrath when he criticized the German military establishment for not giving its U-boat fleet a higher priority. That drew a reprimand from the military's chief of staff, which prompted Hardegen to say, "The Führer has a right to hear the truth, and I have a duty to speak it." Somehow Hardegen managed to survive such a brash public utterance and even remain in the German Navy, let alone remain alive. No longer sent to sea, Hardegen spent most of the rest of the war as chief of U-boat training at a torpedo school. After spending a year in British captivity following the war, Hardegen returned to his home town of Bremen, where he was elected to public office and established a successful oil trading company, an irony since Hardegen's decorated submarine, U-123, had sunk about a dozen oil tankers during his brief but illustrious career as a submarine commander.

❦ ❦

Though Operation Drumbeat had ended and Lieutenant Commander Reinhard Hardegen was no longer a force to be reckoned with, German submarines continued to sink ships close to the American mainland with virtual impunity. In some cases, explosions from burning ships could be heard and even felt on the East Coast. When the Norwegian tanker *Varanger* was torpedoed and sunk about thirty miles off New Jersey on January 14—an attack not attributed to Hardegen's submarine—the ensuing explosion awakened scores of residents and shook houses and other buildings in Sea Island City and was heard about forty miles away in the resort town of Atlantic City. Fortunately, all forty crew members were rescued by two fishing boats. Thereafter, German U-boats began to venture farther to the south. On May 12, an American freighter was torpedoed and sunk in the Gulf of Mexico, about a mile from the mouth of the Mississippi River. Twenty-seven merchant crewmen, including the captain, were killed, while the remaining forty-one aboard leaped from the burning ship and were picked up by a coast guard cutter. Later in May, two more merchant ships were sunk on consecutive days by German submarines, possibly the same one, in the Saint Lawrence River in Canada, killing twenty men.

Most of the submarine attacks, though, were in the western Atlantic, where almost five thousand seamen died and almost four hundred merchant ships were sunk during the first six months of 1942. That prompted the famous historian and essayist Henry Steele Commager to write, "In the spring of 1942, merchant seamen had a higher likelihood of being killed than American troops trapped in the jungles of Bataan. And they died hideously—blown to pieces, frozen solid in icy Atlantic waters or boiled at sea by oil fires that burned with raging force for miles around sunken tankers." And yet thousands of men voluntarily joined the merchant marines, where as civilians they earned far more than sailors in the U.S. Navy but ran the risk of hideous deaths while living in fear of nighttime attacks by German U-boats and Japanese submarines.

❧ ❧

Because of the rampant ship sinkings along the East Coast, most of which were occurring at night, doubts arose about the practicality of playing night games in New York. In early May, while the Giants and Dodgers were playing on the road, floodlights were turned on at the Polo Grounds in Manhattan and at Ebbets Field in Brooklyn while a group of army, New York City, and major league baseball officials went several miles into the Atlantic Ocean to see whether the lights were bright enough to silhouette ships traveling at night off the New York coastline. The group determined that they were, and, as a result, plans for the Giants and Dodgers to play fourteen night games were canceled; instead, the games would start at twilight, usually around six o'clock in the evening. None of the other nine major league teams whose stadiums were outfitted with lights was affected by the decision.

The first twilight game was also the first of sixteen games to raise money for army and navy relief societies and was played at Ebbets Field. In addition to the capacity crowd of nearly thirty-five thousand that turned out on May 8, everyone, including players, coaches, umpires, sportswriters, and team officials, had to buy tickets. Another eight thousand people bought tickets but did not attend, to bring the total proceeds to nearly $100,000 (around $1 million by 2012 monetary standards). Before the game, around two thousand servicemen took part in a ceremony that included a contingent of sailors from the USS *Prairie State*, previously the battleship *Illinois*, but then a training ship in New York, who marched from the center-field gate to home plate accompanied by an army and an American Legion band. Lieutenant Commander Gene Tunney, the former World Heavyweight Champion and head of the navy's physical fitness program, then drew cheers from the crowd in the bunting-bedecked ballpark when he expressed the navy's thanks for the financial support from major league baseball. Mayor Fiorello La Guardia also attracted cheers when he led the crowd in singing "God Bless America," accompanied by Gladys Gooding, who would become as well known as the most popular Dodgers "player" from 1942 until they left for Los Angeles in 1957. Starting in the spring of '42, Miss Gooding played an electric organ that had been installed near the Dodgers' dugout before and during all home games. Gooding had been discovered playing the organ before New York Rangers' hockey games at Madison

Square Garden; in later years she also would play during games played by the New York Knickerbockers of the National Basketball Association. That gave rise to a tricky trivia question as to who had "played" for the Dodgers, the New York Rangers hockey team, and the New York Knicks basketball team. The answer, of course, was Gladys Gooding, whose repertoire of patriotic and popular songs of the forties and fifties was a far cry from the type of deafening recorded music played at most ballparks and arenas in later years.

Of little notice on sports pages the day after the benefit game at Ebbets Field was the box score of a game in Cincinnati between the Reds and the St. Louis Cardinals in which Cardinals manager Billy Southworth sent a thirty-year-old journeyman outfielder and utility man named Coaker Triplett up to bat for twenty-one-year-old rookie Stan Musial, who had gone hitless in his four times at bat. It would not be the first time that Southworth would pinch-hit for Musial, who was in the midst of one of the few slumps he would endure in his twenty-two-year Hall of Fame career. As he did with almost everything, on or off the field, the unflappable and likeable Musial seemed to take being pinch-hit for in Cincinnati in stride. Once Musial cooled off after a fast start, Southworth also began to platoon him and Triplett, with Musial playing against right-handed pitchers and Triplett, a right-handed batter, against lefties. Even though Musial was among the National League's leading hitters by August, Southworth inexplicably continued to platoon him until September, when he went on a tear, hitting over .400 during the month. Until then, apparently, Southworth thought that, as a rookie, Musial might have trouble hitting left-handed pitchers. In fact, he would eventually end his illustrious career having batted over .300 against both right-handers and left-handers. But in 1942, Musial was still relatively unknown. Indeed, Casey Stengel, master of the malaprop and in 1942 the manager of the Boston Braves, often referred to the young outfielder as "Musical." Before long, though, Stengel and just about everyone in baseball would know how to pronounce and to spell Stanley Frank Musial's last name.

⤬ ⤬

May 1942 was an unusual week for at least two pitchers. The Yankees' longtime star hurler Vernon "Lefty" Gomez, who would wind up with a fourteen-year career batting average of .147, low even for a pitcher, shocked Yankee fans and his teammates on May 29 at Yankee Stadium when he got four hits in five times at bat and drove in two runs while winning his first game of the season as the Yanks crushed the Washington Senators, 15–1. Gomez, who would win at least twenty games four times and lead American League pitchers in victories four times en route to the National Baseball Hall of Fame, would get only one more hit the rest of the season, also against the Senators. A favorite of both Yankee fans and his teammates, Gomez was known to stop pitching to gaze at planes passing overhead on several occasions at Yankee Stadium, to the delight of his fans. Because he was from the San Francisco Bay Area like Joe DiMaggio, the Yankee management made him DiMaggio's roommate on road trips during DiMaggio's 1936 rookie year on the grounds that they would have the Bay Area in common and Gomez, six years older and far more worldly than the then-twenty-five-year-old DiMaggio, would serve as a mentor of sorts to the shy, withdrawn, and unsophisticated DiMaggio, who seldom spoke to anyone during his rookie year. Asked by this writer once whether DiMaggio talked to him in the hotel rooms they shared, the droll Gomez said, "Oh sure when we got up in the morning, Joe would say, 'Good morning, Lefty,' and when we were going to bed, he'd say 'Good night, Lefty.'" In subsequent seasons, Gomez recalled, DiMaggio would become more talkative, but not much.

Earlier, on May 13, Boston Braves pitcher Jim Tobin, who had hit only two home runs in five major seasons, including one the day before as a pinch hitter, clouted three homers against the Chicago Cubs and barely missed a fourth when he hit a long drive that was caught against Wrigley Field's left-field wall. He would hit two more home runs in 1942 to give him six for the season—more than many full-time position players hit that year—and partially atone for leading all American League pitchers in losses with twenty-one, which was hardly all his fault, because he had a respectable 3.90 earned-run average. Tobin would end his nine-year big league career with seventeen home runs but with a lowly .137 batting average, which was even lower than that of Gomez, a left-handed batter, who never came close to hitting a home run in 904 times at bat, even though it was only 314 feet down the right-field line at Yankee Stadium. Tobin, who was primarily a knuckleball pitcher, also achieved a measure of renown when, on September 17, 1941, he gave up the first of Musial's 3,630 hits, exactly half of which, remarkably, were at home and half on the road. The hit, a double, came in Musial's major league debut at Sportsman's Park after he had been called up from the Triple-A Rochester Red Wings of the International League, where he had wound up in midsummer after batting .379 and clouting twenty-six home runs with the Cardinals Class-C farm team in Springfield, Missouri. Jumping from Class-C to Triple-A and then to the big leagues in one season was extremely rare, if not unprecedented.

❧ ❧

The benefit game at Ebbets Field on May 8 and subsequent similar events at big league ballparks were part of major league baseball's determination to convince skeptical Americans that there was not only a place for the game during a world war but that it could be beneficial, both as recreation for defense workers, as morale boosters for servicemen, and to a limited degree as a financial resource. Indeed, as the war expanded, even during trying times for the U.S. military, as was the case in 1942, baseball was still doing pretty well after the first month of the country's first wartime season. By then, not much had changed from the year before. The Yankees were still dominating the American League, while their World Series opponents in 1941, the Dodgers, were in first place in the National League. Each of the teams had lost only one regular position player to the draft. For the Yankees, it was first baseman Johnny Sturm, who had hit .239 in his first, and as it turned out only, big league season and who became the first married big leaguer to be drafted. The Dodgers loss was more severe, because they had lost Cookie Lavagetto, their third baseman for the previous five years, who had hit .277 in 1941. However, the Dodgers more than made up for the loss of Lavagetto by obtaining future Hall of Famer Arky Vaughan, a career .318 hitter, from the Pittsburgh Pirates, for whom he had played for ten years, and who in 1935 had led the National League with a .385 batting average. Three quarters of a century later, only one major league third baseman, George Brett, hit for a higher average—.390 in 1980.

Losses to teams in both leagues were minimal. Only one team, Cincinnati, lost as many as two starters to the draft, outfielders Harry Craft and Jimmy Gleeson. Other starters drafted before the 1942 season began were all infielders—Bobby Sturgeon, a shortstop for the Chicago Cubs, and Joe Marty and Burgess Whitehead, both second basemen for the Philadelphia Phils (who had changed their name, at least temporarily, from Phillies) and the Pirates, respectively.

The draft was felt more profoundly in the American League. Besides Hank Greenberg, the Detroit Tigers also had lost outfielder Pat Mullin, who had hit .345 in fifty-four games during his rookie year of 1941, while, in addition to Bob Feller, Cleveland was missing outfielder Soup Campbell. The Washington Senators also were struggling without two starters, All-Star shortstop Cecil Travis and outfielder Buddy Lewis, both of whom eventually found themselves in harm's way, Travis at the Battle of the Bulge in Belgium, and Lewis as the pilot of army air corps transport planes—not that Lewis complained. "Flying to me was the most wonderful thing in the world," he was to say following his discharge in the summer of 1945. "You could say my record in baseball might have been better, but fate injected me into this thing, and I liked it." Lewis especially liked weekends when he was training at an air base in Georgia. "Before we went overseas, they encouraged us to round up a crew and fly anywhere we wanted to, but to let them [his superiors] know where we were going," Lewis said years later. "So on one trip, I told my old teammates I was going to fly over Griffith Stadium in Washington during a game, and I did. We went into a dive and flew so low that we could almost read the players' numbers, and some of the guys waved to me. I think I broke every rule in the book, and I expected to be reprimanded, but no one said a word after we got back."

⁓ ⁓

On the day of the Dodgers–Giants benefit game in May, the biggest naval battle to date was raging in the Coral Sea near the Solomon Islands, northwest of Australia. During the three-day conflict, the U.S. Navy lost the carrier *Lexington*, a destroyer, and sixty-five planes, along with 550 sailors and airmen. In addition, another carrier, the *Yorktown*, was badly damaged but was able to make it to port. The loss of the *Lexington*—the "*Lex*," as her crew called the carrier—left the navy with only two carriers, and one of them, the *Yorktown*, was barely seaworthy and in need of major repairs. The Japanese losses, not quite as severe, included damage to one of two aircraft carriers and the loss of seventy-five planes and, according to the U.S. Navy, about one thousand men. Especially costly to the navy was an air attack on the two Japanese carriers, during which almost fifty American planes and their pilots were lost.

Stories of heroism and remarkable sacrifice from the battle abounded. Edward Flaherty, a twenty-two-year-old electrician mate from St. Louis, told of how he and about a dozen others who survived the sinking of the Navy tanker *Neosho* on May 6 were able to get into a whaleboat after a lieutenant in the boat ordered those who had not been injured to dive into the Pacific. "Lieutenant [Henry] Bradford, a good guy, told all the men not wounded that they must go overboard," Flaherty, who was badly burned, said. "He then dived first and the others followed. The lieutenant and two enlisted men managed to swim through the choppy seas and reach a raft. But I imagine that between ten and fifteen of the others lost their lives."

Flaherty also told of how a pharmacist's mate leaped into the water with a quantity of tannic acid. "He then swam from man to man treating them for their burns," he recalled. "It was the only first aid we got." In all, 179 men lost their lives in the Japanese submarine attack.

Following the Allied defeat in the Battle of the Java Sea, only a month earlier, the Japanese had scored another tactical victory in the Coral Sea engagement. Surely, as Admiral Chester Nimitz, the commander of the U.S. fleet in the Pacific, knew, the Americans could not afford any more such defeats, especially with only three carriers left, including the *Saratoga*, which had been hit by a torpedo and badly damaged in early April and was still being repaired at Pearl Harbor in early May.

A lack of aircraft, especially bombers, also was hurting the American military effort. There were further delays in production because of the efforts of a Senate committee formed and headed by Senator Harry S. Truman that, at Truman's recommendation, had been looking into scandalous inefficiency and profiteering by some manufacturers of aircraft, ships, and various weaponry. After hearing from some of his Missouri constituents about gross extravagance and profiteering at an army camp in Missouri, Truman, on his own, began visiting army installations and defense plants in early 1941 and found that millions of government dollars were being squandered. At Truman's suggestion, the committee, named the Senate Special Committee to Investigate the National Defense Program, was formed shortly thereafter and soon became known as the "Truman Committee," launching the then-little-known senator to national prominence, including the cover of *Time* magazine and of course the presidency. High-ranking defense-plant officials, subpoenaed to testify before the committee, both before and after the attack on Pearl Harbor, admitted that they had cut corners and even used inferior materials, including low-grade steel for ships, in rushing to meet deadlines on the production of planes, warships, tanks, and other war-related products. The disclosures stunned much of the country but confirmed many of Truman's suspicions of corporate greed, even during wartime. One of the most startling disclosures came from Glenn Martin, whose company had been awarded a contract to build B-26 bombers and who admitted that the bombers' wings were shorter than they were supposed to be. Asked by Truman why the wings weren't the proper size, Martin said that by the time it was found they were not long enough, production was too far along and that, besides, the Glenn Martin Company already had the contract. That prompted Truman to tell Martin that, in that case, the committee would see to it that the contract was canceled. Martin thereupon promised the committee that the wings would be fixed. Truman won rave reviews for his committee's work, including one from the influential magazine *The Nation,* which said the country was indebted to Truman and his committee, while *Time* said the committee was "the watchdog, spotlight, conscience, and spark plug to the economic war behind the lines." Indeed, Truman's investigative and revelatory work endeared him to President Roosevelt and was largely responsible for the Democrats picking him to be the running mate for Roosevelt during FDR's successful bid for a fourth term in 1944.

❧ ❧

To help alleviate the shortage of bombers, which was partially due to defective materials uncovered by the Truman Committee,

Henry Ford acceded to a request from President Roosevelt to build a massive production plant in the hamlet of Willow Run in Michigan on property that the automobile magnate owned thirty miles west of his automobile factory in Detroit. The goal seemed unattainable: to build 650 B-24 Liberator bombers each month and hire forty thousand people to do the work. As it was, by June 1942, the Big Three automakers, Ford, General Motors, and Chrysler, already were devoting most of their efforts to producing trucks, jeeps, tanks, and other equipment for the military. By June 1943, approximately 350,000 people had flocked to the so-called "Motor City" to fill available jobs, many of them from the South and including thousands of women, many of whom had never held fulltime jobs before. By the time it was finished in 1942, the Willow Run plant, which was near Ypsilanti, Michigan, encompassed 3.5 million acres, including a mile-long and quarter-mile-wide building that was the world's largest factory structure under one roof and dormitories that could house three thousand workers. By the end of 1944, Willow Run was turning out one bomber an hour for a weekly total of an astonishing 165 a week—well over the original goal. By then, Willow Run employed almost fifty thousand people, including about twenty-five circus midgets to work in difficult-to-reach sections of the bombers, which normal-sized workers found extremely hard to do.

The production accomplishment at Willow Run was extraordinary and led Walter Reuther, the president of the United Auto Workers union, to say after the war, "Like England's battles were won on the playing fields of Eaton, America's were won on the assembly lines of Detroit." That may have been hyperbolic and also arguable, but there was no question that American workers had combined with the country's industrial might to outdo both the Germans and

Japanese in production that may well have made the difference in the outcome of World War II. President Roosevelt never went as far as Reuther in extolling America's assembly lines, although he often referred to them as the country's Arsenal of Democracy, which was pretty close to Reuther's analogy.

By the end of 1942, about two hundred thousand women were holding down government jobs in Washington, D.C., and around two million were working in defense plants and shipyards, usually doing work normally handled by men. Also that year, thousands of women became army and navy nurses and joined the new Women's Army Corps, which came to be known as the WACS, and the Women Accepted for Voluntary Emergency Services, the female equivalent of the navy whose members were called WAVES. A lesser-known, but highly productive women's military group was the Women Air Force Service Pilots, known as the WASPs, which was attached to the army air corps. Also started in 1942, the paramilitary organization attracted more than a thousand licensed women pilots—most of the male pilots in the air force had to be trained to fly—who freed air corps pilots for overseas duty by taking over their duties of flying military planes, including bombers from aircraft factories to military air bases. Other WASPs served as flight instructors or towed targets for aerial gunnery practice.

❧ ❧

There was, of course, no way baseball could compare with what the WACS, WAVES, and WASPs were doing or what was being accomplished at Willow Run or at other defense plants, most of which operated around the clock, seven days a week. But such publications as the *Sporting News* persisted in saying that baseball played an important role as a morale booster. Dan Daniel, a well-known New York sportswriter, was one of the writers who may have exaggerated the game's contribution to the war effort when he wrote in the *Sporting News,* "Baseball marches on in martial tread, cognizant of its duties and its responsibilities, and the hazards which confront it on land, sea, and the air." Some of the players eventually did confront such hazards, but not baseball itself.

∽ ∽

Sometimes, baseball itself got a bit carried away in its effort to link the game with the war effort. One egregious example occurred when, before an exhibition game in Miami Beach in March 1942, the new Philadelphia Phils manager, Hans Lobert, supplied each of his players with a bat and instructed them to march across the field with the bats simulating rifles being carried on the players' shoulders. Lobert's background included seven years as the baseball coach at West Point, and perhaps that had a bearing in his decision. A photo of the stunt was sent to newspapers across the country by the Associated Press and, if anything, subjected the Phils, to both ridicule and bad taste, neither of which they needed, having lost 122 games in 1941, more than any other big league team. As bad, if not worse, were the nine members of the Brooklyn Dodgers who permitted themselves to be photographed during spring training in Havana bearing rifles they were about to use during a turkey shoot. Such photos drew the ire of the *Sporting News*, which had become downright jingoistic during the early months of the war in trying to justify the playing of major league baseball during wartime but obviously realized that such displays only served to hurt the game. In several editorials, the newspaper cautioned against players trying to mimic GIs, as was the case with the Phils, or being photographed, as the group of Dodgers was, with rifles that were going to be used for pleasure.

∞ ∞

As May neared an end, the Yankees and Dodgers held on to their slim first-place leads. Before a Memorial Day crowd of 43,997 at Yankee Stadium, the Yankees split a doubleheader with Detroit (all teams played doubleheaders on Memorial Day and the Fourth of July) amid a panoply of patriotism that included the playing of "Taps," a volley of gunfire by a squad from the Fort Hamilton Army base in Brooklyn, and, as was now customary, the singing of the national anthem. Second-year shortstop Phil Rizzuto, nicknamed "Scooter" because of his five-foot six-inch height and his quickness in the field, had six hits in eight times at bat. At Shibe Park in Philadelphia, another diminutive player of Italian descent, Dominic DiMaggio, also had an outstanding day, hitting safely in seven of ten trips to the plate, while Ted Williams hit his league-leading fifteenth home run as the Red Sox split a doubleheader with the Athletics. At that point of the season, Williams was hitting .333, well behind Yankee second baseman Joe Gordon, who was at .375. Williams also led the American League with thirty-four runs batted in, while Johnny Mize, whom the Cardinals inexplicably had traded to the Giants for three journeymen players in December, was leading the National League with thirty-five. Joe DiMaggio, still mired in a slump, was batting .265, fourteen points behind his bespectacled smaller and younger brother, and still hearing scattered boos at Yankee Stadium. "My timing is off," the Yankee Clipper said with a typical economy of words.

While the doubleheader was going on, about five miles away, sixty-eight FBI agents and local police raided a colony of cabins on the Hudson River waterfront in Edgewater, New Jersey, and arrested an undisclosed number of German aliens and nationals, seizing thirty collapsible rubber boats, a quantity of arms and ammunition, maps of inland waterways, field glasses, cameras, and other paraphernalia. The raid came two months after FBI agents swooped upon the German Seaman's Home in Hoboken, also on the Hudson River waterfront in New Jersey, and apprehended seventy-one German aliens and nationals suspected of being members of a spy ring. Why the FBI suspected the New Jersey residents of being spies, apart from the materials that were found, was never disclosed, nor, so far as is known, was whether any of them were ever prosecuted. The Memorial Day raid served as a striking counterpoint to the patriotic ceremonies being held before the doubleheader at Yankee Stadium and at other major league ballparks on that day. But then, Memorial Day in 1942 was hardly typical, nor, for that matter, was any other day during America's first full wartime year.

3

BASEBALL'S GYPSIES AND THEIR MUDCAT BAND

ON MONDAY, AUGUST 18, 1941, the St. Louis Cardinals were a half game behind the Brooklyn Dodgers in a late-season race for the National League pennant. The Cardinals had split a double-header with the Pittsburgh Pirates the day before and were to open a three-game series with the Boston Braves on Tuesday afternoon. The schedule called for a day off for the Redbirds that Monday, and, having lost star right-fielder Enos Slaughter to an injury, the team would have welcomed a day's rest in Boston after the long train trip from Pittsburgh at a time when plane travel for big league ball clubs was still more than a decade away, and all sixteen teams did virtually all their travel by train.

As usual, though, there were no off days for the Cardinals, who played exhibition games almost every day when no National League game was scheduled during the season in the 1920s, 1930s, and 1940s. And during that third Monday in August 1941, the Cardinals did not go directly from Pittsburgh to Boston but instead, after a twelve-hour overnight trip, stopped in Stamford, Connecticut, a city of fifty thousand at the time, to play an exhibition game that night against a local semipro team. Because the ballpark they played in had no clubhouse, the players had to put on their uniforms at their hotel, as was often the case, and later return to the hotel to change before hurrying to the Stamford train station to catch a midnight train for Boston.

The exhibition game in Stamford, like all the others the Cardinals would play that summer, came about when a local promoter came up with a guarantee that satisfied the team's penurious owner, Sam Breadon. Breadon's reasoning, and that of the team's general manager, Branch Rickey, was that the players could still get a night's sleep on the train to Boston after the game and be in Boston with plenty of time for a game against the Braves the next afternoon at three o'clock. Implicit, too, in their thinking was that the players were lucky to be in the big leagues playing a kids' game during a Depression when millions of American men were out of work.

That all may seem mind-boggling in the 21st century, when many star players use every possible excuse or ruse to avoid playing in the annual All-Star Game and when the Major League Players Association dictates much of what a ball club can do during a season. One thing the Cardinals or any other big-league club could not get away with nowadays would be scheduling exhibitions in towns like Stamford. Breadon's and Rickey's reasoning was that if a small-town promoter like Felix LiVolsi in Stamford could guarantee $1,500 for an exhibition match, why that was almost enough to pay a rookie's salary for the entire season, at least for a Cardinals rookie. Plus, what difference did it make? Such games, which were often played under poor lights and on fields that often did not have dugouts, a clubhouse (as was the case in Stamford), or even fences, were anathema to the players, the manager, and the coaches.

Fifteen years earlier, Breadon, a wealthy automobile dealer in St. Louis, had shown that he would brook no rebelliousness in connection with exhibition games. In 1926 the Cardinals were locked in a pennant battle with the Cincinnati Reds when Breadon booked an exhibition game in New Haven, Connecticut, on an "off day." When Breadon refused a request from player-manager Rogers Hornsby, one of the greatest Cardinals of all time, to cancel the game so that his players could have some much-needed rest, a furious Hornsby sent him a wire saying, "You're more anxious for a few exhibition dollars than a chance to win a championship." Even though the Cardinals went on to win their first World Series, Breadon never forgot nor forgave Hornsby's rebelliousness, and, in what appeared to be an act of vengeance, traded Hall of Famer Hornsby to the New York Giants that winter for Frankie Frisch and pitcher Jimmy Ring, even though Hornsby had won six straight batting titles from 1920 through 1925. During that remarkable stretch, Hornsby had batted over .400 three times, including .424 in 1924, the highest batting average in the 20th and 21st centuries. And he was only thirty years old when he was traded, a move that caused St. Louis fans to hang Breadon in effigy outside his automobile dealership for getting rid of the team's best player and one of the best second basemen of all time. Never one to shy away from his hitting accomplishments, Hornsby, who batted .358 during his twenty-two-year career, said some years after his retirement, "I don't like to sound egotistical, but every time I stepped up to the plate I couldn't help but feel sorry for the pitcher." Given his personality, it's actually highly unlikely that Hornsby, known as the "Rajah," was the least bit compassionate toward pitchers.

Disregarding the players and managers displeasure over playing exhibition games, Breadon continued to book them, even late in the season, with the Cardinals often playing under makeshift lights and then spending the night in Pullman cars en route to the next big league city. "We were like a carnival, playing in towns we'd never heard of," Terry Moore, the Cardinals great center fielder from 1933 through 1948, told me. "We hardly ever had a day off, but few of the players complained because most of us had never been with any club other than the Cardinals, although a lot of the guys prayed it would rain on our scheduled days off. But to us, it was a way of life." At the same time, Moore believed that such exhibitions, especially the ones late in the season, like the one in Stamford in late August 1941, cost the Cardinals the pennant that year. "There's no question in my mind that we would have won the pennant in 1941 if not for all the exhibition games we played," Moore said.

To express their displeasure over the exhibitions, the Cardinals mastered the art of losing baseballs. "We knew they only had a limited amount of balls, so we'd try to lose as many as possible, both during batting practice and during the early innings so that we'd eventually exhaust the supply, and they'd have to call the game," Moore said. "That way we could get some rest at the hotel before heading to the train station."

That's exactly what happened during an earlier visit to Stamford by the Cardinals on August 4, 1938, when they were still the Gas House Gang and the game had to be called prematurely in the ninth inning when the supply of thirty-seven experimental yellow balls— which were easier to see under the few arc lights that were placed around the field on flat-bed trucks—ran out with the Cardinals holding a 20–4 lead over a local team made up primarily of factory workers, most of whom had worked all day. As he usually did in exhibition games, Frisch, who became the manager in 1933, started all his regulars except for Elwood "Preacher" Roe, a twenty-five-year-old left-hander who had just been brought up from the minors. Aided by the poor lights, Roe struck out almost every batter he faced until, mercifully, Frisch removed him from the mound after he had pitched four innings and put him in right field. "The way he was throwing, the ball looked like a yellow pea," the Stamford All-Stars shortstop, Tommy Pantas, said some years later. As it developed, Roe appeared in only one game for the Cardinals in 1938 before being sent back to the minors, where he languished for five years before returning to pitch for eleven seasons with the Pittsburgh Pirates and the Brooklyn Dodgers. As a starter with the Dodgers, Roe won ninety-three games, including twenty-two in 1951, and lost only thirty-seven. Stamford fans who were there in 1938 still remembered him best, though, for mowing down almost every hitter during the four innings he pitched.

As much as they disliked having to play in exhibition games, the Cardinals always went all out, even when they were in a pennant race. "We didn't know any other way to play," Moore said, "and we felt we owed it to the fans to play well." A good example of that all-out type of play came during the first inning of the Cardinals' second visit to Stamford, when lead-off batter and third baseman Jimmy Brown hit a line drive to left center field and, while trying to stretch it into a triple, dived head-first into the third base but was called out; and during their 1938 visit to Stamford, the Cardinals scored twenty runs on twenty-one hits, including home runs by future Hall of Famers Johnny Mize and Joe Medwick, in taking a 20–1 lead into the last half of the ninth inning. Let up? As Terry Moore said, they didn't know how to, even scoring seven runs in their last time at bat. And all four of the runs they gave up were yielded by the irrepressible Pepper Martin, who was an infielder and only pitched during exhibition games, often throwing pitches between his legs and over his back.

The Cardinals were an especially big attraction during the raucous Gas House era in the 1930s, especially between innings, with their Mudcat band, which included the team's most colorful player, Pepper Martin, who played the harmonica and guitar; pitcher Lon Warneke, who later became an umpire, who strummed a guitar and sang; Bill McGee, who, naturally, fiddled; pitcher Bob Weiland, who blew into a jug that somehow added to the musicality; and outfielder Frenchy Bordagaray, who played a contraption that included a washboard, a car horn, a whistle, and an electric light. Martin also was prone to borrowing flashlights from fans, and, while playing in the outfield (though he was primarily an infielder) he would wave the flashlight skyward while pursuing a fly ball to dramatize the inadequate lighting. If it wasn't a circus, it was close; and, like a circus, it was entertaining.

Not surprisingly, because most of them were from the South, the Mudcats specialized in country music. While traveling on trains, the group, to the delight of most passengers who knew who they were, would often parade through the cars playing. "Most of the time, they'd practice in our private cars for hours at a time," said Mickey Owen, a second-year Cardinal catcher in 1938 who was traded to the Dodgers in 1941. "Some of the guys got a kick out of the music while a few hated it. But if you didn't like it, there was no stopping Pepper and rest of the Mudcats. Sometimes they'd be practicing on the train, and Pepper would say, 'Let's go,' and they'd go marching through the train, playing away. It was really something to see." And, apparently, to hear.

At times, the Mudcats, or at least their notoriety, proved too much for Frisch, who managed the Cardinals through 1938, with the first five years being while he was still playing second base. During the summer of 1938, the Cardinals were on their way to play their Triple-A farm club, the Rochester Red Wings, when the cars carrying the team passed a billboard that read, "COME OUT TO RED WING STADIUM TONIGHT TO SEE PEPPER MARTIN AND HIS MUDCATS." In smaller type below, the sign read, "AND ALSO SEE JOHNNY MIZE AND JOE MEDWICK AND THE REST OF THE ST. LOUIS CARDINALS." Seeing the sign, Medwick, unhappy at playing second fiddle, so to speak, to a wacky musical group of teammates, snapped, "What the hell are we anyway—a baseball team or a minstrel show?" Frisch also did not appreciate his ballplayers getting second billing to the Mudcats. "I'm the only manager in baseball traveling with a goddamn orchestra," Frisch, no lover of the Mudcats' repertoire, said on seeing the sign. "And I don't like it." As it developed, the Mudcats outlasted the old Fordham Flash (Frisch, a native New Yorker, had been a football, baseball, and basketball star at Fordham) with the Cardinals, because he was gone by the 1939 season and the Mudcats played on until Martin retired at the end of the 1940 season, although he would return during the wartime player manpower shortage in 1944 to play—but only baseball—in forty games for the Cardinals.

The Cardinals were hardly the only big league team that played exhibitions during the season. Other teams that did the same, though, only played some of their minor-league affiliates. But the Cardinals played just about anywhere so long as the price was right. If they weren't exactly America's team, the Cardinals, as the Gas

House Gang, were the most colorful and one of the best. As one of the two westernmost teams in the major leagues (the St. Louis Browns were the other), the Cards, as they were also called, had perhaps the largest geographical support, which encompassed most of the southwestern states and even downstate Illinois. Furthermore, their radio broadcasts from the 1940s on had the largest radio audience of any other big league club. And their frequent exhibition game appearances, particularly during the Gas House Gang era, also endeared them to fans in the Midwest and the Northeast. Even some members of the New York media became Cardinal fans while growing up in New York, such as Bill Gallo, a longtime sports cartoonist and columnist for the New York *Daily News.* Another member of the New York media, Art Rust, Jr., a popular black radio reporter and sports talk-show host, was also a Cardinal fan, although to some people that might be hard to understand. "As a kid, I'd wait outside the Polo Grounds to get autographs of some of the Cardinals after they'd played the Giants," Rust once told me:

> Most of them were southerners and a few would rub their hands across my head and tell me it was for good luck, while some of the other players laughed. I didn't like being made fun of, but they'd give me autographs and the fact that I'd be there whenever they came to New York, some of them would recognize me, and I stayed a fan. Looking back years later, I realized that's the way it was in the forties and fifties.

Some other well-known media figures, while not necessarily Cardinal fans, became big fans of Stan Musial, who always did extremely well at Ebbets Field, where the nickname, Stan the Man, was bestowed him. It was done at least in part by admiring Dodger fans, some of whom would say, "Here's that man again" when Musial came to bat.

"While growing up in Brooklyn, I saw Musial play at Ebbets Field as a kid and later as a sportswriter, and I became a big Musial fan," said Dave Anderson, who first covered Musial as a sportswriter for the old *Brooklyn Eagle* and later was a Pulitzer Prize–winning sports columnist for the *New York Times*. Anderson also recalled how for years the Cardinals would ride the subway from Ebbets Field to their hotel in Manhattan, as they also would do after playing the Giants at the Polo Grounds. "One day, while I was in the same subway car as some of the players, I got Marty Marion's autograph," Anderson said, referring to the Cardinals shortstop of the 1940s and 1950s. "I still remember how Marion drew a small circle on top of the i in his last name. Years later, while on an assignment in St. Louis, I mentioned it to him when he was the manager of the restaurant at Busch Stadium where the Cardinals played, and he couldn't believe I remembered that from so many years ago."

The Cardinals, not surprisingly, also endeared themselves to the South, because they usually had more players from southern states than other big league teams. Of the thirteen position players on the 1942 team, nine were Southerners, and perhaps the best player on the 1941 team, Johnny Mize, was from Georgia. Most of the nine pitchers in 1942 were also Southerners. Furthermore, almost all the players were from the vast Cardinal farm system, including all eight position players and seven of the nine pitchers. By contrast, the Cardinals archrival during the early 1940s, the Brooklyn Dodgers, usually started only two players from their farm system: shortstop Pee Wee Reese and outfielder Pete Reiser, who won the National League batting title in 1941 when he was just a twenty-two-year-old rookie. At that, Reiser, who was from St. Louis, had also been in the Cardinal farm system until 1938, when Baseball Commissioner Kenesaw

Mountain Landis, in a crackdown on the farm system that Branch Rickey had devised, declared that about one hundred Cardinal farm-hands, including Reiser, would become free agents, whereupon Reiser signed with the Dodgers. Another Dodger outfielder in 1942, the sullen and pugnacious Joe Medwick of Carteret, New Jersey, also had come up through the Cardinals farm system before spending eight years and part of a ninth with the Cardinals, during which he batted over .300 every season, including 1937 when, in his best season ever, he won the Triple Crown with a batting average of .374, 154 runs batted in, and thirty-one home runs, which tied him with Mel Ott for the National League lead. He also led the National League in hits, runs scored, doubles, total bases, and infielding percentage among outfielders, with a .988 percentage. A charter member of the Gas House Gang, "Muscles" Medwick, as some sportswriters called him, also was the only player removed from a World Series game by a baseball commissioner. During the seventh game of the 1934 World Series, with the Cardinals leading the Tigers in what would be the final score, 11–0, Tiger third baseman Marv Owen did not take kindly to how Medwick slid into third base, and a scuffle ensued between the two. When Medwick, who had a reputation as a brawler, went out to his position in left field, he was bombarded with fruit and bottles, delaying the game and prompting Commissioner Landis to order Medwick taken out of the game for his own protection.

In a surprise development in 1940, Rickey traded the twenty-eight-year-old Medwick, an eventual Hall of Famer from Carteret, New Jersey, to the Dodgers. That trade broke Medwick's heart, as did another trade that sent Enos Slaughter, who had spent thirteen highly productive years with the Cardinals, to the New York Yankees in 1954 when Slaughter was thirty-four years old and was on the downside of his Hall of Fame career. The photo of a crestfallen Slaughter sobbing at his Cardinals' locker after he'd been informed of the trade is one of the most touching pictures ever taken of a major league player. Rickey's trade of Medwick (he had left the Cardinals fourteen years before the Slaughter trade) was based on his policy of trading away star players who he felt had their best years already behind them. That was true of Medwick, although he would still bat over .300 four times while playing for the Dodgers and the New York Giants before returning to St. Louis to close out his career in 1947 and 1948, retiring with a .324 career batting average. But the trade of Mize in 1942 by Rickey seemed to make little sense, because "the Big Cat," as he was nick-named, was only twenty-nine years old and had hit over .300 in all six of his seasons with the Cardinals. He had also led the National League in hitting in 1939 with a .349 batting average and in home runs in 1939 with twenty-eight and in 1940 with forty-three, when he also led in runs batted in (137). Big as he was at six-three and 215 pounds, Mize was hardly slow, as he proved by leading the National League in triples in 1938 with sixteen. Mize certainly wasn't traded because of an attitude problem, because he was quiet and well-liked, not to mention well-respected by his Cardinal teammates, as he would be with the Giants and later the New York Yankees. One of the most powerful hitters in baseball, Mize became a Paul Bunyan–esque figure during the Cardinals exhibition game in my hometown of Stamford, Connecticut, in 1938 when, during batting practice, he hit about a half dozen balls over a stand of trees in right field—a distance of well over four hundred feet, and something no one else had ever done—as a crowd of about four thousand looked on in amazement. For good measure, Mize hit another over the distant trees during the game. Not to be outshone, Joe Medwick also hit a homer over the canvas enclosing what was normally an open ball field during the one-sided game. So although Pepper Martin and the Cardinal Mudcats made the crowd laugh throughout the game, Mize and Medwick drew oohs and aahs for their display of long-ball hitting, typical during their exhibition appearances.

⚬⚬ ⚬⚬

If the Cardinals always included almost all Southerners in the 1940s, they also included probably the lowest-paid players. Enos Slaughter told me once that when he was promoted from the Cardinals Triple-A farm team in Columbus in 1938, he was paid $400 a month, the same as he had been paid while playing for the Columbia Red Birds in the American Association. Musial's salary had gone from $150 to $400 a month in 1941 when he went from Class C, the second-lowest level in the minor leagues, to $400 with the Triple-A Rochester Red Wings, the same prorated salary he received during his two weeks with the Cardinals. In 1942, his first full year in the majors, Musial signed for $700 a month, which added up to $4,200 for the season, the equivalent of about $60,000 in the 21st century, less than Yankee star Alex Rodriguez was making a game in 2011. For the Cardinals, that was typical for a first-year player, even one as promising as Musial.

Regarding all the exhibition games and the relatively low pay the Cardinals' players earned, Moore said, "Nobody complained, at least not to Branch Rickey or Sam Breadon, because we were all just glad to be in the big leagues. And a lot of the players knew that if they did complain that they'd probably be let go." Then, too, of course, there was nothing the players could do about it, because the teams controlled their destiny, and free agency was about two decades away. That, of course, was not the case in later years, when even journeyman players earned more than $1 million a year.

One of the highest-paid players in major league baseball in 2011 was Cardinals first baseman Albert Pujols, who received $14,508,395 for batting .299, hitting thirty-seven home runs, and knocking in ninety-nine runs. By contrast, in 1948, Stan Musial received $31,000 (roughly $300,000 in 2012) for batting a league-leading .376, hitting thirty-nine home runs, driving in 131 runs, and leading the National League with 230 hits. Musial, whose highest salary was $100,000 in the late 1950s (about $1 million in 2012) and who played in the pre–free agency era, remained with the Cardinals until he retired after the 1963 season, his twenty-second with the team, and it seemed likely that even given the choice to move elsewhere, Musial would have stayed with the Cardinals. Pujols, meanwhile, turned down an offer from the Cardinals in late 2011 that would have paid him $200 million over a ten-year period and signed a ten-year contract with the American League's Los Angeles Angels of Anaheim, who play about thirty miles from Los Angeles, that will pay him $254 million, or more than $25 million a year.

❧ ❧

If the Cardinals were mostly all products of the team's far-flung farm system, whose Triple-A teams were in Columbus, Ohio, and Rochester, New York, so were the Yankees. In 1942, seven of the eight position regulars were from the team's farm system—the exception was first baseman Buddy Hassett, who came to the team that year for what would be his last season after playing for the Dodgers and the Boston Braves. The irony there was that Hassett was one of only two Yankees from New York, the other being shortstop Phil Rizzuto, who would spend his entire thirteen-year career with his hometown team while on his way to the National Baseball Hall of Fame. Like the Cardinals, most of the Yankee pitchers were also from the team's farm system. But that was not the case in Brooklyn, whose pitching staff included only one player, Ed Head, who hadn't played for any other team and wouldn't during his five-year major league career.

Once the Dodgers obtained a player in a trade, though, he usually stayed for a long time. Good examples include first baseman Dolph Camilli, outfielder Dixie Walker, and catcher Mickey Owen. Later in the forties, when Brooklyn had established a good farm system, the team brought up such eventual stars as Gil Hodges, Jackie Robinson, Duke Snider, Roy Campanella, Carl Furillo, and pitchers Sandy Koufax, Ralph Branca, Don Newcombe, Carl Erskine, Clem Labine, and Johnny Podres, most of whom helped the Dodgers win their first pennant in 1955.

The young Cardinal team of 1942 was something special, and very likely the best Cardinal team of all time. More than ten years later, Enos Slaughter, who had played with Hall of Famers Mickey Mantle, Yogi Berra, and Phil Rizzuto, among other outstanding Yankee players, said he thought the '42 team was the best he had played on during a career that stretched from 1939 through 1959. Slaughter pointed out that it didn't have an established star, except for pitcher Mort Cooper, and with an average age of twenty-five and with no player over twenty-nine at the beginning of the season, it was the youngest team in the big leagues. Also, one of the hallmarks of Cardinal teams had always been speed, and the '42 team, with the addition of the fleet-footed Musial, was probably the fastest. And no outfield in the National League could compare defensively with Slaughter, Moore, and, when he began to play on a regular basis during his rookie year,

Musial. Further, the six-foot three-inch Marty Marion, who came to be known as "the octopus" because of his long gangling arms that stopped almost any ball hit between second and third base, was probably the best shortstop in the league, and indeed perhaps the best shortstop never to make it to the National Baseball Hall of Fame. And in Walker Cooper, the Cardinals had the best young catcher in the National League, along with a pitching staff whose oldest starter, Mort Cooper, Walker's brother, was only twenty-nine.

As the westernmost team in the National League, the Cardinals often had to undergo the longest road trips, sometimes spending almost two days on trains en route to Boston. But as Stan Musial, who played during both the train and plane eras, once said, "The long time we spent on trains brought us closer together than teams are today, and I'm glad I was around when we traveled by train." It also meant that sportswriters who covered the teams on a regular basis also spent far more time with the players they were writing about. Traveling on the same trains and eating, drinking, and playing cards with the players in the three or four cars usually set aside for a team meant there was a much closer relationship between many of the writers and players. But that also turned out to be a drawback, because most writers were far less inclined to be critical of players on teams they covered. As a result, any criticism of a player—and there was very little of it—was usually muted. Another reason, perhaps, was that not many players were making more money, or even as much, as some of the writers. Today, by contrast, the gulf between what players and sportswriters make is vast, and they seldom see each other outside a ballpark. Yankee writers all knew about Babe Ruth's sybaritic nocturnal behavior but never wrote about it, because they not only liked the Babe but spent time with him riding the rails. Nowadays, because they tend to live in disparate worlds, many sportswriters, particularly those who work for tabloid newspapers, would almost be forced to report on Ruth's womanizing and drinking, because most of it was so flagrant and also would be fodder for television and sensationalistic newspapers, not that it probably would have bothered the Babe.

Apart from long train trips, the Cardinals, like the St. Louis Browns, often had to play their home games on a sun-baked diamond in the hottest city in the major leagues, with the temperature often rising close to 100 degrees, at a time when most games in the early 1940s were still being played in the heat of the afternoon. Ignoring that factor, many players in later years were prone to express the view that players of that era had an advantage in playing most of their game during daylight when, in fact, it tends to be much cooler, and thus more comfortable, during night games. Ted Williams also injected another element that modern-day players don't seem to consider. "We almost always played doubleheaders on Sundays and holidays, and quite often the second game would run past sunset," Williams told me in May 1991 on the fiftieth anniversary of his .406 season, when he was reunited with Joe DiMaggio at Fenway Park:

> I remember games occasionally going past eight o'clock and with no lights it could be difficult to see, especially if you were batting against someone like Bob Feller who was throwing almost a hundred miles an hour. More than a few times I turned to the plate umpire and said, 'Don't you think we ought to call this one because of darkness?' They usually didn't, and we kept on playing as it was getting dark. Much as I liked to play during the day, I was glad when we got lights and could put them on when games ran late and you had trouble seeing the ball when you were at the plate.

Williams neglected to mention another disadvantage to playing day games that went beyond twilight: Players did not start wearing batting helmets until the mid-1950s, which made batting against a Bob Feller or a Hal Newhouser in the gloaming a somewhat unsettling experience. Then, too, there were the long, enervating train trips on unair-conditioned trains, which lasted up to twenty-four hours, and, as Terry Moore recalled, often left players covered with coal soot by the time they awoke in the morning.

❧ ❧

As May came to an end, Williams was still terrorizing American League pitchers, while DiMaggio remained in a slump and was still hearing catcalls and boos. Meanwhile, the country got a boost of sorts with the opening of the movie *Yankee Doodle Dandy*, based on the life of song-and-dance man and composer George M. Cohan and starring native New Yorker James Cagney. Long renowned for his gangster portrayals, Cagney demonstrated his remarkable diversity and talents as a singer and dancer with a portrayal of Cohan that *New York Times* movie critic Bosley Crowther called "an unbelievably faithful characterization and a piece of playing that glows with energy" and "as warm and delightful a musical picture as has hit the screen in years." The movie, which had its premiere at the Hollywood Theater on Broadway, was filled with a patriotic score that included such stirring Cohan classics as "You're a Grand Old Flag" and "Over There," which lifted the spirits of Americans across the country at a time when they needed a boost. It also won Cagney the Oscar in 1942 for Best Actor.

The country was to get an even bigger lift in June 1942, and it would come thousands of miles from Broadway.

4

TURNING POINT IN THE PACIFIC WAR?

THE MAN WHO planned the attack on Pearl Harbor, Admiral Isoroku Yamamoto, one of Japan's most powerful military figures, felt from the beginning that Japanese forces had to move swiftly in the Pacific against the much smaller and largely decimated U.S. fleet if Japan were to win the war. "I shall run wild for six months or a year, but I have utterly no confidence for the second or third years of the fighting," said Yamamoto privately before the December 7 attack on Pearl Harbor. Yamamoto, who had studied at Harvard and served as a naval attaché in Washington, was convinced that if the war lasted more than a year, the United States would gain the upper hand.

In accord with Yamamoto's plan, Japanese forces quickly conquered the Philippines, Malaya, Singapore, the Dutch East Indies, and Borneo. His next goal was the American possession of Midway atoll, about thirteen hundred miles from Oahu and a launching pad for U.S. bombers. Three previous aerial attacks on Midway, including one the day Pearl Harbor was attacked, had been repulsed by U.S. forces, but Yamamoto's latest plan was for a massive air and sea assault on the island. Coinciding with the Midway attack would be an assault on, and ultimately conquest of, the Aleutian Islands in Alaska and most likely all of Hawaii, New Caledonia, the Fiji Islands, Samoa, the Solomon Islands, and possibly Australia. By then, he felt, the United States might surrender. Attacking Midway, Yamamoto felt, would extend Japan's defensive perimeter to almost twelve thousand miles. That grand plan, in the aftermath of the demoralizing American raid on Tokyo, Yamamoto was convinced, would destroy much of what little was left of the U.S. fleet in the Pacific.

In May 1942, a Japanese armada that included eleven aircraft carriers carrying almost seven hundred planes, eleven battleships, a dozen cruisers, and forty-five destroyers headed for Midway in two waves, separated by about two hundred miles. However, American cryptographers had decoded the Japanese plan, and by the time Japanese bombers launched their attack on U.S. forces on Midway, a much smaller American fleet was waiting for that vast naval armada. The best that Admiral Chester Nimitz, commander of the U.S. Pacific fleet, could assemble were three aircraft carriers, including the *Yorktown*, which had been repaired in less than a week after almost being sunk in the Coral Sea; eight cruisers; fourteen destroyers; and not a single battleship. Totally outmatched in terms of ships, planes, and manpower, all the Americans had going for them was the element of surprise. Also waiting for the Japanese attack were about one hundred relatively old marine planes, along with artillery and rifles dating from World War I. It most certainly looked like a mismatch.

At the beginning it was, as the Japanese struck first, with more than one hundred bombers and fighters from four carriers attacking Midway at 5:00 a.m. on June 4 and inflicting considerable damage, but not on the coveted airstrip. In the air, Japan's famed fighter planes known as Zeros easily outfought the much slower Brewster Buffalo fighters launched from Midway. Waiting until all the Japanese planes were back on the decks of the three carriers, Admiral Raymond Spruance, the commander of the U.S. task force, dispatched around fifty torpedo planes and dive-bombers to attack the three Japanese carriers. However, none of the planes succeeded in hitting any of the carriers, and around thirty-five American aircraft were shot down. By that time, it appeared that a Japanese victory was imminent. But Spruance immediately counterattacked, sending a second wave of thirty-five bombers from the carriers *Enterprise* and *Yorktown* toward the Japanese armada. This time, the attack was successful. Scoring hit after hit with its bombs, the Dauntless dive-bombers not only destroyed scores of fueled Japanese planes on the carrier decks but eventually sank four of the six carriers, all of which had launched planes for the attack on Pearl Harbor. A number of the other ships in the Japanese armada also were hit and either sunk or damaged. An American rout was on.

By the time the naval battle ended two days later, in addition to the four carriers that had been sunk, a Japanese heavy cruiser and three destroyers had been sent to the bottom of the Pacific, while two, possibly three, battleships and a light cruiser had been damaged along with four transport or cargo ships, one or two of which may have also been sunk. In addition, more than four thousand Japanese sailors and airmen had been killed, and around 350 planes were destroyed. Meanwhile, apart from the loss of the *Yorktown* and the destroyer *Hammann*, the American fleet had lost 150 planes and 307 men.

"Pearl Harbor has now been partially avenged," Nimitz said at the end of the battle, the biggest yet in the Pacific.

Yamamoto, in his quest for an early victory, knew that time was on the side of the United States, aware that if Japan's aggressive advances were halted, the power of American industry could very well turn the tide in America's favor. Indeed, during the remaining three years of the war in the Pacific, the Japanese would build only three more aircraft carriers, while the United States, which had lost so much of its fleet at Pearl Harbor and in the Battle of the Coral Sea, would produce sixteen, along with far more other warships, merchant vessels, tanks, and other weapons and war materials. Meanwhile, the damage inflicted by U.S. forces at the Battle of Midway had enabled the U.S. Navy to at least reach parity with the hitherto superior Japanese Naval force.

In what was believed to have been a diversionary maneuver to the Midway attack, on June 3, a relatively small Japanese force had invaded two islands in the Aleutian Islands chain in Alaska, which was then a U.S. possession, the day before the Battle of Midway began. As at Midway, the Japanese suffered a crushing defeat, losing 4,350 men—about half its total invading force—along with seven warships and nine cargo transport ships. By comparison, the United States lost 1,481 men, one destroyer, and two transport ships during the air, sea, and land fighting, which didn't end until the summer of 1943.

If those victories gave a huge lift to American morale, the news continued to be bleak along the East Coast and as far south as the Gulf of Mexico, where, from January to June 1942, almost four hundred cargo ships and tankers had been sunk, the vast majority of them in the Atlantic Ocean, including many within thirty miles of the U.S. shoreline. That spring, the architect of the German U-boat campaign, Admiral Karl Donitz, said, "Our U-boats are operating so close to the American coast that bathers and sometimes entire coastal cities are witnessing the drama of war." Donitz was right. Indeed, not even beachgoers were safe from the U-boats' depredations. In mid-March 1942 spectators watched in fascination as a U-boat pursued two tankers in broad daylight off the coast of Atlantic City. Finally, one of the tankers was hit by a torpedo, exploded, burned, and sank. Two days later, beachgoers saw a submarine, perhaps the same one, chase a tanker even closer to shore and fire a torpedo. The "fish," as torpedoes were called, missed the tanker but headed straight for shore, where it hit a beach and exploded. Fortunately no one on the beach was hurt, but it showed that even people on shore were not immune from danger from the marauding, and virtually uncontested, German submarines. Something had to be done to spot the rampaging U-boats, and, with only about twenty small ships, most of them the size of coast guard cutters, and around one hundred old planes, the navy was incapable of coping with the German "wolf packs." Also, it wasn't until May 1942 that convoys of navy sub chasers ranging from 100 to 175 feet, coast guard cutters, and other patrol craft were assigned to accompany cargo ships and tankers, along with small patrol planes and blimp, in the western Atlantic. Later, navy "armed guard" crews that consisted of an officer, about twenty gunners, a radioman, and a signalman were assigned to most large merchant ships. Hanson Baldwin, the military analyst for the *New York Times*, wrote on August 15 that the convoy system had been so effective that between May 14 and the end of July, "only four ships out of almost eighteen hundred con-voyed had been sunk." Until the convoy system was established, some of America's richest yachtsmen, aware of the dire situation off the East Coast, stepped into the breach by offering the services of their multimillion-dollar yachts. The government accepted the offer, and by June yachts owned by the likes of Vincent Astor, William Vanderbilt, and Huntington Hartford, all members of the "Cruising Club of America," began to patrol the Long Island shoreline and New York harbor in search of German U-boats. Taking a cue from the wealthy sailors, whose yachts were equipped with machine guns and rifles, scores of citizen pilots volunteered to patrol the New York and New Jersey coastline in their small red, blue, and yellow aircrafts, which carried depth charges and small bombs. About the same time, President Roosevelt halted a shipment of seventy search planes that had been built for the British and had them diverted for use along the East and West coasts, where they were needed as much, if not more so, than in England. At the suggestion of their teams' management, no doubt many major league players, includ-ing the entire twenty-five-man Boston Braves squad, signed on as aircraft spotters, scanning the skies for planes of any kind and then notifying authorities. So far as is known, none of the players, or any other spotters, ever spotted a plane with a swastika or a rising-sun symbol on a fuselage.

Considering what was happening right off the East Coast, in the Pacific, in Europe, and in North Africa, big league players knew that they were lucky to be playing baseball and that ducking an inside head-high fastball without a helmet was a lot safer than being on a warship off Midway, in a tank in France or Italy, or aboard a mer-chant ship in the Atlantic.

5

BASEBALL AT MIDNIGHT

MILES FROM MIDWAY atoll, big league baseball continued to thrive, drawing crowds comparable to the last peacetime season of 1941. At the beginning of June, the defending champion New York Yankees led the Detroit Tigers by eight games, while in the National League, the Brooklyn Dodgers were six games ahead of the St. Louis Cardinals. Both batting leaders were surprises. Second baseman Joe Gordon of the Yankees, best known for his fielding prowess and home-run power who had never batted higher than .284 in four previous major league seasons, was leading the American League with a .380 average, three points higher than his Boston Red Sox counterpart and future Hall of Famer Bobby Doerr. Leading the National League was catcher Babe Phelps of the Pittsburgh Pirates, who, in what would be the last of eleven big league seasons, was hitting .373, thirty points better than Dodger outfielder Pete Reiser. Phelps's average, like Doerr's, would soon drop precipitously.

Perhaps the biggest surprise, though, was Joe DiMaggio's protracted slump. By June 6, when Gordon's average had climbed to .391, DiMaggio, who had hit .357 in 1941, was batting .266, forty-two points lower than his younger brother, Dominic, and sixty-one points below Ted Williams, who was at .327 and leading the American League with fifteen home runs and fifty-five runs batted in. No one could ascribe Gordon and Phelps's averages to wartime pitching, Because, apart from Bob Feller and Hugh Mulcahy, every starting pitcher in 1941 was still pitching during baseball's first wartime year. Joe DiMaggio, still the target of occasional boos, particularly at Yankee Stadium, could attest to the still-high quality of big league pitching in 1942.

Baseball fans woke up on June 1 to the biggest surprise development of the season when they read that Red Sox first baseman Jimmy Foxx had been sold to the Chicago Cubs for $10,000 ($140,000 in 2012). In his eighteenth big league season and with a career batting average of .332, the thirty-four-year-old Foxx was one of baseball's premier sluggers, who had driven in more than one hundred runs thirteen years in a row and who on June 16, 1938, set a major league record when he was walked six times in one game. That year, Foxx was named the American League's Most Valuable Player for the third time after he batted .349, hit 50 home runs, and drove in 175 runs. But he had hit only nineteen home runs in 1941, his lowest total in thirteen years, and was batting only .274 after having led the American League in batting twice and in home runs four times, including hitting fifty-eight in 1932, only two fewer than Babe Ruth's record of sixty, set in 1927. Though Foxx, known as "Double-X," had still managed to hit .300 in 1941, it was evident that the Red Sox had planned to turn twenty-five-year-old Ulysses (Tony) Lupien of nearby Chelmsford, Massachusetts, who had joined the team in 1940 after captaining the baseball team at Harvard, into their future first baseman. Still, Foxx accepted a contract that slashed his salary in half, from $20,000 to around $10,000 for the 1942 season, not uncommon at the time but utterly impossible today. Apparently, at the insistence of Red Sox owner Tom Yawkey, Lupien had started the season at first base, only to be replaced by Foxx because of his weak hitting. However, Lupien had regained the position again after Foxx fractured a rib a week before he was traded. As it developed, Lupien was no Jimmy Foxx. He finished the 1942 season with a .281 average but with only three home runs. After batting .255 and hitting only four home runs during 1943, Lupien was traded to the Philadelphia Phillies following the end of that season. Three years later, he was gone from the major leagues, with a six-year career average of .268 and eighteen home runs, fewer than Foxx was to hit in thirteen of his twenty big league seasons, which would end in 1945 with a .325 career batting average and 534 home runs, second at the time to Ruth and more than enough to get him elected to the National Baseball Hall of Fame. More than a few of Foxx's home runs were titanic blasts, including one that landed in the third deck of the left-field stands at Yankee Stadium, which was estimated to have traveled almost five hundred feet. "He was so strong that he had muscles in his hair," Lefty Gomez, the Yankee pitcher who yielded that home run, once said.

In truth, Foxx was definitely on his last baseball legs when Yawkey sold him to the Cubs after he had cleared waivers in the American League, meaning no team was interested in signing him, even at $10,000 a year. Yawkey's judgment was borne out when Foxx, in seventy games for the Cubs in 1942, mainly as a pinch hitter, batted .205.

After sitting out the 1943 season, Foxx appeared in fifteen games for the Cubs in 1944 and had only one hit in twenty times at bat for a .100 batting average. His next and last major league season in 1945 was spent with the Philadelphia Phillies, where, appearing in eighty-nine games, the thirty-seven-year-old Foxx batted .268 and hit his final seven home runs. Foxx, who had pitched briefly in the minors, also appeared as a reliever for the Cubs in nine games, posting a creditable 1.22 earned-run average.

Later, Foxx spent two years as a minor league manager, managed the Fort Wayne Daisies in the All-American Girls Baseball League, and was the head baseball coach at the University of Miami. Tom Hanks' portrayal of a manager in the women's league in the film *A League of Their Own* was largely based on Foxx, including the former slugger's purported propensity for alcohol, which some believed affected his play during his last few years in the big leagues.

❧ ❧

On June 3, as the Battle of Midway was winding down, Mel Ott, in his first year as player-manager of the New York Giants and his seventeenth with the team, set a new National League record when he drove in run number 1,583. Setting an excellent example for his players, the thirty-three-year-old Ott, who came up to the Giants when he was sixteen years old, was on his way to leading the league with 30 home runs, with 118 runs, and with 109 walks, while also batting .295. The five-foot nine-inch 170-pound Ott, one of the most popular players ever to play for the Giants, would lead the National League in home runs six times, despite his small stature and a quirky habit of lifting his right leg as he swung (Ott was a left-handed batter). He would finish his twenty-two-year Hall of Fame career in 1947 with a .304 career batting average and 511 home runs, while also serving as an outstanding outfielder.

A perennial All-Star, Ott was among four Giants named to the team again by National League managers. It wasn't until 1947 that fans were permitted to vote for All-Star teams, although they lost that right for twelve years in 1957 when Cincinnati fans stuffed ballot boxes, voting for Reds' players for every position except the first baseman (first baseman George Crowe must not have taken kindly to the vote) when only Frank Robinson deserved to start. The Dodgers had the most players named, seven, including six position players, but not first baseman Dolph Camilli, the league's Most Valuable Player in 1941 and who was leading the league in home runs when the selections were announced. Five Cardinals were picked, including the Cooper brothers: "pitching battery" Mort Cooper and his younger brother and catcher Walter Cooper. By June 25, when the All-Star team was announced, Mort Cooper had a 10–1 record with six shutouts, with all his victories coming in complete games. Going the distance was hardly rare at the time, as it is today, because most winning pitchers pitched all nine innings and often even more when games went into extra innings. Most big league teams had one primary relief pitcher who was usually only called upon when a starter began to get hit hard and not to preserve his arm, as is the case today.

Nine members of the New York Yankees were named to the American League All-Star team, including second baseman Gordon, the league's leading hitter; Joe DiMaggio; shortstop Phil Rizzuto; catcher Bill Dickey; and, inexplicably, his backup, Buddy Rosar, who was hitting .205. DiMaggio's younger brother, Dominic, whose batting average was forty points higher, also was picked; the oldest of the three DiMaggio brothers playing in the major leagues, Vince, an outfielder for the Pittsburgh Pirates, was not. Other Red Sox chosen were Ted Williams, Bobby Doerr, and pitcher Ted Hughson. War or no war, the two All-Star teams were almost identical to those picked during the peacetime season of 1941, indicating again that draft boards and the armed forces were being extremely generous to major league baseball, if indeed not showing favoritism toward the two big leagues.

One of those favored to a considerable degree by the military was Williams, and he heard about it from Fenway Park fans, especially when they got the impression that he was either not hustling or sulking. On July 1, Red Sox playing manager Joe Cronin fined Williams $250 for not hustling during a game against Washington on June 30 in Boston when he seemed to be going through the motions during two at bats and sulking, apparently after spectators along the left-field line and in the bleachers had booed him. "Williams said they can't boo him," said an irate Cronin, who removed Williams from the game after the fifth inning for his lackadaisical play. "Well, it's the privilege of fans who pay their way in to boo any one they think is not doing his best. If Williams wants to play for the Red Sox, he's going to hustle or he won't be in there."

After arriving at Fenway Park the following day, a somewhat contrite Williams told reporters, "I know it was all my fault. Joe did the right thing in taking me out of the game. I'm just childish enough and thick-headed enough and screwy enough to let those wolves in left field get under my skin. What I should do is bring out twenty-five pounds of hamburger and invite them down to enjoy it." It was hardly an apology to the fans in left field or any other part of Fenway, and his remarks about "those wolves in left field" would only exacerbate his fragile relationship with them, especially during a year when the United States was at war and Williams was being very well paid to play baseball and to stay at first-class hotels.

Eventually, Williams hit on a way to at least partially cope with booing fans. Asked by this writer years later whether Williams had given him any tips on playing left field when he joined the Red Sox in 1961 and eventually replaced Williams in the outfield, Hall of Famer Carl Yastrzemski laughed and said, "Yeah. He told me to put cotton in my ears which he said he eventually did . . . and I did. After all, following Ted Williams in left field wasn't easy." Seven days after being reprimanded and fined by Cronin, Williams did something that was even more surprising than reacting to critical fans when he bunted successfully in the eleventh inning of a game against Detroit at Fenway Park. The bunt, which Williams laid down on his own and which evoked a roar from the crowd, advanced fellow outfielder Pete Fox to second, with Fox eventually scoring the winning run on a sacrifice fly by Cronin. It would be four more years before Williams would bunt again, and for the last time, against the St. Louis Cardinals during the 1946 World Series, when he beat out the bunt down the third-base line while the Cardinals were in the "Boudreau shift." "I got four hits that day, which was very unusual, and we won the game," recalled Joe Garagiola, the Cardinals catcher that day, "but the next day the headlines in the Boston papers were all about Williams bunting." In what would be his only World Series, Williams managed only four other singles to go with his successful bunt in twenty-five times at bat for a .200 average.

Another tempestuous big leaguer, Dodger manager Leo Durocher, also was fined the same week as Williams. In Durocher's case, he was fined $50—a piddling amount even in 1942—and suspended for three days by National League President Ford Frick for throwing a towel on the field before a doubleheader with the Cincinnati Reds at Ebbets Field after an argument with home-plate umpire Tom Dunn. Fines were hardly new to Durocher, who also was thrown out of about a half dozen games in 1942.

❧ ❧

Because of the ban on night games in New York, Ott's Giants, like their archrival Brooklyn Dodgers, would instead play five twilight games that would start between 6:00 and 7:00 p.m. but would have to end an hour after sunset, usually around 9:30 p.m., under an agreement with the army. That usually meant that the lights could be turned on for about an hour. The rule would result in considerable confusion and, not surprisingly, some teams' stalling while leading or trailing, because scores would revert to the end of the previous inning when the lights had to be turned off—and no exceptions were made. Even though the annual All-Star Game was always played in the afternoon, the 1942 game on July 6 was rescheduled to start at twilight—in this case, 6:30 p.m., at the Polo Grounds, ostensibly so more defense-plant workers could get to see the game, which raised $95,000 (almost $1 million by 2012's monetary standards) for the so-called armed forces "Bat and Ball Fund." This was also the time when a citywide blackout was scheduled to begin. What made it even more unfortunate was that the start of game was delayed by rain for fifty-three minutes, but less than ten minutes after that, American League All-Stars had won, 3–1, and the lights went out all over the city, including at the Polo Grounds. For twenty minutes, players sat in darkened dugouts and fans remained in the stands, with the only signs of light coming from the lighting of cigarettes in an era when smoking was not only tolerated but, in many circles, including the movies, considered fashionable. Strangely, Yankee manager Joe McCarthy used his starting lineup for all nine innings and only used two pitchers. The other fifteen American League All-Stars might as well have stayed home. By contrast, Leo Durocher, the National League skipper, used almost all his position players and three pitchers. McCarthy's strategy, though not appreciated by spectators hopeful of seeing other members of the American League squad, still was successful as the American League won, 3–1.

By winning, the American League won the right to play in a second All-Star Game the following night in Cleveland against an all-star team made up primarily of former big leaguers then in the service. As expected, the game was one-sided, with the American League All-Stars winning, 5–0, with the team's three pitchers yielding only four hits to players, who, apart from starting pitcher Bob Feller, would not have made either major league All-Star team in 1942. Feller, the major attraction, mainly because of his stardom as a Cleveland pitcher, lasted only one and two-thirds innings, during which he gave up three runs and four hits in the game played before a crowd of sixty-two thousand that raised $100,000 for the servicemen's Bat and Ball Fund.

Until he went aboard the battleship *Alabama* and saw action in the Pacific, Feller seemed to be pitching as much while he was in the navy as when he was with the Indians. One of his appearances was at the Polo Grounds on Sunday, June 14, three weeks before the first All-Star Game, during a fund-raising entertainment gala for "Army and Navy Relief" that drew more than twelve thousand spectators while competing with a Yankee game across the Harlem River. In a five-inning game between Feller's Norfolk Naval Training Station team and an army all-star squad, for which former Philadelphia Phillie Hugh Mulcahy did the pitching, Feller shut out the soldiers while striking out seven and giving up only three hits as the sailors won, 4–0. Stars from a variety of other sports and from the entertainment world also performed during the fund-raiser. Heavyweight champion and member of the U.S. Army Joe Louis boxed four rounds with his former sparring partner, George Nicholson; world record-holder Cornelius Warmerdam, the first man to pole vault over fifteen feet, soared fourteen feet eight inches over the bar before missing at fifteen feet two inches; tennis stars Alice Marble and Don Budge lost a one-set tennis match to two relatively unknown players; Ed (Porky) Oliver, a member of the Professional Golf Association tour, won a golf pitching contest; and the "South" beat the "North," 5–1, in the somewhat obscure—at the time—game of lacrosse, which most of the spectators had never seen before and knew nothing about. As if that weren't enough, dancer Ray Bolger did a boxing pantomime routine in which he feigned knocking himself out, and a team of chorus girls from the Broadway show *By Jupiter* defeated a group of Conover models in a relay race. Old-timers, who had seen nothing but baseball and football games and an occasional boxing match at the old ballpark, no doubt found some of what they were seeing hard to believe, while aware that they were doing so for a good cause.

If the two All-Star Games ran relatively long because of frequent player changes, a game between the Yankees and Tigers a week later at Yankee Stadium turned out to be the fastest of the 1942 season. With Hank Borowy, one of two former Fordham University pitchers on the staff—Johnny Murphy being the other—allowing only two singles, the Yankees beat Detroit, 3–0, in a game that was over in one hour and twenty-four minutes, about an hour faster than most big league games played in the 21st century. But then a game that exceeded two hours was a rarity in the 1940s, while practically no major league games were finishing in fewer than two hours by the 1970s.

❧ ❧

Although twilight baseball leagues were common throughout the country among amateur players who had to work during the day, they became a novelty in the major leagues in 1942. Such games, which usually started between 6:30 and 8:00 p.m., were scheduled for two reasons: because of a ban on night games at the Polo Grounds and Ebbets Field in New York and in the hope of drawing more daytime "defense workers" at some other big league ballparks.

The few twilight games played in New York drew only slightly more spectators than weekday afternoon games. An exception was a benefit game for the Army Emergency Relief Fund on August 3 between the Giants and Dodgers, which drew a record crowd of almost fifty-eight thousand at the Polo Grounds. As the deadline approached, the Giants were trailing, 7–4, in the last half of the ninth inning with two men on base and no outs when the home-plate umpire called the game because the 9:30 deadline had arrived. Thus the score reverted to the last of the eighth inning, with Brooklyn winning, 7–4. Most Giants' fans went wild, furious that the home team would not get a chance to win the game after having led by three runs. After the game, Giants owner Horace Stoneham announced that following another twilight game the next evening, the rest of the planned twilight games at the Polo Grounds would be shifted to the afternoon, because "playing against the clock is too tough a proposition."

The following night it was the Dodgers turn to lament twilight games. With the score tied, 1–1, in the top of the tenth inning, Pee Wee Reese hit an inside-the-park home run into the spacious Polo Grounds outfield to give the Dodgers a 5–1 lead. However, those four runs were nullified when, with the Giants at bat in the bottom of the tenth, time ran out an hour after sunset, and the game was called with the score reverting to what it was after nine innings. This time, it was the Dodger fans who erupted with boos.

In addition to the ban on late-night baseball at two of the three New York ballparks, weather also became a wartime casualty, or at least talking on the radio or writing in a newspaper about the weather at a sports event did. Under a gentlemen's agreement of sorts, sports announcers were not permitted to discuss the weather, even if it was having a bearing on a sports event, such as a snowstorm during a football game or a rain delay. The military's theory was that talking about the weather, especially on the radio, could be of aid to the enemy, in this case, the Germans or Japanese. Red Barber, who became the Brooklyn Dodgers radio announcer in 1939 but also broadcast college and professional football games, recalled how, during a radio broadcast of a National Football League Championship Game between the Chicago Bears and the New York Giants at Wrigley Field in Chicago exactly two weeks after Pearl Harbor, he mentioned that the Giants' center was using a towel, whereupon the broadcast was interrupted, after which Barber received a phone call instructing him not to mention anything relating to weather. In that particular instance, Barber recalled, the teams were playing in mud, leading an army officer monitoring the broadcast to assume that it was raining and that listeners, including perhaps spies and saboteurs, would also assume the same. Later, the broadcast was interrupted again after Barber described how one of the teams "had an advantage" because they were driving towards the goal line. That, of course, implied that the team had the wind at its back. "The same man called me back and said I was referring to the wind, although I never mentioned the wind," Barber said. "But that's how sensitive the military was about the weather."

Even sportswriters, writing about a game that would appear in newspapers the following day, did not usually mention the weather even though it might well have changed by the time when the papers came out. If a game was interrupted by rain, a writer would note that it was interrupted but not mention the rain. And if a game was postponed because of rain, writers merely wrote that the game was not played and would be made up at a future date or use such vague term as "the game was postponed because of weather" or the teams "were idled," as a *New York Journal-American* sportswriter wrote when a Giants game was postponed because of rain in mid-July 1942. Writers also were forbidden to mention weather forecasts for upcoming games.

Newspapers also frequently called upon citizens to obey dimout or blackout regulations. For example, the *New York Times* ran periodic notices on the front page informing readers that all windows and doors had to be shaded, because light "contributes to the glow in the night sky over the city that has been found to silhouette ships at sea." Along that line, the *Times* reminded readers of the army's slogan relating to dimout regulations: "If in doubt, put it out." Most New Yorkers, like most people elsewhere along the East and West coasts, abided by the dimout regulations.

By the All-Star break, Ted Williams had taken the batting lead in the American League, which would seesaw back and forth between him and Joe Gordon for the rest of July, while Pete Reiser held on to the lead in the National League. The twenty-three-year-old Reiser, in his third season with the Dodgers, had led the National League in batting in 1941 with a .343 batting average and was regarded as probably the best young player in the game, but his bravado in the outfield would ultimately shorten his career. On July 19 in a game against the Dodgers at Sportsman's Park in his hometown of St. Louis, Reiser crashed into the center-field fence after catching, but then dropping, a drive by the Cardinals' Enos Slaughter and had to be carried off the field with a concussion and hospitalized overnight. It was not the first, nor would it be the last, time that the talented young Dodger would collide with an unpadded outfield fence, usually made of concrete or bricks, as is the case at Wrigley Field in Chicago. Hard outfield walls, coupled with the absence of "warning tracks" in front of outfield walls, dirt or rubberized surfaces that are now commonplace in all big league ballparks, explained why most outfielders shied away from pursuing balls they knew were going to hit the wall.

❧ ❧

By the 1980s, major league players were not only fraternizing before and after games but during games and could often be seen talking and laughing with one another on the base paths. Not so in the forties, when there were only sixteen teams, compared with thirty by the beginning of the 20th century, and competition for roster positions was fierce. Much as they did in the twenties and thirties, players often slid high and hard into second base, and pitchers were far more inclined to brush back hitters, particularly Dodger pitchers, who were ordered to do so by the former St. Louis Cardinals Gas House Gang shortstop Durocher. In a game between the Dodgers and Cubs at Wrigley Field on July 14, six batters had to hit the dirt to avoid being hit by pitches. The "bean ball war" began after Leo Durocher went out to the mound to talk to Dodger pitcher Kirby Higbe following back-to-back home runs by Cubs outfielder Lou Novikoff and Jimmy Foxx in the fourth inning. After Durocher had returned to the Dodger dugout, Higbe's next pitch sailed behind the back of Cub slugger Bill Nicholson. In the next inning, in obvious retaliation for Higbe's brush-back pitch, Cub pitcher Hiram Bithorn knocked down Higbe with a pitch thrown directly at him and later sent Joe Medwick to the ground with a high and inside fastball. An enraged Durocher unleashed a torrent of invective at Bithorn, after which Birthorn, on leaving the mound, fired a baseball at Durocher in the Dodger dugout, which was deflected by Dodger catcher Mickey Owen. Cubs relief pitcher Frank Erickson picked up where Bithorn left off when he knocked down Dodger second baseman Billy Herman twice and brushed him back a third time in the sixth inning. That only inspired the former Cub second baseman and future Hall of Famer, who paid back Erickson with a home run into the left-field bleachers that gave the Dodgers a 9–3 lead and, eventually, a 10–6 victory. Despite the victory, the Dodgers lost a half game in the standings after the Cardinals swept a doubleheader that same day, which left Brooklyn seven and a half games in front of St. Louis.

❦ ❦

Occasionally, some of the strong service teams played one another before major or minor league games. For instance, the

Norfolk Naval Training Center team played several games at Yankee Stadium and at Municipal Stadium in Cleveland, where Norfolk's star pitcher, Bob Feller, had pitched for the Indians. On July 25 at Ruppert Stadium in Newark, home of the Yankees perennially powerful Triple-A Newark Bears, Feller struck out thirteen batters in six innings in a game between the Norfolk navy team and the a team from the Quantico marine base in Virginia. Feller was the main draw in a doubleheader that also included a game between the Bears, who included six future major leaguers, and the Toronto Maple Leafs, which drew a crowd of sixteen thousand, larger than the average big league contest in 1942. Adding to the attraction was the appearance of Babe Ruth and Dodger President Larry MacPhail as umpires for the game between the service teams. As at many such events, the proceeds went to a service-related fund, in this case, the Navy Relief Society and the American Red Cross. Feller, to his credit, eventually told his superiors at Norfolk that he had joined the navy not to play baseball but to fight the Germans or the Japanese. At his request, he underwent gunnery training and in September 1942 went aboard the battleship *Alabama* as a chief petty officer in charge of a gun crew and saw considerable action in the Pacific. Despite four years in the navy, Feller was as good as, if not better than, ever when he rejoined the Indians after the war. On April 30 at Yankee Stadium, Feller threw his second no-hitter—he would pitch one more in July—and went on to win twenty-six games to tie Hal Newhouser of the Tigers for the American League lead. He also led the league in strikeouts with 348, one fewer than the major league record at that time, and in complete games with thirty-six, while finishing third with a 2.18 earned-run average—all of that after serving four years in the navy, most of it aboard the *Alabama* in the Pacific.

Although big league salaries remained about the same as the previous year, there was a wide disparity between what Joe DiMaggio and Ted Williams made and how much journeymen and rookies earned. Nothing was more indicative of how little some players made than a mid-season decision by twenty-eight-year-old catcher Buddy Rosar, in his fourth year as a backup to Yankees Hall of Fame catcher Bill Dickey, to leave the Yankees abruptly and without permission, while Dickey was sidelined with an injury, on July 18 to take a test to become a policeman in his hometown of Buffalo, New York. Absent without leave for three days, Rosar forced the Yankees to sign thirty-five-year-old catcher Rollie Hemsley, who had recently been released by the Cincinnati Reds. Catching both games of a doubleheader in Cleveland the next day, Hemsley left the Indians management wondering why it had waived him out of the league after four years when he hit safely five times. Rosar, who was earning about $10,000, around $5,000 over the approximate minimum big league salary, rejoined the Yankees in Cleveland three days later after the club announced he would be fined $250.

"This is a sane desire for protection," Rosar said in explaining his decision to apply for a job as a Buffalo cop. "Baseball is my meat and drink right now, but no one can say when I'll go out there and meet with an accident that might end my baseball days."

Still, most people thought his action was strange, especially since he was playing for baseball's world champions. Almost needless to say, most Buffalo policemen would have been more than glad to change jobs with Rosar, as most likely would most American men in the armed forces. Overshadowing Rosar's brief defection was DiMaggio's latest hitting streak, which reached eighteen on July 21 as the Yankees beat the Indians, 8–3, in a night game in Cleveland, where his remarkable fifty-six-game streak had ended a year earlier, thanks to two great defensive plays by Indians third baseman Ken Keltner. However, the latest streak was in jeopardy when DiMaggio came up to bat for the last time in the ninth inning without a hit. But the Yankee Clipper came through, ripping a single to drive home the third run of the inning. As had his momentous streak of a year earlier, this one ended in Cleveland when DiMaggio failed to get a hit in three official times at bat, flying out three times, walking once, and being hit by a pitch. Nevertheless, the Yankees won their eleventh game in a row when they beat the Indians, 5–1, to extend their lead over the Red Sox to twelve games, despite four more hits by Hemsley, who was cheered loudly by his former fans, many of them wondering why the Indians ever let him get away at the end of the 1941 season.

By the end of July, the Yankees had extended their American League lead to thirteen games over the Red Sox, while in the National League the Cardinals were eight and a half games behind the Dodgers. Reiser led the National League in batting with a .353 average, followed by lumbering veteran catcher Ernie Lombardi of the Boston Braves at .338, while Ted Williams's .351 was tops in the American League, trailed by Yankee second baseman Joe Gordon, who was hitting .339. Williams also led both leagues in home runs, with twenty-three, and runs batted in, with ninety-eight. Though still being platooned in left field with journeyman Coker Triplett, Stan Musial, with an average of .320, was now fourth in batting in the National League, behind former Cardinal outfielder Joe Medwick and ahead of teammate Enos Slaughter. Besides his batting talents, Musial also was dazzling fans with his speed on the bases and in the outfield, where he often ran down and caught balls that most other outfielders could not reach.

If the big leagues were much like they were in 1941, both in personnel and quality of play, life away from major league ballparks was not. Merchant ships were still being sunk by German U-boats at an alarming rate along the East Coast, most of the country was now confronted with a meat shortage, German forces were advancing in Russia, and the Japanese controlled much of the Aleutian Islands. The Japanese also were threatening U.S. bases in Port Moresby and New Guinea in the Southwestern Pacific, which they hoped to use as bases from which to attack Australia and, eventually, India. Meanwhile, New York City held its first surprise citywide air-raid drill and blackout starting at 9:50 p.m. on July 31 and ending twenty-five minutes later. Sirens throughout the city's five boroughs sounded the alert, halting all mass transit service, including the city's vast subway network, and enveloping the city in a surreal darkness. Mayor La Guardia, who toured parts of the city with army officials, pronounced the blackout "an excellent performance." Only fifteen arrests were made during the blackout, mostly of people who refused to comply with orders to turn off their lights. Among those arrested was sixty-two-year-old Robert Howard, who was charged with disorderly conduct for dancing in the street while waving a lighted flashlight at the corner of Ninth Avenue and Fifty-second Street in Manhattan. Precisely what Howard was celebrating was not determined, but given the way things were going for the United States, there was little to celebrate eight months into World War II.

6

PISTOL PETE AND LEO THE LIP

THE TWO TEAMS at the top of the National League standings during the first four months of the 1942 season could hardly have been more different. The Brooklyn Dodgers, the defending league champions, who had led since late April, were, apart from center fielder Pete Reiser and rookie pitcher Ed Head, a veteran team, all of whom had been obtained in trades except for shortstop Pee Wee Reese who had been bought from Louisville of the Southern Association. Catcher Mickey Owen and left fielder Joe Medwick had previously played for the Cardinals, first baseman Dolph Camilli for the Cubs and Phillies, second baseman Billy Herman for the Cubs, third baseman Arky Vaughan for the Pirates, and right fielder Dixie Walker for the Yankees, White Sox, and Tigers. Except for Head, all the starting pitchers had been with at least two other teams, including starters Whitlow Wyatt, Curt Davis, Kirby Higbe, and Larry French. And this was at a time when, for the most part, lineups remained constant over a period of years, primarily because players were bound to teams, because it was well before the free-agency era when players began to move from team to team, sometimes as many as a dozen times.

Apart from third baseman Cookie Lavagetto, the team was intact from the 1941 season and, if anything, had been strengthened with the addition of Vaughan and pitcher French, who would win fifteen games. French's acquisition had bolstered an outstanding pitching staff headed by Higbe and Wyatt, who had tied for the league lead in victories in 1941 with twenty-two. Wyatt also had led in shutouts with seven. By contrast, every one of the Cardinals, except for pitcher Harry Gumbert, had never played for another major league team and had come up through the team's farm system. Of the eight starting position players, only one, second baseman Jimmy Brown, was over thirty, while, except for Reiser, Reese, and Owen, all the Dodger regulars were at least thirty years old, as were pitchers Wyatt, Davis, and French. Of the Cardinal starting pitchers, only Gumbert, at thirty-two, was over thirty.

None of that mattered to Dodger fans, among the most loyal, if not *the* most loyal, in baseball, despite the Dodgers having won only three pennants: in 1916, 1920, and 1941 (but no World Series), while Charles Ebbets was the owner and Wilbert Robinson the manager. They were also the most ardent and boisterous, led by Hilda Chester, a heavyset middle-aged woman and a Dodger fan since the days when the team was the Robins, who sat in the center-field bleachers banging on a frying pan, ringing a cowbell, and exhorting the Dodgers with her piercing voice, which could be heard throughout the ballpark. "There could be thirty thousand people there yelling at once, but Hilda was the one you'd hear," Pete Reiser once said. Chester was so beloved that after she suffered a heart attack in 1941, Leo Durocher and several Dodger players visited her in the hospital, where Durocher, no sentimentalist, gave Chester a lifetime pass in the grandstand. She never used it, though, because she preferred sitting with her friends in the bleachers, where, after a visiting player had made an out, she often would let loose with her trademark chant, "Eat your heart out, you bum!" Then there was the Dodgers "Symphony," (pronounced sim-phoney), an assemblage of a half dozen musicians who would traipse through the stands, serenading both the team and its rabid fans and playing "Three Blind Mice" when the umpires came out before a game at a time when only three umpires worked big league games except during the World Series.

Cozy as it was, Ebbets Field, named for the team's second owner, Charlie Ebbets, who had it built in 1913, could not have been a more appropriate ballpark for the Dodgers, with a grandstand that was closer to the field than any other major league stadium, and where fans seated in the upper deck could literally look down on their heroes or "Brooklyn Bums," as sports cartoonist Willard Mullin of the *New York World Telegram* and *Sun* referred to a character who was supposed to personify the Dodgers from the late 1930s into the 1950s. Adding to the ballpark's charm was the forty-foot-high concave right-field fence, with its huge scoreboard, clock, and signage, which included a thirty-foot-long, three-foot-high sign for a Brooklyn clothing store under the scoreboard that promised a new suit to any batter able to hit it on the fly. So far as is known, the only batter to do so, on June 6, 1937, was Woody English, a shortstop for the Dodgers, who had been traded to Brooklyn by the Cubs that year. Because the sign was at ground level, outfielders were almost certain to catch fly balls before they could hit the three-foot-high sign. Whether English ever got a free suit is not known, but Carl Furillo, an outstanding right fielder for the Dodgers from 1946 until 1960, was given one by the store owner, Abe Stark, for "protecting" Stark's sign for so many years until the Dodgers moved to Los Angeles in 1958.

Situated snugly in a residential neighborhood, Ebbets Field also possessed the most distinctive and stately entrance in the major leagues, with a twenty-seven-foot-high rotunda, whose Italian-marble interior, chandeliers in the form of twelve baseball-bat arms holding twelve glass-shaped baseballs, and twelve gilded ticket windows gave the ballpark a regal touch.

It's safe to say that the Dodgers were the pride of Brooklyn and symbolized the borough. Indeed, many people throughout the country thought Brooklyn was a city unto itself, as it had been until 1898, when it became New York's fifth borough. Most likely that was because the team was listed in the major league standings as "Brooklyn." Because every other major league team was listed by its city's name when the Dodgers were in Brooklyn, that led many people to assume it was a city, and with more than two million people living there, that belief was understandable. Through thick and thin, and mostly thin during the 1920s and 1930s, Dodger fans remained extremely loyal and devoted to the team. Some of them remembered the team when its nickname was "Robins," in honor of Wilbert Robinson, who was the manager from 1914 through 1931 when it reverted to Dodgers, as it had been from 1911 to 1913 after having been the Brooklyn Superbas and, before that, the Brooklyn Bridegrooms from its founding in 1890 until 1898. To many fans, the team was sort of an extension of their families—thus the close bond. And the players reciprocated that loyalty and devotion, with many of them lining up along the first-base railing not only to sign autographs but to chat with fans, some of whom could be neighbors they recognized. Practically all the players lived in Brooklyn and could be spotted in stores, restaurants, bars, and walking to and from Ebbets Field. Writer Stanley Englebardt, who grew up in Brooklyn, recollected how second baseman Eddie Stanky, who played for the Dodgers from 1944 through 1947, often would come to his family's apartment to play cards with Englebardt's father and a few other family friends, including Milt Shulman. "My father met Eddie through Milt Shulman, a big Dodger fan, who let Eddie and his wife share the Shulmans' apartment during the season," Englebardt, a longtime writer for *Reader's Digest,* recalled in October 2011. "Remember, the players weren't making much money then, and in Brooklyn they were very close, even friendly, with the fans."

Through the dark days of the 1920s and 1930s, some writers called the Dodgers "the daffiness boys." That was mainly because of gaffes in the field and not due to the players themselves, except for Babe Herman, an outfielder and the team's best hitter of that era, and Casey Stengel, who played for the Dodgers from 1912 through 1917 and managed the team from 1934 through 1936. The colorful Stengel, who had his greatest success as a manager with the Yankees from 1946 through 1960, ingratiated himself with the fans because of his flamboyant umpire baiting, his mispronunciation of some of his own players' names, and his malapropisms in public and in the press. Some of his antics became legendary, such as when, after arguing with an umpire at Ebbets Field, he took off his hat and a bird flew out, drawing a roar from the crowd. Herman also became a fan and sportswriter favorite because of his hitting—during a thirteen-year career he batted .324—and his unpredictable behavior on the field, such as when he slid into third base when it was already occupied and when a fly ball hit him on the head. Then there was the time he took a cigar out of his jacket pocket, and a sportswriter asked if he needed a light. "No thanks, it's already lit," Herman replied, whereupon he put the cigar in his mouth and began to puff away.

No one on the 1942 Dodgers came close to Stengel or Herman in flaky behavior. For the most part they were very businesslike on the field. For color you had to turn to the fiery Durocher and the team's volatile president, Larry MacPhail, who was forever firing Durocher (usually when he was drunk, which was often) and then rehiring him the next day or forgetting that he had fired him during what became an extremely symbiotic relationship. Their main concerns off the field were pitchers Kirby Higbe and ace reliever Hugh Casey, both of whom liked to drink a lot, gamble, and chase women. In his book *Bums,* Peter Golenbock quotes first baseman Howie Schultz, who roomed with Higbe for a while, as saying that when the Dodgers arrived in a city for a series, Higbe would immediately order two bacon, lettuce, and tomato sandwiches and two shots of Southern Comfort. "That was his arrival snack all the time," Schultz told Golenbock. Schultz also recalled that Higbe occasionally asked him if he snored, whereupon Schultz would say, "You better ask someone else." That was because, as Schultz said, "I didn't see much of old Hig."

If Higbe liked to drink a lot, the big burly Casey liked to drink even more. Carl Furillo, who joined the Dodgers in 1946 and became an outstanding right fielder, told Golenbock about one of Casey's quaint travel habits when the Dodgers went on the road: "A normal guy would have a little handbag and a toothbrush or maybe a shirt or something. Not him. He'd have two quarts of whiskey in it."

It wasn't Casey's drinking as much as it was Ernest Hemingway's that led to a memorable impromptu boxing match at the writer's home in March 1942, when the Dodgers did their spring training in Havana for the second year in a row. Hemingway got to know Durocher and many of the players while attending their practices and preseason games in Havana and took them skeet-shooting and rolled dice with them at legal casinos in pre-Castro Cuba. Occasionally, Hemingway would also invite the players to his home outside Havana. One night that March, after a night of heavy drinking, Hemingway, who fashioned himself a good boxer, challenged a reluctant Casey to box with him, "just to spar and fool around a little bit," as Billy Herman was to recall. "Papa," as Hemingway was called, picked the wrong Dodger to spar with. Casey could be friendly one minute and moody the next, but he was good with his fists and flattened more than a few barflies during barroom arguments, and in one instance he threw a man through a plate-glass window at a Brooklyn saloon. Not that any of that would have mattered to the cocky Hemingway.

As Casey was putting on a pair of boxing gloves, Hemingway hauled off and hit the 210-pound Casey, sending him crashing onto a tray filled with glasses and ice and into a book stand. After getting up, Casey finished putting on the gloves and, without saying a word, began belting Hemingway, knocking him down several times. "Hemingway would no sooner get up than Hugh would knock him down again," Herman said. "Finally he got up this one time, made a feint with his left hand, and kicked Casey in the balls."

At that point, the Dodgers figured they had had enough of Hemingway's hospitality and headed back to their hotel. The next day, an embarrassed Hemingway came to the ballpark and went around apologizing to everyone, especially Casey. "I don't know what got into me," he said, according to Herman. "But I know exactly what got into him. About a quart, that's what." During the remainder of spring training, Durocher, a nocturnal creature of the first order himself, made sure that none of the Dodgers had dinner and drinks any more at Papa Hemingway's.

Hemingway had a knack of trying to pick fights with the wrong people. Once when retired heavyweight champion Gene Tunney was visiting Hemingway at his stateside home in Key West, Florida, Tunney began to demonstrate a boxing maneuver when Hemingway threw a punch at Tunney that hit him in the chest. Without a word, Tunney responded with a right cross that deliberately missed Hemingway's jaw by about three inches. "If you ever try to do that again, next time I won't miss," a furious Tunney said. Despite the incident the two men remained friends, and Hemingway never tossed a punch at the former champion again.

Ironically, both Hemingway and Casey ended their lives the same way—by shooting themselves. Casey killed himself in 1951, two years after he had retired as a Dodger, while talking to his estranged wife on the telephone from an Atlanta hotel room, apparently because his wife had refused to reconcile with him. He was only thirty-seven years old. Hemingway killed himself ten years later, in 1961, when he was sixty-three and reportedly suffering from depression.

⚜ ⚜

For all of his brilliance as a baseball man, MacPhail could spin out of control when he had had too much to drink, which was often. The main target of his drunken fury was Durocher, whose main vices were gambling, hanging around with shady characters, and pursuing women, even when he was married to movie actress Laraine Day. Growing up in a tough neighborhood in West Springfield, Massachusetts, Durocher became a gambler and pool hustler in his teens while tending to develop relationships with other pool hustlers, card sharks, and racketeers. Joining the powerful New York Yankees in 1928 as the team's starting shortstop—he turned out to be the best in the American League—Durocher alienated teammates with his cockiness and his flamboyant clothes, despite his fierce competiveness as a player. Some teammates also suspected Durocher of stealing money from their clothes in the locker room. Babe Ruth, who liked just about everyone, disliked Durocher intensely and suspected him of stealing his valuable wristwatch and told him so. Durocher in turn called Ruth a baboon and implied to Yankee teammates that the Babe was African American. In 1938, the year Durocher was traded to the Dodgers by the Cardinals and Ruth had become the Dodgers' first-base coach, Durocher loudly suggested in the clubhouse that Ruth did not know the team's signs. As a furious Ruth began to move toward him, Durocher shoved him hard, knocking Ruth into a locker. Fortunately for Durocher, Dodger players and coaches had to separate the two before Ruth had a chance to respond. Most of the Dodgers thought that Ruth, bigger and stronger, could have killed Durocher, which, some felt, would not have been a bad idea. Indeed, some of the Dodgers preferred having let Ruth go at Durocher. Most player fights are broken up quickly, especially when they're among teammates, and many of the players knew that Durocher was aware of that and that it was why he struck first. When Durocher became manager the next year, there was no way Ruth was going to return to the Dodgers as a coach. As it turned out, it was Ruth's last job in baseball. The Yankees, never known for sentiment, had never offered him one, and never would, despite his immense popularity with Yankee fans and his enormous contributions during his fifteen glorious years with the team. But then this was the same organization that also never offered jobs to Joe DiMaggio or Mickey Mantle, their two biggest stars after Ruth and Lou Gehrig, and fired another one of their best and most popular players, Yogi Berra, sixteen games into the 1975 season.

∞ ∞

A protégé of Branch Rickey, with whom he had gone to law school at the University of Michigan, Larry MacPhail had been recommended for the position of general manager by Rickey when "the Mahatma," as he was called, was the general manager of the Cardinals. After serving as a captain in the army during World War I, MacPhail practiced law and sold real estate and cars before Rickey got him the job as general manager of the Cardinals' Triple-A team in Columbus, which he built into the most successful franchise in the vast Cardinal chain. At Rickey's recommendation, MacPhail was then named general manager of the Cincinnati Reds, where he persuaded a Cincinnati businessman, Powell Crosley, to buy the financially strapped team. While in Cincinnati, MacPhail not only established a winning team but also convinced Crosley to hire Red Barber to broadcast the Reds' games on radio and to install lights in 1935, which made the Reds the first major league team to play night games. But he argued often with Crosley and wore out his welcome in 1937 when, while drunk, he punched Crosley out during an argument. Again, his mentor, Rickey, got MacPhail back on his feet when he recommended that the Dodgers, then on the verge of bankruptcy, hire him as president and general manager. When MacPhail hired Durocher, then thirty-three years old, as the Dodgers' playing manager in 1939, it was evident that it would be a combustible and fractious relationship in light of their fiery personalities and huge egos. And it was, with MacPhail firing Durocher about a half dozen times during the four years they were together, a period marked by angry quarrels, disagreements over personnel, and more than a few fistfights. Erratic as the relationship was, it worked pretty well. With a team largely assembled by MacPhail and skillfully managed by the mercurial Durocher, the Dodgers won their first pennant in twenty-one years in 1941, MacPhail's fourth on the job. By then, he had proven himself anew as both an excellent judge of baseball talent and highly creative. In addition to making Durocher the manager, MacPhail bought a half dozen minor league teams, hired sixteen scouts, and persuaded Red Barber to leave the Reds to become the Dodgers' radio broadcaster. Over a four-year period, MacPhail essentially brought in a brand-new team. Among the players he bought or traded for from 1938 to 1941 were pitchers Whittlow Wyatt, Kirby Higbe, Curt Davis, Larry French, Hugh Casey, and eight position players who would become regulars—first baseman Dolph Camilli; second baseman Billie Herman; third baseman Arky Vaughan; shortstop Pee Wee Reese, the onetime marble champion from Louisville, Kentucky; outfielders Joe Medwick, Dixie Walker, Pete Reiser; and catcher Mickey Owen. In bringing in Barber to broadcast Dodger games, MacPhail defied an agreement of the three New York teams, reached just before MacPhail arrived, to ban radio broadcasts of games on the grounds that such broadcasts hurt attendance. On the basis of his, and Barber's, experience in Cincinnati, he knew that, in fact, broadcasts would help promote a team and increase attendance. And, in Brooklyn, as in Cincinnati, MacPhail was right, as Dodger attendance increased from 650,000 in 1938 to almost a million in 1939, Barber's first year, and the Dodgers outdrew both the Yankees and the Giants. Despite his southern accent, Dodger fans, and other Brooklynites, too, loved Barber for his low-key delivery, his homespun charm, and his distinct expressions—such as the "ducks are on the pond" and the "bases are FOB," for full of Brooklyns, both of which meant the bases were loaded.

MacPhail's main acquisition, in 1938, was Reiser. The nineteen-year-old Reiser, a left-handed hitter who became a switch-hitter during his sixth major league season, was the best prospect in the lot, as Rickey, who discovered him playing amateur ball in St. Louis, knew. Not wanting to lose him for good, Rickey, to whom MacPhail was beholden, asked his protégé if he could sign Reiser and then hide him in the Dodgers farm system for a few years, then trade him back to the Cardinals. That was both illegal and unethical, but that didn't stop MacPhail from signing Reiser for $100 and sending him to Superior, Wisconsin, in the Class-D Northern League. But when Durocher saw Reiser in spring training in 1940, he insisted on keeping him on the roster for opening day, whereupon MacPhail fired him again, after which Leo the Lip responded by punching MacPhail, who then sent Reiser to Elmira, a Dodger Double-A farm team in upstate New York. Once again, MacPhail relented and rehired Durocher, who eventually convinced MacPhail to bring back Reiser, by then tearing up the Eastern League. An immediate sensation while playing third base and then replacing Durocher, still the playing manager, at shortstop when he broke an ankle, Reiser could do it all—hit for power and average, fly around the bases, and, after being converted to an outfielder, run down almost every ball hit in his vicinity, often with reckless abandon. After hitting .293 in fifty-eight games in 1940 while playing short-stop, third base, and the outfield, Reiser was made a full-time centerfielder the next year, which in the long run did not turn out be a good idea. Meanwhile, MacPhail apologized to Rickey for not keeping his word about eventually trading him back to the Cardinals, but Rickey understood, especially after MacPhail paid the Cardinals an extra $250,000 for Reiser in a deal in 1940 that sent Medwick and Curt Davis from the Cardinals to the Dodgers. Rickey was not quite as understanding when Reiser batted a league-leading .343 in 1941 as the Dodgers beat out the Cardinals in a close pennant race. Reiser—who was dubbed "Pistol Pete" four decades before the nick-name would be applied to basketball star Pete Maravich—would eventually get to play for Rickey, but by then he would not be the same player he was in the early 1940s. As it developed, Reiser would have a meteoric and potentially Hall of Fame career that would be slowed and then ended because of his propensity for crashing into concrete outfield fences.

After clinching the pennant in the last game of the season when they beat the Boston Braves in Boston while the Cardinals were los-ing, the Dodgers were on their way home when MacPhail sent a wire requesting that the train stop at the 125th Street station before it went on to Grand Central Terminal. MacPhail had gone to the station in Harlem so that he could be aboard the train when it was greeted by hundreds of fans at Grand Central. When a conductor asked Durocher if it was all right to stop at 125th Street—Durocher always insisted that he was not told about the wire—Durocher said no, because several players asked if they could get off there so that they could get home earlier and he didn't want them to do so. As it was, Durocher later said that he saw MacPhail on the platform as the train roared past the 125th Street station. "I knew there'd be hell to pay because we didn't stop once I found out MacPhail had sent the wire asking that the train stop there," Durocher said years later. Sure enough, that night MacPhail summoned Durocher to a meeting at the Hotel New Yorker in Manhattan, screamed at him for not letting the train stop at 125th Street, and told him he was fired even though the Dodgers were scheduled to start the World Series against the Yankees two days later. At about two o'clock the next morning, the phone rang in Durocher's hotel room. It was MacPhail. "I want to talk some things about the World Series with you in the morning," MacPhail said.

"Okay," Durocher replied before turning over and going back to sleep. The call, even at two in the morning, came as no surprise to Leo the Lip, nor did the fact that he had been rehired again.

7

THE DONORA GREYHOUND

EXCEPT FOR STAR players whose salaries usually leaked out, most big league teams in the 1940s did not let it be known how much they were paying their players. Still, it was common knowledge that the Yankees, who usually led both leagues in attendance had the biggest payroll, as they do during the 21st century. Likewise, no one outside baseball knew which team had the smallest payroll, although it is very likely that it was the St. Louis Cardinals. The highest paid player on the Cardinals was pitcher Mort Cooper, who was earning $12,000 in 1942 (about $165,000 by 2012 monetary standards). As a result of the relatively low salaries in the forties, most players held jobs in the off season that ranged from teaching to driving a truck for the city, as Sibby Sisti (an infielder for the Braves in Boston for eleven years and then for two years after they moved to Milwaukee in 1953) did every winter in his native Buffalo. "The weather usually was pretty bad, but the pay was about the same as

I made playing for the Braves," Sisti once told me. "I sure couldn't live on what I was making for the Braves."

But then as Terry Moore, the great Cardinal center fielder and captain in the late 1930s and 1940s, once said, "Most of the guys loved the game so much, they probably would have played for nothing." That may have been an exaggeration, but then Enos Slaughter told this writer that before he was called up by the Cardinals in 1938, he was paid $400 a month, the same he had received his last season with the Cards Triple-A team in Columbus, Ohio.

As a rookie in 1942, Stan Musial earned $4,200 (about $160,000 by 2012 monetary standards), which was a lot more than the $65 a month he earned his first two years as a minor league pitcher and occasional outfielder for the Williamson, West Virginia, Red Birds of the Mountain State League in 1938 and 1939. Two other rookie teammates of Musial, pitcher Ernie White and third baseman George "Whitey" Kurowski, received about $4,000 in 1942. An outstanding high school baseball and basketball player, Musial had passed up a basketball scholarship at the University of Pittsburgh and signed with the Cardinals at the age of seventeen after his junior year at Donora High School in western Pennsylvania. In high school, Musial had played baseball on a team that included Buddy Griffey, an outstanding all-round athlete and the father of eventual Cincinnati Reds' star Ken Griffey and grandfather of Ken Griffey, Jr. Another Donora native, Steve Filipowicz, was also briefly an outfielder in the National League, including parts of two seasons with the New York Giants, with whom he played for 1945 and 1946. Also, in 1945, as a first-round draft pick out of Fordham, he was a fullback and defensive back for the New York Football Giants, who at the time also played at the Polo Grounds.

Though Musial had attracted the Cardinals' attention because of his pitching prowess, he won only fifteen games while losing eight during his two years with Williamson and batted .258 the first year and .352 the second. Because of his wildness on the mound, his manager during his second year at Williamson, Harrison Wickel, told the Cardinals that Musial was "the wildest pitcher I've ever seen," and recommended that he be released. Fortunately for the Cardinals, Branch Rickey disregarded that recommendation and Musial was sent to the Daytona Beach Islanders in Florida, also a Class-D club, in 1940, where he won eighteen games and lost five while hitting .311. Recognizing Musial's batting ability, manager Dickie Kerr also played him in the outfield in between pitching starts. Kerr, a St. Louis native, was a five-foot seven-inch left-handed rookie pitcher on the infamous Chicago White Sox team, eight of whose players, including "Shoeless" Joe Jackson, were accused of taking money from a New York gambler to throw the World Series to the Cincinnati Reds in 1919. Kerr won thirteen games that year and twenty-one the next season and was not involved in the scandal. Indeed, with players behind him who weren't trying to win, Kerr won two of the three games the White Sox won in the best of nine Series, the first of which was a three-hit shutout.

When the left-handed Musial was hurt when he landed on his left shoulder while diving for a ball in the outfield late in the season, he planned to return home, knowing he couldn't pitch any more that year. But Kerr persuaded him to remain with the Islanders as an out-fielder, telling him that, because of his hitting, he still had a future in baseball. Aware that Musial, who had married his high school sweetheart Lillian Labash in Daytona Beach in May, was feeling the financial pinch, Kerr took the Musials into his own home to live for the rest of the season. Almost twenty years later, Musial heard that Kerr, who had been a father figure to him in Daytona Beach, had fallen on hard times and bought him a $20,000 house in Houston. Coincidentally, Kerr died in 1963, the year Musial retired with a .331 major league career batting average.

A full-time outfielder in 1941, Musial hit a league-leading .387 with twenty-six home runs in eighty-seven games with the Class-C Springfield Illinois Cardinals in the Western Association. Promoted to the Cardinals Triple-A Rochester Red Wings in July, Musial batted .326 and was called up in mid-September by the Cardinals, then in a tight pennant race with the Dodgers. He did not disappoint, collecting twenty hits in forty-seven at bats and striking out only once while posting a .427 batting average. Despite Musial's outstanding play, the Cards finished two and a half games behind the pennant-winning Dodgers. From mediocre minor league pitcher who had been on the verge of being released in 1939, Stan Musial, in the late summer of 1941, had demonstrated that he belonged in the big leagues as an outfielder, whose hitting, fielding, and speed in the outfield and on the bases would earn him the nickname "The Donora Greyhound."

Third baseman George (Whitey) Kurowski, like Musial, who was also of Polish descent, was also a rookie and had been called up from Rochester late in the 1941 season, in his case to play in five games. So, too, were pitchers Johnny Beazley, who would win twenty-one games during his first big league season; and Howie Pollet and Murray Dickson. The two oldest players on the opening-day roster, thirty-three-year-old sidearm pitcher Lon Warneke and thirty-six-year-old backup catcher Gus Mancuso, were both traded during the season to teams they previously had played for: Mancuso to the Giants in May and Warneke to the Cubs in July, both for cash. Trading Warneke, the Cardinals last link to the Gas House Gang and its Mudcat band, raised eyebrows, since he had won seventeen games in 1941 and had a 6–4 record when he was dealt to the Cubs on July 8. Apparently, Rickey sensed that "the Arkansas Humming Bird," as Warneke was called because of his singing talents, might be on the downside, and he appeared to be. He won five and lost seven with the Cubs, admittedly a weak team, in 1942, and then went 4–5 in 1943, and, after serving in the Army in 1944 and part of 1945, won one game and lost one in 1945, his last season.

Rickey rarely held on to players who were in their thirties, especially when, like Warneke, they were among the highest-paid players on the team. (Warneke was believed to have been making about the same $12,000 as Mort Cooper.) As a rule, Rickey traded players who he felt were just past their peak but were still market-able. He wasn't always right, particularly in the cases of future Hall of Famers Joe Medwick and Johnny Mize. In 1941, Rickey also traded twenty-five-year-old Mickey Owen to the Dodgers, where Owen became one of the best catchers in the National League. That trade made more sense, since, by 1941, the Cardinals had Walker Cooper, also twenty-six, who was a better hitter if not a better catcher.

As for the Cardinals' persona in 1942, it was no Gas House Gang, the colorful and rollicking cutups of the 1930s who were personified by Leo Durocher, Pepper Martin, Medwick, Warneke, and manager Frankie Frisch. Most of the 1942 players, like Musial, were quiet, unassuming, disciplined, and in general easy for manager Billy Southworth to handle. No other team in baseball had a bigger radio audience than the Cardinals, whose games were carried on KMOX in St. Louis, whose powerful signal was able to reach most of their fan base that ranged from southern Illinois to the Southwest.

Along with a very strong pitching staff, the Cardinals had one of the best outfields in baseball, with Musial in left (when Coaker Triplett wasn't playing), Terry Moore in center, and Enos Slaughter in right field. Though overshadowed by Joe DiMaggio, who was regarded as the nonpareil of center fielders, Moore was probably as good in the field although not as a hitter, while Musial and Slaughter, like Moore, were fast and outstanding fielders with good arms. In the slender six-foot three-inch Marty Marion, in his third season with the team, the Cardinals had perhaps the best shortstop in the league. While managing the Boston Braves, Casey Stengel once said after a game against the Cardinals, "He robbed us of base hits all day. On one play, I swear he had three extra arms." Alluding to Marion's long reach, Stengel added, "The guy's uncanny. All he has to do is throw his glove on the field, and the Cardinals have an infield." Years later, former Cardinal catcher and broadcaster Joe Garagiola, who played with Marion in the mid-and late 1940s and in 1950, said, "Everyone raves about Ozzie Smith [the Cardinal shortstop in the 1970s and 1980s whose play earned him the nickname of "Wizard"], but they never saw Marty Marion play."

As a manager, Billy Southworth was the antithesis of Durocher. A former outfielder with five teams during a thirteen-year big league career, during which he batted a highly respectable .297, Southworth had ten hits for the Cardinals when they beat the Yankees in 1926 for their first World Series Championship in the 20th century. Southworth first managed the Cardinals in 1929, his last year as a player, and returned in 1940 after managing in the Cardinals' farm system and battling a drinking problem that was exacerbated by a number of personal losses Southworth would suffer. His first wife, Lida, had lost twins in childbirth after their son, Billy, was born, and then died of a cerebral hemorrhage in 1932.

A soft-spoken, warm, and paternalistic figure with a sharp baseball mind, Southworth was a perfect fit as manager of the young Cardinals team in 1942, counseling players who were having personal problems and encouraging them when they were having trouble on or off the field. Three years later, in yet another personal tragedy, Southworth was devastated when his son, Billy, Jr., a promising minor league player who had flown numerous bombing missions in Europe after becoming the first professional baseball player to enlist when he joined the army air corps in December 1940, was killed when the B-29 bomber he was piloting crashed into Flushing Bay near La Guardia Field in New York on February 25, 1945, while on a training mission. Five other crewmen died in the crash, while five survived. A major at the time, Southworth was twenty-seven years old. Billy Southworth Sr. also had a daughter by his second wife, whom he married in 1935.

By 1945, Southworth had come to be regarded as one of the best managers in baseball, a friendly and likeable skipper, though a hard taskmaster with a record that few of his contemporaries could ever match. But none of his success as a manager could assuage the loss of his son, of whom, understandably, he was extremely proud. Southworth had always referred to his players as "my boys" and did so even more frequently after his only son was killed.

8

PLAYING IN THEIR BROTHER'S SHADOW

IF RED SOX center fielder Dom DiMaggio was overshadowed by his big brother Joe, that was at least double the case for Vince DiMaggio, also an outfielder, who played for five big league teams from 1937 through 1946. The oldest of the brothers, Vince was not as big as Joe, who was a year younger, but bigger than Dom, who was born five years later. Primarily a power hitter, Vince was best known for striking out and led the National League in that category six times during a ten-year career with the Braves, Cincinnati Reds, Pittsburgh Pirates, Philadelphia Phillies, and the New York Giants. Though Joe played three more years, Vince struck out more than twice as often—837 times, while Joe fanned only 369 times. In 1939, when Vince led the National League with a record 134 whiffs while hitting .228, brother Joe, who led the American League with a .381 average that year, fanned only twenty times. Vince's best year was 1940, his first season with Pittsburgh, when he batted .289, which would be his best average during a ten year big league career, and hit nineteen home runs. That year, and five others, Vince was among the National League's top-ten home-run hitters. Like his younger brothers, Vince was an outstanding outfielder with a very strong arm and somehow managed to make it on the National League All-Star team in 1943 and 1944, even though he batted under .250 both of those seasons.

Like Joe and Dominic, Vince DiMaggio played in the Pacific Coast League, including three years with the San Francisco Seals. After leaving the major leagues in 1946 with a career batting average of .249 and 125 home runs, Vince returned to the minors for five years, the last two as a playing manager, before retiring at thirty-eight, hoping to pursue a career in opera but never quite making it. Joe and Dominic may have been better ballplayers, but even they agreed that Vince's baritone was far and away the best voice in the DiMaggio family.

Much more of a contact hitter than brother Vince, Dom DiMaggio never struck out more than sixty-eight times in a season during his eleven-year major league career, all of which would be spent with the Red Sox, and he would finish with a career batting average of .298. In 1948, he hit safely in thirty-four consecutive games, before the streak was broken when brother Joe caught a sinking line drive hit by Dominic in the eighth inning. His hit streak was still a Red Sox record as of 2011. Unlike Joe's if-looks-could-kill glare after Dominic robbed him of a hit during his streak in 1941, Dommy wasn't bothered because he was convinced he couldn't match his older brother's phenomenal achievement.

Because of his small stature and his scholarly mien, enhanced by the eyeglasses he had worn since he was a child, Dom DiMaggio was called "the Little Professor." That was understandable, because he hardly looked like a professional athlete and was often mistaken for a member of the Red Sox staff or a sportswriter. Yet, Ted Williams called Dominic, who became a seven-time all-star, "the best lead-off man in the American League." Williams also appreciated the youngest of the big league DiMaggios for his speed and skill as a center fielder, who often ran down and caught balls in left-center field, which Williams, an average outfielder, could not have reached. "He was the easiest outfielder I ever played with," Williams once said. "When he called 'mine,' you didn't have to worry about the rest of the play." Williams, who batted third in the Red Sox lineup, had a high respect for Dom's judgment and would often badger him with questions about a pitcher. "What's he got, Dommy? What's he throwing?" Williams would ask as they crossed paths after Dominic had batted. Williams did so because he was aware that Dominic, like himself, was both very perceptive and highly analytical. In many instances, Dom DiMaggio's insight and subsequent responses to Williams's questions would pay off and help the Splendid Splinter when he went to bat. Thus, the Little Professor not only aided Williams in the outfield, he also helped him at the plate.

For all of Joe DiMaggio's fame as a great outfielder, most baseball experts felt that Dominic was the better outfielder, because he could cover more ground and had a stronger arm than his bigger and older brother, as did brother Vince. Yet, at times the comparisons between him and his superstar brother seemed to rankle Dom DiMaggio. "Yes, he's my brother, and I'm his brother," Dominic said more than a few times. "It's been a struggle all my life. I've always been Joe's kid brother." In a lighter vein, he said, "The only two things

I can do better is play pinochle and speak Italian." For the first two months of the 1942 season, though, Dominic was a better hitter, too, outhitting Joe by around twenty points.

Dominic was the youngest of nine children born to fisherman Giuseppe and Rosalie DiMaggio in the San Francisco Bay area. "I think Pop's pride and joy was Dom," Joe once said. "When Dominic was in short pants, Pop wanted him to become a lawyer 'because he wears glasses.'" Dominic preferred becoming a chemical engineer, but because of his own baseball talents, he followed in the footsteps of Joe and Vince. He started out as a shortstop, but minor league managers, fearful that a bad bounce could break Dom's glasses and injure him, shifted him to the outfield. It was a very smart move.

Unlike Vince, after he left the Red Sox in 1953, Dom went into business, starting two highly successful manufacturing companies in the Boston area, where he lived until his death at the age of ninety-two in 2009. Demonstrating his business acumen, he was part of the original ownership of the New England Patriots (then the Boston Patriots) in 1960, buying 10 percent of the team for $25,000 and selling it six years later for $300,000. Then in 1977, after Red Sox owner Tom Yawkey died, Dom DiMaggio headed a syndicate that tried, unsuccessfully, to buy the Red Sox. By then, Dom was a multi-million-dollar businessman, married, and the father of three children. "I never encouraged my two sons to get into baseball," he said. "I knew it would be twice as hard on them as it was on me. The Joe DiMaggio legend was just too strong." So, he could have added, but wouldn't, would have been his own as an outstanding Red Sox player.

Like his more famous brother, Joe, Dom DiMaggio also spent three years in the military but, unlike Joe, never complained about missing three big league seasons. Indeed, when he tried to enlist in the navy during the 1942 season, Dom DiMaggio was classified 4-F because of poor vision. But he persisted, and by October 1942, he managed to convince the navy to take him. "I had to fight my way into the navy," Dominic said. "They rejected me because of my eyesight, and for the longest time I told them I wanted to be in the navy. I was not about to sit out the war." Like most major league players, including brother Joe, Dom DiMaggio spent his time in service playing baseball at the Norfolk Naval Training Station and then serving as the playing manager of a naval depot team in Australia.

Returning to the Red Sox at the age of twenty-nine in 1946, Dom showed he hadn't lost anything, hitting .316—one of four times he would bat over .300 during his twelve major league seasons. His biggest disappointment that season came in the eighth inning of the seventh game of the World Series against the Cardinals at Sportsman's Park in St. Louis. With the Red Sox trailing, 3–1, and with two outs and men on second and third, Dom DiMaggio hit a drive against the bleacher wall in left center field, scoring both runners to tie the score. But while running to second base, he pulled a hamstring muscle and had to leave the game. Williams then popped out to end the inning for the Red Sox. Then in the last half of the ninth, with Enos Slaughter on first base after a single, Harry Walker hit a drive to left center that Leon Culberson, who had replaced DiMaggio in center field, ran down at the wall and threw to shortstop Johnny Pesky in short left field. Disbelievingly, Pesky heard his teammates screaming, "Home! Home" and whirled around to see Slaughter racing all the way home from first base, whereupon he fired the ball home, only to have Slaughter slide in safely in what became known in baseball lore as "the mad dash home." Slaughter said later that if Dom DiMaggio had still been in center field, he never would have tried to make it home. "Not with his arm," Slaughter said of the Little Professor.

In an interview in January 2012, the Red Sox Hall of Fame second baseman Bobby Doerr, who played with Dom DiMaggio, told me from his Oregon home, "Dom DiMaggio was a great player and should be in the Hall of Fame."

9

THE U-BOAT COMMANDER
FROM THE BROOKLYN
NAVY YARD

BY MIDSUMMER OF 1942, far fewer cargo ships and tankers were being sunk off the East Coast, mainly because they were being protected by newly built destroyers, corvettes, and other navy and coast guard vessels, along with gunners from the navy's Armed Guard program. But there was still high drama elsewhere in the Atlantic involving German submarines and American convoys. Typical, perhaps, was a battle between about a dozen U-boats and about half that number of American destroyers escorting a convoy of cargo ships in the North Atlantic in early August:

> "I was on lookout in the bow when the action started," said John Tattersall, a merchant seaman from Haverhill, Massachusetts. "First thing I knew, I saw flares go streaking up and then in the light I could see a whole pack of submarines. After calling the skipper, I saw one ship go blasting up sky-high,

then another one roared up right after that, and after that there were three subs right off the starboard bow. I thought for sure we were goners. But then the gunners on our ship get one sub and then another and they blew up so close that pieces of one of the subs landed on our deck. But then two torpedoes hit us, and the ship started to split in two just as we were swinging the lifeboats out. At that point, we went over the side like monkeys."

After being adrift for about two hours in a sea filled with debris from the wreckage of several sunken submarines and ships, John Tattersall and the rest of his shipmates were rescued by a navy corvette. Meanwhile, most of the German U-boats in the wolf pack had been sent to the bottom of the Atlantic by navy depth charges, the customary weapon against enemy submarines. "I don't know when she'll sail, but my next ship will have me out there again soon," the seaman said after arriving back in Massachusetts. "But there's a war going on out there, and this country's got to win."

Many of the U-boat commanders spoke fluent English, some because they had lived and worked, and even studied, in the United States. In one instance, following the sinking of an American cargo ship, the U-boat surfaced, and the captain came out of the conning tower to talk to a number of seamen in lifeboats. "Are any of you guys from Brooklyn?" he asked in perfect English, which was tinged with a slight Brooklyn accent. Several of the seamen said they were from New York, and two said they had worked at the navy yard, whereupon the U-boat skipper said, "I lived in Brooklyn for a couple of years and worked at the Brooklyn Navy Yard. I might have worked with you guys." He then wished the crewmen good luck and closed the conning tower hatch, after which the submarine submerged and disappeared.

In another instance in early June, the crew of a German submarine picked up two of thirty-two survivors of an American merchant ship after it was torpedoed in the Caribbean with the loss of fifteen men. "The Germans took us into the cub and washed the oil off us with rags," nineteen-year-old Cornelius O'Connor said after being rescued along with a twenty-four-year-old by a Brazilian merchant ship, taken to a port in Brazil, and then flown back to the United States. "The captain gave us rum, tea, graham crackers, water, and black bread." Asked by the captain how the American people felt about the war, O'Connor said Americans were convinced they would win the war. "But then he said the Germans were stronger than Americans though and were going to win," the young American seaman replied. About two hours later, the submarine surfaced, and the two seamen were given a life raft, four gallons of water, and a bailing can and told them to head south for six miles to find other members of their crew. Using their shirts as sails and rowing, they were picked up five days later by the Brazilian freighter. "The German captain treated us well, speaking English all the while, and shook our hands before putting us on the raft," O'Connor said after returning home. "To the rest of the sub's crew, we were like a sideshow attraction that they just stared at."

Two other merchant seamen whose ship was torpedoed and sunk in the western Atlantic also were treated in a civil manner while spending some time aboard a German submarine. After being picked up by the U-boat while thirty-seven survivors of their ship were being tossed about in lifeboats, Captain Robert Perry and his chief engineer, M. V. Walter, were given some food and drinks and then lectured by the sub's skipper, who told them, "Roosevelt is a dangerous man to have at the head of your country." Several times during his lecture, the commander also blurted out, "To hell with Roosevelt," after which his twenty-one-member crew would repeat in unison, "To hell with Roosevelt." Eventually, the submarine captain and his crew released the men, putting them in a life raft and wishing them luck. They, too, were later rescued by a passing merchant ship.

Another U-boat commander also had harsh words about the American president after his sub torpedoed and shelled an American merchant ship in the Gulf of Mexico on May 16. Twenty-one of those aboard, including five gunners of a navy armed guard crew, were killed, while twenty-six others survived. Among the survivors were a couple from Mount Cory, Ohio, and their sixteen-month-old son. While they were in a lifeboat, the captain of the submarine came out on deck and, addressing the survivors in the water in an apologetic tone, said, in broken English, "You can thank Mister Roosevelt for this. I am sorry."

At least one U-boat captain was even apologetic about sinking a cargo ship off the northern coast of South America in early August, killing three people. Thirty others survived and were rescued. One of them, William Hicks, the ship's radio operator, recalled how the commander of the submarine came out on the deck to talk to the survivors in nearby lifeboats. "He kept asking us if we needed anything," Hicks said. Then he said, "Sorry I had to torpedo you." The captain then wished the survivors luck and went back down below.

Another U-boat commander was equally as apologetic. When his cargo ship was torpedoed off the Florida coast in July, seaman Morgan Seifert of New York, who was at the ship's wheel, was practically blown out of his shoes. Trapped in a cable that took him forty feet under water, he finally managed to get loose and to swim to the surface and then to a life raft. "My foot was bleeding badly, and I screamed for help," he said, "and the sub which had surfaced hoisted me aboard. "While he was being treated for his wound, the sub captain said, in perfect English, "I have nothing against the United States. It's only my personal feelings against President Roosevelt and Secretary Knox," which was a reference to Navy Secretary Frank Knox. "Here, have some schnapps," the captain said as he extended a glass of whiskey to the twenty-year-old seaman. Then, as Seifert was being lowered into a life raft, the sub commander gave him some water and hardtack, usually hard biscuits or bread. "Remember, none of that food or water goes to Secretary Knox," the sub skipper said with a smile. Seifert's raft and a second raft, carrying a total of eighteen survivors—nineteen others had been killed—then was adrift in heavy seas and broiling sun for nineteen days before they were picked up by a passing merchant ship.

Not all German U-boat commanders were as solicitous. Following another attack on a merchant ship in the Gulf of Mexico in May, fifteen crew members managed to get off the vessel in a lifeboat. As another twenty-four were clambering into another lifeboat, the German captain called out, "Is everyone off the ship?"

"No!" the seamen shouted back.

"We heard a laugh, and something that sounded like 'okay,'" one of the survivors in the first lifeboat recalled. But the laughter was followed by a treacherous and horrific act as the nearby submarine fired a torpedo into the second lifeboat, shattering the boat and catapulting bodies into the water as their shipmates in the first boat looked on in horror. All but two of the twenty-four seamen in the second boat were killed, and those who survived were badly injured.

By the end of July, U-boat attacks had destroyed more than four hundred tankers and cargo ships, with the loss of several thousand lives in the western Atlantic. However, German submarines had stepped up their attacks in the Caribbean and in the Gulf of Mexico. In early August, thirty-two men, including two U.S. Coast Guard signalmen, were killed when two small Cuban merchant ships were torpedoed and sunk in the Gulf of Mexico. Twenty-seven survivors were rescued and taken to Key West, Florida.

By then it had become apparent that many of the German wolf-pack commanders knew about some ship movements. Hans Guliksen, captain of a Norwegian cargo ship that was torpedoed in the western Atlantic in July with the loss of one life, told of how the attacking submarine came alongside the thirty-one survivors in lifeboats and demanded to know the name of the ship, its tonnage, and its nationality. Guliksen knew he had no choice but to provide the answers and did just that. On the basis of that information, the U-boat commander told the Norwegian captain that he knew the port from which they had sailed and their destination—and he was right.

Earlier in July, following the sinking of a combination American merchant and passenger ship off the Atlantic Coast, which claimed nine lives, the captain, William McDonough, said he thought the attacking submarine had advance knowledge of his ship's course. "In my opinion, there was a lot of monkey business about this torpedo-ing," McDonough said. "I feel that the crew of the submarine knew we carried a valuable cargo and also that the destination and route were known to them."

McDonough may well have been right. By then, it was known that some German nationals living in the United States were providing vital shipping information to the Nazis. Some were bartenders who garnered the information while overhearing merchant seamen, and sometimes navy sailors, talking at bars while on shore leave about their ships' projected movements. Others were dockworkers or had other jobs that brought them into close contact with both merchant seamen and U.S. sailors. That eventually prompted a pithy but accurate slogan that began to appear at bars, restaurants, and other public places around the country, but particularly in port cities on the East and Gulf coasts. It read: "Loose lips sink ships," which became perhaps the best-known slogan of the war.

10

RIDING THE RAILS

IF HARDLY ANY American civilians were traveling by ship in 1942, more Americans than ever were traveling by train, including hundreds of thousands of servicemen. So, too, were big league baseball teams, which were still doing so until the 1950s. As the western-most teams, the St. Louis Cardinals and the St. Louis Browns logged the most miles, sometimes spending up to twenty-four hours or more on trips from St. Louis to Boston. "It resulted in a far greater camaraderie than you have on ball clubs today, because you spent so much time together," said Don Gutteridge, who spent five years with the Cardinals during the Gas House era and then four years with the Browns during an eleven-year career that ended with brief stays with the Red Sox and the Pirates and a two-year stint as manager of the White Sox. "We ate together in the dining car, played cards together, slept together in the Pullman cars, and talked baseball by the hour." Enos Slaughter, a teammate of Gutteridge when both played for the Cardinals in the late 1930s, agreed: "They talk about family on some clubs nowadays, but when you traveled by train, you really were a family." Slaughter rode trains during eighteen of the nineteen years of his Hall of Fame career. "Now players drive to an airport, get on the team plane, maybe go to sleep, fly to wherever they're playing next, and go to their hotel room, and then to the ballpark the next day. Now, especially at home, a lot of players only get to see each other at the ballpark."

Former Red Sox second baseman Bobby Doerr said he much preferred traveling by train than flying. "Near the end of my career, we had a choice of flying or going by train, and I'd always go by train," Doerr said. "It was much more relaxing than flying, and it brought the players closer together. When we were traveling between Chicago and St. Louis, I loved just sitting and looking out the window at farmland. It was both enjoyable and relaxing."

Most baseball teams chartered three private cars—two sleeping cars and a dining car, which also served as a lounge—that could be coupled to a regular train. In 1942 and the subsequent three years of the war, though, teams shared diners and club cars with sometimes awestruck riders, who couldn't believe they were eating in the same car as Ted Williams or Joe DiMaggio. For the most part, the players kept to themselves, but there were exceptions. "If Pepper Martin heard there was, say, a group of Shriners or Boy Scouts on the train, he'd go down and talk to them, play his harmonica, and sign autographs," said catcher Mickey Owen, who spent several seasons playing with Martin on the Cardinals in the late 1930s. "Sometimes, he'd bring the Mudcats along. The Mudcats also would break out their instruments and practice for hours on train trips, and sometimes they'd go marching through the train, playing and attracting crowds. It was really something to see." And no doubt to hear.

Though the Gas House Gang had a reputation for being a rollicking collection of characters, it had its share of internal strife. Owen recalled how, during a game of poker aboard a train, Paul "Daffy" Dean, the younger brother of Dizzy Dean, with whom he played for the Cardinals from 1934 through 1937, implied that Joe Medwick had not anted up. "Joe was furious and said to Paul, 'Are you calling me a thief?'" Without waiting for an answer, Owen said, Medwick, always ready for a fight, punched Dean in the nose. "Blood spurted from Paul's nose, and I think Joe felt he had killed him," Owen said. "But Paul never flinched, and Joe backed off, realizing that Paul had taken his best shot without going down. Paul then jumped on Joe and began to bang away before some of the guys pulled him off. It was totally out of character for Paul, who was a quiet, easygoing guy, not at all like Dizzy, and never got into fights."

Getting into fights was not out of character for Pete Gray, the one-armed outfielder, who spent the 1945 season with the Browns. "Pete was a helluva ballplayer but had a chip on his shoulder a mile wide," said infielder Ellis Clary, who was a teammate of Gray in 1945. Clary recalled a near fight involving Gray on a railroad station platform in Toledo. "We were waiting for a train after playing an exhibition game against our Toledo farm club," Clary said. "There was a barrel of fish on the platform, and someone took one of the fish out of the barrel, then sneaked up behind Pete, and put the fish in his left pocket, where he kept his cigarettes. When Pete reached in the pocket for his cigarettes and found the fish, he went right at Sig Jakucki, a big pitcher who outweighed Pete by about fifty pounds and was always pulling pranks on him. Pete suspected that Jakucki had done it and hauled off and punched him in the chest. If some of the guys hadn't grabbed Sig, he might have killed Pete on that platform." Despite such incidents and Gray's tendency to rebuff any efforts to make things easier for him in general, he appeared in seventy-seven games and got fifty-one hits in 234 times at bat while striking out only eleven times and batting .218, a higher average than that of many big league outfielders with two arms who three and four decades later were earning more than $1 million and not necessarily performing as well in the outfield.

An even more memorable fight than the one between Gray and Jakucki occurred on a train carrying the Yankees from Kansas City to Detroit after they had clinched the American League pennant in 1959. The Bronx Bombers were celebrating the occasion with champagne that night when Ralph Houk, then a coach with the Yankees, prepared to light up a victory cigar. As he did, relief pitcher Ryne Duren sneaked up behind him and playfully, or at least playfully to Duren, squashed the cigar in Houk's face. According to some accounts, Houk, who was renowned for his quick temper, responded by decking Duren with a punch. Other witnesses said Houk, who had served at the Battle of the Bulge and was known as the Iron Major—having been a major in the army—floored Duren with the back of his hand.

For younger players, the train carrying a team could sometimes be a classroom of sorts. "A lot of the veterans would take young players aside on the train and tell them what to expect from other teams they were going to face," Don Gutteridge said. "At the beginning of my career, I learned an awful lot from some of the older guys while riding the trains."

Owen's recollections were similar. "I recall sitting on the train with pitchers like Lon Warneke and Curt Davis, who would tell me about different hitters," said Owen, an outstanding catcher, although best remembered for letting a pitch from Hugh Casey get away from him that cost the Dodgers a win in the 1947 World Series. "Sometimes, especially during the war, you'd find yourself on trains with other teams. I remember how, once, when I was a young catcher with the Cardinals, Jimmy Wilson, a great catcher who was managing the Phillies at the time, spent an hour with me in the washroom showing me the best way to put a tag on a runner. He was the best tagger I ever saw, and he helped me tremendously."

But in addition to the long hours, train travel had some other drawbacks. "When I came up [in 1935], the trains were not air-conditioned," said Terry Moore, who played for the Cardinals from 1935 through 1948. "We'd spent a lot of time in the diners, which were cooled by ice. But on hot nights, we'd open the windows to get some air and then wake up covered with soot and cinders from the locomotives."

Mel Allen, who broadcast Yankee games in the 1940s and 1950s, said, "The train was a rollicking clubhouse. Casey Stengel would roam through the cars, delighting passengers with his stories or making speeches in the dining car that just about everyone on the entire train could hear. And everyone, the players, coaches, managers, writers, and broadcasters, spent a lot of time together on the train trips."

Jack Lang, who covered the Dodgers and later the New York Mets for the defunct *Long Island Press* and later for the New York *Daily News*, said his job was both easier and more difficult in the train-traveling days. "The players were far more accessible on the trains," Lang told me years ago. "In a way, they were a captive audience, and the writers got to know them much better." But when it came to filing stories, things were less rosy for the beat writers. "Quite often you'd have to hurry to catch the train after a game, so you'd have to write your story on the train. Fortunately, if you were writing for a morning paper, you still had time, since most games were played in the afternoon," Lang recalled. "If you left Cincinnati, for example, you'd have an hour and a half to get your story done before the train reached Indianapolis, where a Western Union operator would be waiting. So you had to have the story done by then, because there was no other way to file your story."

Planes, of course, occasionally encounter turbulence, but then trains also could have their rough moments, as Hall of Fame shortstop and later manager Lou Boudreau recollected. "The train would go around a bad curve, and it would wake you up," Boudreau said. "Or you'd be awakened while the train was going along a bad stretch of track."

Like Pepper Martin and Casey Stengel, Babe Ruth also liked to roam through a train. "Babe loved people, and he'd wander through the train, talking to passengers, who loved meeting him," said Jimmy Reese, who roomed with Ruth in 1930 and 1931 when he was a utility infielder for the Yankees. "I'll never forget the time Jake Ruppert [then the owner of the Yankees] was aboard the train, and Babe picked him up and threw him into an upper berth," Reese, a longtime coach for the then-California Angels, said. "No one else would have ever dared to do a thing like that." By the 1950s, most players had their own roomettes aboard the team trains. But in the earlier years, players slept in upper and lower berths in Pullman cars. "The veterans got the lower berths, and the younger players the uppers," said Reese, who was still hitting fungoes for the Angels while in his mid-eighties. "But when I was with the Yankees, Babe had his own drawing room on the train, something that, as a rule, only managers and coaches had."

Ruth was the central figure in one of the legendary episodes of baseball train travel. "The Yankees were about to leave Shreveport, Louisiana, during a spring training trip in 1925, when, suddenly, the Babe came running through the train, followed by a woman with a knife," recalled Red Foley, a former baseball writer for the New York *Daily News.* "When he got to the observation car at the end of the train, he jumped off and onto the platform to escape the woman, who was still right behind him. She finally got off, too, and then Babe managed to jump on the train as it started leaving the station."

Dave Anderson, then a young sportswriter for the old *Brooklyn Eagle*, also found himself pursued on a train, albeit in a less dangerous fashion, by no less than one of his all-time favorite athletes, Jackie Robinson. "I was talking to Roy Campanella [the Brooklyn Dodgers Hall of Fame catcher] in the Dodgers' clubhouse after a close game that the Dodgers had lost to the Giants," Anderson recalled:

> Jackie was still furious about an umpire's call and that shrill voice of his became louder and louder. Finally, Campanella said, and he said it quietly, "Oh, Robinson, why don't you shut up," and I used the quote in my story the following day. That night we were leaving by train on a road trip when somebody told me on the railroad platform at Penn Station that Robinson was looking for me. I asked why, and he told me it was because of the Campanella quote. I had thought the quote was funny, since I don't think Campy was really serious when he said it. But I was told that Jackie didn't see it that way. A short while later while I was in my roomette in one of the three cars the Dodgers usually had on a train, I heard Jackie's voice loud and clear from one of the other cars, and then nearer and nearer, saying "Where's that Dave Anderson? I'm going to kick his ass." He finally got to my roomette, where I was sitting down with the door was open, since I knew there was no point in trying to hide. Jackie, obviously very mad, stared down at me, and said, "You made me look bad in front of my teammates by using that quote, and I'm going to kick your ass." I told Jackie to take it

easy and that Campanella was smiling when he said it, and readers probably understood that he wasn't being serious. But Jack said he didn't think so, and I kept saying I thought they would, after which he finally left. He never mentioned the quote again, and we had a good relationship from then on.

Anderson said he treasured the memory of the incident, because, as he said in his book *Sports of Our Times,* "For once I had seen Jackie Robinson the way his opponents often had—in full flame out."

For Don Gutteridge, who never had to worry about being pursued on a train by Jackie Robinson, traveling by train was a joyful experience, especially at night. "I still remember the clickety-clack sound of the train on the tracks," Gutteridge said years ago. "It was the most marvelous sound to go to sleep by, and I never slept better than on the train. It took a lot longer than it does by plane, but I loved traveling across the country by train. Someday I'm going to get back on the train and take some of the same long trips that we did many years ago. I bet I'll sleep better than ever."

11

SABOTEURS LAND ON LONG ISLAND

WALKING ALONG A lonely Long Island beach in the dark of night, young John Cullen sometimes wondered whether he had made a mistake in joining the coast guard shortly after Pearl Harbor rather than the navy, where, he thought, wartime might be more exciting. Cullen knew the fashionable Hamptons area well, having grown up in the New York City borough of Queens, about a hundred miles from where he was based at the coast guard station in Amagansett, then a quaint fishing village but which by the beginning of the 21st century had become part of the ultrafashionable and chic "Hamptons," which included the towns of Southampton, East Hampton, and Montauk on Long Island's so-called east end along the Atlantic Ocean.

Because of top-secret information the U.S. government had received about German plans to land saboteurs on the East Coast, President Franklin Roosevelt ordered that a series of old life-saving stations on Long Island be reactivated as coast guard stations and a fort be established just west of the Montauk Lighthouse, which included four sixteen-inch gun emplacements and one six-inch battery. In addition, the president ordered that the coast guard establish patrols around the clock in such beach areas as Long Island, where the government believed German saboteurs might try to land. Cullen was one of the coast guardsmen assigned for such a task, walking eastward about three miles to the next station in the town of Napeaque, just west of Montauk, and then back to his station in Amagansett. Though the beaches were deserted at night, lights flickered from fishermen's cottages, vacationers' bungalows, and homes of year-round residents beyond the beaches' dunes and high grass. After an hour's break, Cullen, carrying only flares and a flashlight, would do another tour, as would the other coast guardsmen, none of whom, inexplicably, carried weapons, at stations along the Long Island beaches. It was lonely and boring duty, especially late at night when fog often enveloped Long Island beaches, and Cullen sometimes had to use his flashlight and walk alongside the water to see where he was going.

Saturday, June 13, 1942, was such a night, "so foggy that I couldn't see my shoes," Cullen recounted. He had set out on patrol around midnight and had covered about three hundred yards in a pea-soup fog, with no moon, and certain that the only sounds he would hear would be the foghorn from the historic 145-year-old Montauk lighthouse at the far east end of Long Island. On such nights, Cullen would walk even closer to the water, because the firmer sand gave him better traction. Encountering anyone, especially on such a night, was very unlikely. "Once in a while you might run into somebody, but it was extremely rare," he said years after

World War II had ended. When he did, he would order them off the beach while citing beach curfews that were in effect, usually an hour after sunset.

But this night would be different—very different—and one that Cullen would never forget.

Suddenly, Cullen came upon three men, one at the water's edge in civilian clothes and wearing a fedora hat and two others, a bit farther back, in bathing suits and up to their knees in the water.

A startled Cullen called out, "What's the trouble?"

No one answered, and the man in civilian clothes kept walking toward him, at which point Cullen pulled a flashlight from his hip pocket.

Thinking Cullen may have been reaching for a gun, the man called out, "Wait a minute. Are you the coast guard?"

"Yes," Cullen responded. "Who are you?"

"Fishermen," the man in the fedora said. "We were on our way from East Hampton to Montauk when our engine failed and we ran aground."

Cullen found it hard to believe that fishermen would run aground, even in a fog, only five miles into their trip, and with fifteen miles to go, and also would be fishing so close to shore. It all didn't figure.

"Come up to the station and wait for daybreak," Cullen replied. "I'll get you all some coffee."

"Wait a minute. You don't know what's going on," the man, who appeared to be about forty years old, said. "How old are you, and do you have a mother and a father? I wouldn't want to have to kill you."

Hearing that veiled threat, Cullen knew that these definitely were not fishermen, and probably not Americans, either. "I'm twenty-one," Cullen answered, "and yes, I do have a mother and father."

At that point, a third man in a bathing suit appeared, dragging a canvas bag, and spoke to the apparent group's leader in German.

Furious at him for doing so, the man in the fedora said, "Shut up!"

By now there was no doubt in Cullen's mind that he was dealing with German saboteurs.

"What's in the bag?" Cullen said while trying to remain calm.

"Clams," the man in the bathing suit replied.

That made no sense, either, Cullen knew, because there were no clams for miles around. He also knew that fishermen in the area were not inclined to wear fedora hats and bathing suits.

"Yes, that's right," the spokesman for the group said.

By now, Cullen realized he was in a very tenuous and probably dangerous situation. His concern was intensified when the spokesman said, "Why don't you forget the whole thing?" He then reached into his pants pocket and pulled out a wad of bills. "Here's some money—$100," he said.

"I don't want it," Cullen answered.

Drawing more money out, the man said, "Then take $300."

Thinking fast, Cullen decided it would be best to take the money.

"Okay," he said.

After giving the young coast guardsman the money, the man, staring at Cullen, said, "Now look me in the eyes. Would you recognize me if you saw me again?"

The spokesman then took off his hat, revealing a streak of gray hair in the middle of his dark hair. Recognizing him would not be hard, Cullen realized, because along with the gray-streaked hair he had large ears and a large hooked nose.

But again, Cullen realized it was best to be prudent, even if it meant lying. "No, I wouldn't," he said.

With the stranger apparently satisfied with Cullen's actions, Cullen decided to walk away, then turned around and walked backwards, fearing he might be shot in the back. After crossing the dunes and tall grass in the rear of the beach, Cullen began to run to the coast guard station just beyond the dunes. Meanwhile, knowing their time may have been limited before other coast guardsmen descended on the beach, the saboteurs began digging several holes in the sand near the dunes and buried four wooden cases containing explosives, detonators, materials for incendiary bombs, and clothing. They then left, hoping that a map and other directions they had would lead them to the Amagansett station on the Long Island Rail Road line, about a half mile away.

Back at the coast guard station, Cullen informed a skeptical boatswain's mate and longtime coast guardsmen, Carl Jenette, who was on duty, about what had happened. Finally convinced, Jenette called several superiors who lived nearby, one of whom notified the FBI in Manhattan. Jenette then awakened the other six men on duty in the two-story wooden building in the station. He handed out .30 caliber rifles to Cullen and the other six men and gave them instructions on how to use them. None of them had ever carried a weapon before. With Cullen leading the way, they hurried to the beach, wondering whether more saboteurs had landed or were on the verge of doing so. They soon thought that might well be the case. Arriving on the beach at about 2:00 a.m., Cullen and the other coast guardsmen detected an odor of diesel fumes and heard what appeared to be the roar of an engine starting up. Looking out over the water, they were able to see a long and slender dark object a few hundred yards off shore. "John said the whole beach rumbled," his wife, Alice, said years later. Fearing that it might be a submarine with another landing force, Chief Boatswain's Mate Warren Barnes ordered all the coast guardsmen to take posts behind the dunes with their rifles and to be prepared to resist a landing party. As it developed, the submarine had transported the four saboteurs from Germany and then became stuck on a sandbar at low tide after having two crewmen take the four men ashore in a rubber dinghy. After being lodged on the sandbar for almost three hours and fearful of being spotted, the U-boat commander, Hans-Heinz Linder, prepared to have the crew abandon ship and then scuttle the sub with explosives. But shortly before 3:00 a.m., the submarine finally got underway after it had been lifted by the incoming tide and headed out to sea. Had the U-boat remained stuck, all fifty crew members would have been captured before dawn and the submarine impounded, making what was developing into a sensational story even bigger. Cullen and the other coast guardsman weren't the only ones to have seen the submarine. Chief Radio Man Harry McDonald also had spotted it from the naval radio station nearby. He quickly called the main coast guard district headquarters but was ignored. He then called a nearby army station and was also given a brush-off. "What are you trying to do, start something?" he was asked.

After changing into dry clothes on the beach and burying their wet garments in the sand beyond a dune, the four saboteurs walked quickly toward the nearby Montauk Highway and then headed for the train station. Amazingly, no one in the coast guard or FBI thought of searching the highway, a logical place for the saboteurs to have headed, or posting coast guardsmen at the train station. Arriving at the station shortly after daybreak, they boarded the first train of the day, which left at 7:00 a.m. for the three-hour trip to Penn Station, about 125 miles to the west. Paying for their train fares was not a problem, because the saboteurs had been provided with almost $100,000 in cash to use during their mission, which was scheduled to last for two years. Following only two weeks of training at a farm school for saboteurs in Germany, the four men, all in their mid- and late thirties, were given precise instructions where they were to detonate bombs and to wreak other havoc at such installations as the Hell Gate railroad bridge that extends from the Bronx to Queens, the Pennsylvania Railroad terminal in Newark, a number of factories and water works between New York and Chicago, and several department stores, including the famous Macy's store in Manhattan, where seaman Cullen had worked as a delivery man before joining the coast guard the day after the Japanese attack on Pearl Harbor. But as they rode toward New York, they realized that because of their encounter with Seaman John Cullen and the possibility that the U-boat had been spotted, it was highly likely that their cache of explosives and other materials would be found in four wooden crates beneath the sands of a Long Island beach and that their mission might already be doomed.

By the time the saboteurs had boarded the Long Island Rail Road train, the armed coast guard party on the beach at Amagansett had given up its short search, but with Cullen's help, along with a discarded bathing suit and a pack of German cigarettes, had found the spot where the Germans had buried their cache of materials. The question now, the coast guardsmen wondered, was where had the German saboteurs gone? Had they merely checked out the nearby Montauk Highway, they would have easily found out. In the meantime, calls were made to FBI headquarters in New York and Washington, and by later that morning, a widespread search had begun in nearby Long Island shorefront towns. Particularly surprisingly was that no German collaborators, of which there were hundreds, if not thousands, in the metropolitan New York area, were nearby to pick up the saboteurs by car. Back at the Coast Guard station, John Cullen counted out the money that the stranger had given him and found that it added up to $260 and not the $300 that the stranger had said it was. It turned out, he had short-changed Cullen, which prompted Cullen to smile. Cullen knew that it could have been much worse; he could very well have been killed.

The following day, a Sunday, Cullen, in civilian clothes, led FBI agents—who had arrived in Amagansett late Saturday night, about nine hours after Cullen had encountered the saboteurs—on a search of bars and restaurants in Amagansett and surrounding towns for the saboteurs. With descriptions of the saboteurs that had been furnished by Cullen, FBI agents in New York also began looking for the saboteurs in Manhattan hotel lobbies, restaurants, and bars, particularly in the heavily German Yorkville section of Manhattan. By late Sunday, as it developed, George Dasch, the saboteur leader, was looking for the FBI while out on the town with the rest of his group.

❧ ❧

All four of the saboteurs were familiar with the United States, because they had all lived there and spoke fluent English. The leader, thirty-eight-year-old George Dasch, had returned to Germany in May 1941 after living in the United States for eighteen years and primarily working as a waiter and a salesman. As a waiter, he had spent time waiting on guests at the Sea Spray Inn in East Hampton and the Irving Hotel in Southampton, very close to where he and his three fellow Germans had landed.

One of the saboteurs, Ernest Burger, had even become an American citizen while working in Detroit and Milwaukee as a machinist from 1927 until 1941 and for a while had been a member of the Michigan National Guard. The third member, Robert Quirin, also came to the United States in 1927 and worked as a mechanic and painter in Syracuse and Schenectady in upstate New York, marrying another German national in New York City in 1930 after applying for citizenship. The fourth and final member, Heinrich Heinck, who was also married, worked in New York as a machinist from 1926 to 1939, when he also returned to Germany. Before they left, both Quirin and Heinck had become members of the pro-Nazi German-American Bund, but that hardly focused suspicion on them, since thousands of other Germans living in the United States had done the same before the United States entered the war after Pearl Harbor. Both their wives were in Germany when the two men left on their highly secretive mission.

Before changing trains in Jamaica, a part of the borough of Queens, the four saboteurs went on a shopping spree in stores nearby, buying suits, shirts, and shoes among other items, some of which they put on in the store, after which they discarded the still-damp clothes they had had on before leaving the beach at Amagansett. On arriving in Manhattan almost ten hours after they had landed in Amagansett, the group split up in pairs and checked into two separate hotels just off Broadway on the West Side of Manhattan. That afternoon, they went out on the town, touring Times Square and Rockefeller Center, eating at restaurants, and arranging to meet at prescribed times over the next few days at the city's famous Horn & Hardart automats and even at Grant's Tomb, a tourist attraction on Riverside Drive that overlooks the Hudson River. While crossing Fifth Avenue early that afternoon, they stopped to watch, along with about two million others, a huge "New York at War" parade, which included about 250,000 marchers, floats, tanks, and heavy artillery, while fighter planes and bombers flew overhead. The irony that they would be doing so on the same day they had arrived in the United States to ostensibly wreak havoc on certain American facilities was not lost on the four saboteurs. Had they wanted to catch a movie later that day, they could have seen the eventual Oscar-winning film *Yankee Doodle Dandy*, with James Cagney; Charlie Chaplin in *The Gold Rush*; *Mrs. Miniver*, with Greer Garson and Walter Pidgeon; Rita Hayworth in *My Gal Sal*; Shirley Temple in *Miss Annie Rooney*; or Alfred Hitchcock's *Saboteur*, which would have been an appropriate choice. Or if they preferred to see a stage play, they could have gone to see *Arsenic and Old Lace*, Noel Coward's *Blithe Spirit*, or *Porgy and Bess*, with music by George Gershwin.

While eating at an automat a few blocks away from the "New York at War Parade," Dasch, who knew the city better than the others, said with a wan smile, "Aren't you glad to be back in the United States?" All four chuckled at the remark, knowing that they had indeed returned. But given the episode on the beach at Amagansett and the unlikelihood of returning to get any of their supplies, there was hardly much to laugh about.

If the saboteurs bought any of the New York newspapers the next day, they might have found it interesting, and perhaps ironic, that on the day they had landed on Long Island and been confronted by a young coast guardsmen, former world heavyweight boxing champion

Jack Dempsey had been sworn into the coast guard as a senior lieu-tenant. The forty-six-year-old Dempsey, whose attempt to enlist in the army in January had been turned down because of his age, was to become the physical director at the Manhattan Beach Coast Guard station in Queens. After being sworn in, Dempsey said, "I'm happier than the day I won the world title," which was July 4, 1919.

That Sunday, only a day after landing, the saboteurs' mission began to unravel when Dasch told Burger in their hotel room that, from the outset, his intention was to disrupt their plot so that more Germans could realize the evils of Nazism. If Burger was surprised to hear that, then so was Dasch when Burger said he also wanted their mission to fail and had deliberately left German cigarettes on the beach so that the coast guard could find the explosives and other weapons. Later in the day, Dasch clumsily tried to surrender. Contacting the FBI office in Manhattan by phone, he told an agent that he wanted to talk to FBI Director J. Edgar Hoover. The agent told Dasch that Hoover was based in Washington and, chalking up Dasch as a crank caller, hung up on him. After enjoying Manhattan for five more days, Dasch took a train to Washington on Friday and went directly to the FBI offices to surrender. That turned out to be the beginning of the end of what had become a fools' errand that had been entrusted to a group of unreliable and uncommit-ted misfits. The following day, the three remaining saboteurs, who had spent most of their time eating, drinking, and sightseeing, were arrested in Manhattan by FBI agents who no doubt had been led to them by Dasch. The arrests, along with John Cullen's happenstance encounter with the four saboteurs, were disclosed at a news confer-ence by Hoover, who implied that the plot had been foiled entirely by the FBI, which of course was not the case and which infuriated the coast guard. It was not the first time Hoover had taken credit for what another agency, in this case the coast guard, had actually accomplished, and it most certainly would not be the last.

At any rate, one week after landing on Long Island, all four saboteurs had been arrested. Expected by the German High Command to shock Americans by blowing up bridges, railroad terminals, and other targets, the saboteurs had spent practically all their time visiting tourist sites, eating and drinking without having to worry about money, visiting family members and friends, and in general enjoying the Great White Way. Convinced that their days on the run were probably numbered, it could well have been a fatalistic matter of eat, drink, and be merry, for tomorrow we may die, which if they were caught they knew was highly likely. The saboteurs also knew that had they been captured in German military uniforms, they would have had to have been treated as prisoners of war and held at a POW camp in the states but that by wearing civilian clothes, they would be regarded as spies and quite likely would be executed. To say the least, they knew their prospects were very bleak. For a while at least, they were able to get by in New York just fine because of their ability to speak good English, and, when necessary, to identify themselves by displaying fraudulent Selective Service draft cards that they all had. All the while, none of them, and especially Dasch and Burger, was in any hurry to blow anything up, assuming they even could have done so.

∞ ∞

Four days after Dasch, Burger, Quirin, and Heinck landed on Long Island, four other German saboteurs in civilian clothes made their way to shore in a dinghy from a submarine that had surfaced about five hundred yards off Port Vedre in Florida. They had better luck than their brethren on Long Island. After burying explosives and other equipment and materials into the sand for later retrieval, they managed to get to nearby Jacksonville, from where they took a train to Cincinnati. By prearranged plans, two saboteurs then went to Chicago and the other two to New York, with one going to Chicago and another to New York to see the wives they had left behind when they returned to Germany. Like the four men who had landed on Long Island, all four had spent considerable time in the United States. One, Herbert Haupt, the youngest at twenty-two, had been brought to the states by his parents as an infant and became an American citizen when his father was naturalized in 1930. While attending high school in Chicago, Haupt was a cadet officer in the U.S. Reserve Officer Training Corps. After working as an optical apprentice, he went to Mexico in June 1941, then traveled to Japan, and then to Germany by ship. After going to Chicago following the Florida landing, Haupt visited his parents and reconnected with an old girlfriend, Gerda Stuckman, proposing to her after a few dates. Haupt obviously was being optimistic about his group's mission and apparently did not expect to get caught. The other three, all in their thirties, had come to the United States in the late 1920s and early 1930s and worked at various jobs. Two married in the United States, including the leader of the Florida group, Edward Kerling, who later worked as a butler and chauffeur and his wife as a maid in Short Hills, New Jersey, and Greenwich, Connecticut. While in the United States, Kerling became active in the German-American Bund and was a guest of the Hitler regime at the 1936 Olympics in Berlin. Like the other two, he returned to Germany by ship for sabotage training.

Although the Florida group's landing and travel to the Midwest went smoothly, their freedom was short-lived, largely, it is believed, because of information provided to the FBI by Dasch after he had turned himself in. Two were captured by the FBI on June 23, six days after they had landed in Florida, while the other two were seized in Chicago on June 27. Once again, Hoover implied that the FBI was entirely responsible for the arrests. Most of the approximately $150,000 that the German government had given to the saboteurs was seized by the FBI. In addition, eight men and six women in New York and Chicago were arrested by the FBI, which charged that they had served as contacts for the eight saboteurs after they arrived in the United States. Among them was the wife of Edward Kerling, the leader of the group that had landed in Florida, and the parents of Herbert Haupt.

Following a monthlong trial before a seven-member military commission in Washington, in which John Cullen was the prosecution's first witness, the eight saboteurs were found guilty and sentenced to die in the electric chair. Six of them did, on August 8 in the District of Columbia jail, while Burger received a life sentence and Dasch a thirty-year term for assisting the FBI in the arrest of the other six saboteurs. Both those sentences were commuted after the war by President Harry Truman, and Burger and Dasch were allowed to return to Germany. The entire misadventure was a huge embarrassment to the German government and to Adolf Hitler, who had encouraged it. How the Germans had selected such people as Dasch and Burger for the assignment when they obviously were temperamentally and emotionally ill-suited for it was difficult to understand. Seemingly their only qualifications were that they could speak fluent English and had all lived in the United States for a while and were familiar with the country's culture. Otherwise, there seemed to have been very little to recommend them for such a dangerous and complex task, and as a result the ill-fated venture turned out to be a massive failure for Germany and especially for its intelligence service.

Not surprisingly, President Roosevelt wanted a high-profile trial of the saboteurs, and he got it, with stories of the trial on front pages of newspapers throughout the country and much of the world. Roosevelt felt, too, that executing the six men would send a message to Germany that would deter any similar ventures. The message apparently registered, since there were no further known incidents of attempted sabotage. The only comparable incident occurred on November 29, 1944, when two men, one of whom, William Colepaugh, had grown up in Niantic, Connecticut, and had attended the Massachusetts Institute of Technology (MIT), were taken ashore from a submarine in Frenchman's Bay near Hancock, Maine, on a cold and snowy wintry night. Colepaugh was an unlikely German spy, because he could not speak English, although his mother was of German descent. After getting a job on a Swedish ship in early 1944, he went to the German consul's office in Lisbon, Portugal, and offered his services. The second agent, Erich Gimpel, was a professional spy, making them an odd couple for such a venture, whose mission was to act as spies and not to conduct any sabotage. Carrying $60,000 and two pieces of luggage, they managed to make it to New York by train, but Colepaugh, like Dasch and Burger, the two German saboteurs who had landed on Long Island the year before, had a change of heart and, like Dasch had done two years earlier, turned himself in to the FBI on December 26. He then helped the FBI track down Gimpel, who was captured on December 30. The agents were both charged with espionage and sentenced to death, but after the war, President Truman commuted their sentences to life in prison. However, Colepaugh was released after serving seventeen years and then settled in King of Prussia, Pennsylvania, before retiring to Florida. Gimpel served ten years in prison and then was deported to Germany in 1955. From all accounts, their mission, like the one by the four saboteurs who had landed on Long Island, was an abject failure. Once again, it seemed, the Germans had picked the wrong men. Not only did they appear to be incompetent and to lack commitment, but one was quick to turn on the other in an effort to save his own skin.

Meanwhile, John Cullen would emerge as an American hero for what he accomplished on an American beach not far from where he grew up. No longer would he have to walk patrols on foggy nights. Instead, over the next three years, the coast guard would have Cullen appear at parades, war-bond rallies, and the launching of a number of newly built coast guard vessels. For a while, he also would serve as a driver for several high-ranking coast guard officers and for Fred Vinson, the secretary of the Treasury, which had jurisdiction over the coast guard at the time. "They became good friends," Cullen's wife said in referring to her husband and Vinson, who later became the chief justice of the U.S. Supreme Court. The highlight of 1942, though, would be his marriage in October to Alice Nelson, whom he had been dating for four years. They would settle down on Long Island and raise two children while he worked as a sales representative for a milk company after briefly returning to work for Macy's. Following his encounter with the saboteurs, Cullen was promoted to coxswain and later to chief boatswain's mate, the highest reenlisted rank in the navy and coast guard. He also received the

Legion of Merit, a high military honor that is awarded for exceptionally meritorious conduct. Cullen and his wife eventually moved to Chesapeake, Virginia, to be near their daughter's children. It was there that he died in 2011 at the age of ninety, still a coast guard legend.

"Right up until the time he died, John still had nightmares about what happened on the beach at Amagansett," Mrs. Cullen said during an interview in October 2011. "He never really got over what happened that night in 1942. John knew that Dasch and the others had been ordered to shoot and kill anyone they might come across after landing on Long Island, but that for some reason Dasch let John go."

12

THE "MIGHTY-MITE" YANKEE SHORTSTOP FROM BROOKLYN

HAD GEORGE DASCH and the other three saboteurs who landed on Long Island been baseball fans, they might have enjoyed seeing Yankee right fielder Tommy Henrich, who was of German descent, hit a game-winning home run at Yankee Stadium in the Bronx after they had arrived in New York on Saturday, June 13. Henrich, nicknamed "Old Reliable" for his consistency at bat and in the outfield, would not last through the season, though, because he would be called up by the coast guard in late August. They also would have been able to watch the Yankees sensational young shortstop Phil Rizzuto, now in his second season, make a rare error but handle nine other chances in the field flawlessly.

Rizzuto was a rarity, both because he was a native New Yorker and because as a teenager, he was only about five feet three inches tall and weighed about 130 pounds. No big league team had recruited him, although he had been an outstanding player at Richmond Hill High

School in Queens and had been scouted by the St. Louis Cardinals and Boston Red Sox while still in high school. But in 1935, when Rizzuto was sixteen, his coach, Al Kunitz, arranged a tryout for his star shortstop at Ebbets Field in his native Brooklyn. Extremely quick, agile, and sure-handed at shortstop, Rizzuto impressed Dodger scouts with his fielding and hitting. But the Dodgers' crusty manager Casey Stengel felt that Rizzuto was not big enough or strong enough to withstand the rigors of a 154-game schedule (plus, in the case of the Yankees, almost always a World Series) and, even more, having much bigger base runners crashing into him while trying to break up double plays. "Casey took one look at me, and said, 'Listen, kid, you better go and get yourself a shoe-shine box. That's the only way you'll make a living.'" Rizzuto recalled years later. "I was crushed."

At least that's the account Rizzuto always gave. Another account, which appeared in a book by writer Gene Schoor, a friend of Rizutto, said Stengel was not present during the Ebbets Field tryout. According to Schoor, the tryout, which involved about 150 prospects, was conducted by two of Stengel's coaches, Otto Miller and Zach Taylor. After Rizzuto had outrun all the other would-be big leaguers during sprints from left field to first base, he finally got a chance to hit, or at least thought he did. However, the first pitch thrown to Rizzuto by one of the prospects hit him in the back and sent him sprawling. In pain but determined to impress Miller and Taylor, Rizzuto could barely swing his bat and waved weakly at several pitches, missing all of them. At that point, Miller said to him, "Okay, sonny. That's it. Sorry but you're not ready yet, little fellow."

Near tears and devastated, Rizzuto then went home with an uncle who had driven him to Ebbets Field. Years later, after Rizzuto had joined the Yankees, Stengel said he was embarrassed to find out that his coaches had let Rizzuto get away without watching him at shortstop, according to Schoor.

Later that summer, Kunitz, Rizzuto's high school coach, still convinced that Rizzuto had major league potential, arranged for another tryout, this one at the Polo Grounds, home of the New York Giants. But after a brief look at Rizzuto at bat and in the field, Giants' coach Pancho Snyder also dismissed Rizzuto, telling him he was too small to make it to the big leagues. Disappointed but not disillusioned, young Rizzuto remained hopeful while playing in amateur leagues in Brooklyn, Queens, and on Long Island for the rest of the 1935 and 1936 seasons, sharpening his skills and eventually adding another ten pounds to his small frame. A second opportunity developed in 1937, when Rizzuto, then twenty, was invited to a weeklong tryout session at Yankee Stadium in the Bronx. Rebuffed at first by a security officer who refused to let Rizzuto inside the stadium the first day of the tryout, feeling he was too small to be a baseball player, Rizzuto impressed the Yankees' top scout, Paul Krichell (who years later would scout and sign Mickey Mantle) and Art Fletcher, one of manager Joe McCarthy's coaches, who conducted the tryout, particularly with his dazzling play at shortstop and his surprisingly strong arm.

"You could play a game every day during the tryout, and it was a good thing I could bunt and steal, although I did hit one in the seats down the left-field line, and so the Yankees signed me to a contract," said Rizzuto, who almost always deprecated his abilities as a player. After the tryout, an ecstatic Rizzuto boarded the elevated train beyond the center-field bleachers at the original Yankee Stadium, anxious to get home to tell his parents about the contract and how he would now be part of an organization that once included Babe Ruth and Lou Gehrig and in 1941 had three other Italian Americans: Joe DiMaggio, Frank Crosetti, and pitcher Marius Russo, the only other New Yorker on the team, who was also from the borough of Brooklyn and, coincidentally, had also played baseball at Richmond Hill High in Queens. (Another Italian American, Yogi Berra, would join the team in 1946.) Just maybe, Rizzuto thought, he might eventually be able to succeed Crosetti at shortstop and play in front of the great DiMaggio. That night, Rizzuto received a phone call from a Red Sox scout who offered him a contract. The call had come one day too late, and the Red Sox eventually would have to settle for Johnny Pesky, which of course wasn't bad at all. As it developed, Pesky would join the Red Sox a year after Rizzuto came up with the Yankees and would lead the American League in hits his first three years in the big leagues.

The year Rizzuto signed with the Yankees, the Bronx Bombers would win their second of four consecutive American League pennants and World Series, which made Rizzuto all the happier and the envy of his Brooklyn, Queens, and Long Island teammates. That summer of 1937, Rizzuto would be assigned to the Yankees Class-D Bassett Furniture Makers in Virginia in the Bi-State League, where he would hit a very respectable .310 in sixty-seven games. Moved up to the Class-B Norfolk, Virginia, Tars of the Piedmont League the following year, Rizzuto batted .336 in 112 games while delighting fans with his acrobatic fielding and his speed. In 1939, Rizzuto, now one of the Yankees' hottest prospects, at that time playing with the Kansas City Blues, the Yankees' Double-A affiliate in the American Association, where he hit .316 in 135 games, followed up that impressive season with an even better one with the Blues in

1940, when, as far and away the most popular player on the team, he batted .347 with a league-leading 201 hits, including ten home runs in 148 games.

As good as the world-champion Yankees were, there was no longer any way they could not bring Brooklyn's Phil Rizzuto back to New York, along with his Kansas City teammate, second baseman Jerry Priddy. When Rizzuto, now twenty-four, told his parents of his promotion to the Yankees, his father, Philip Senior, a streetcar motorman, broke open a bottle of homemade wine (it was during Prohibition) to celebrate with his wife, Rose, and a few relatives while anxious to get to work the next day to tell his co-workers, many of them Yankee fans.

When he reported to the Yankees spring training camp in St. Petersburg, Florida, Rizutto knew he would have to compete with veteran Frank Crosetti, who was thirty and starting his tenth year as the team's starting shortstop. Though a good shortstop, Crosetti was a weak hitter, whose career batting average was .241 and had hit a low of .194 in 1940 when the Yankees' streak of four straight pennants and World Series had been ended by the Detroit Tigers. However, with such hitters as DiMaggio, Bill Dickey, Charley Keller, Joe Gordon, George Selkirk, Tommy Henrich, Red Rolfe, and, up until 1935, Babe Ruth, the Yankees could afford Crosetti's low batting average.

During the month and a half leading up to the season opener, it became apparent that Rizzuto was a better hitter and as good, if not better, than Crosetti in the field. And on opening day in Washington on Monday, April 14, Rizzuto was not only at shortstop but batting leadoff. For a rookie, it was an especially memorable and moving day in Washington, because players of both the Yankees and Senators lined up along both foul lines during pregame ceremonies that included a considerable amount of patriotic pageantry and then rushed over to the box where President Franklin Roosevelt was to throw out the first pitch. Though he went hitless in his first game and the second the following day at Yankee Stadium, Rizzuto shone in the field, handling all seven chances flawlessly and participating in two double plays with Gordon while being greeted warmly by a hometown crowd of slightly more than forty thousand. Describing Rizzuto's play as "scintillating," John Drebinger wrote in the *New York Times* that in the fifth inning, Rizzuto "got a double play off so fast he looked to have it [the ball] on its way before he actually got his hands on it."

Rizzuto finally got his first hit, and two more, the next day, when the Yankees lost their second straight game to the Philadelphia Athletics at Yankee Stadium. As a number of sportswriters often would do during Rizzuto's first two seasons, Drebinger alluded to Rizzuto's short stature when he wrote about his stretching an apparent single into a double: "Of course since he is built close to the ground, it is difficult to tell where the little fellow's running stops and his sliding starts." In other accounts, Rizzuto would be called the mighty mite, the half-pint shortstop, and so on, none of which bothered Rizzuto, who was living out a dream by playing with the Yankees. Rizzuto even had to laugh off comments by some Yankee teammates. After getting his first look at Rizzuto in training camp, Lefty Gomez, the team's principal jester, asked rhetorically why the Yankees had to bring up a Lilliputian. Gomez, like the rest of the Yankees, soon came to like Rizzuto immensely, both because of his ability in the field and at bat as well as his likeable personality. DiMaggio, in particular, took a liking to the newest Yankee starter, often asking him to join him for dinner or a movie. It seemed like an unlikely friendship, one of baseball's biggest stars from San Francisco and a still relatively unknown rookie from Brooklyn. When his hitting streak ended in Cleveland on July 17, a disconsolate DiMaggio asked Rizzuto to wait for him before leaving the ballpark. Then as they walked back to their downtown hotel in silence, DiMaggio suddenly stopped in front of a bar and grill. Turning to Rizzuto, he asked, "Do you have any money?" Rizzuto said that he did. "How much?" DiMaggio inquired.

After counting what he had in his wallet, Rizzuto said, "Eighteen dollars."

"Let me have it," DiMaggio said, which Rizzuto did, whereupon DiMaggio started walking towards the bar and grill, which was uncharacteristic of the intensely private DiMaggio. As he did, he turned and said to Rizzuto, "Go back to the hotel. I'll see you later." Rizzuto, of course, did exactly that.

Years later, I asked Rizzuto whether DiMaggio ever paid him back the $18, and the Scooter said he hadn't.

"Did you ever ask him for the money?" I inquired.

"Noooo," Rizzuto said, characteristically drawing out the vowel "o" and smiling. "I'd never do that."

As it was, Rizzuto, with an empty wallet, had to ask one of his Yankee teammates for a loan to pay for his dinner that night in Cleveland.

Succeeding as he did, Rizzuto demonstrated anew that, of the country's three major sports, size means little in baseball, unlike in basketball and football, where height (in basketball) and weight (in football) are almost prerequisites. In future years, players even shorter than Rizzuto would have solid big league careers. Among them were outfielder Albie Pearson, who was to play with four teams during a nine-year career, and Freddie Patek, who would last fourteen years, most memorably as the shortstop for the Kansas City Royals during their glory years in the 1970s. Both players were five-foot-five, an inch shorter than Rizzuto, and weighed fewer than 150 pounds. The shortest pitcher in modern times was five-foot six-inch left-hander Bobby Shantz, who lasted sixteen years while pitching for six teams and in 1952 led the American League in victories with twenty-four.

In earlier times, there were even shorter players, but then men in general were shorter when they played in the early part of the 20th century and in some cases in the latter part of the 19th century. Among them were Hall of Famers Wee Willie Keeler, who was five-feet four and a half inches tall, which explains his nickname; and Rabbit Maranville, who was five feet five inches tall. Like Rizzuto, they rarely hit home runs. The shortest slugger was five-foot six-inch Hack Wilson, who led the National League in home runs four times, including 1930, when he hit fifty-six home runs, which at the time was second only to Babe Ruth's sixty, which Ruth belted in 1926. But then Wilson weighed 190 pounds, about 50 pounds more than Keeler and Maranville.

❧❧ ❧❧

Yankee manager Joe McCarthy had planned to play another rookie, Gerry Priddy, at second base alongside his Kansas City teammate Rizzuto while moving Joe Gordon to first base, even though Gordon was one of the best fielding second basemen in the league. However, Priddy had missed the opening game with an injury, and after seeing how well Rizzuto and Gordon worked together in the first two games, McCarthy kept Gordon at second. Priddy wound up playing all four infield positions but in only 115 games for the Yankees over two seasons and was traded in 1943 to Washington, where he became a starter for three years, and later played with the Detroit Tigers and the St. Louis Browns. Rookie Johnny Sturm would become the regular first baseman in 1941 but hit only .239 before being drafted into the army, never returning to the major leagues. Sturm would be succeeded in 1942 by another New Yorker, Buddy Hassett, who had spent three years each with the Dodgers and the Boston Braves after starring in both baseball and basketball at Manhattan College and spending three seasons in the Yankee farm system. After one year with the Yankees, Hassett joined the navy and served as a lieutenant aboard the aircraft carrier during the invasions of Iwo Jima and Okinawa in the Pacific. Hassett, by then thirty-four, tried to regain his first-base position when he returned from service in 1946 but was released by the Yankees. He then played one season with the Newark Bears, the Yankees Triple-A farm team in the International League, and two more in the minors as a playing manager before returning to Newark as manager in 1949 and then managing in Colorado Springs, Colorado.

From the very beginning, Yankee fans, especially the many of Italian extraction, became enamored by Rizzuto, and they had plenty of good reasons. He had an ebullient spirit and a ready smile, was spectacular at shortstop, began to hit well as the season pro- gressed, and was a rarity in that he not only was a hometown New Yorker (as was Gehrig) but was even smaller than most of the Yankee fans. Before long, Rizzuto was nicknamed "Scooter," and it both seemed to fit him and lasted through his later days as an iconic and idiosyncratic Yankee broadcaster given to malapropisms, birthday greetings to Yankee fans, and his signature expression of "Holy cow."

Indeed, Rizzuto would wind up as one of the team's most popular and beloved players of all time, as much for his unique broadcasting style and his ability to succeed despite his size as for his skills as a player, joining a pantheon that included Ruth, DiMaggio, Gehrig, Mantle, Berra, and Derek Jeter. And like Ruth, DiMaggio, Gehrig, Mantle, and Berra, he would wind up in the National Baseball Hall of Fame, as, no doubt, will Jeter, who at the time that this book was written is still an active Yankee. Because of Rizzuto's slow start at the plate, McCarthy often played Crosetti at shortstop, leading Rizzuto to believe he might wind up on the bench or back in Kansas City or in Newark. But by June, Rizzuto began to hit consistently and would cement his hold on the shortstop position for eleven years, except for the three years he spent in the navy during World War II.

Apart from Rizzuto and Sturm, the Yankees' starting lineup in 1941 would be the same as the year before and would again live up to the nickname "Bronx Bombers," as DiMaggio, Keller, and Henrich all hit more than thirty home runs and Gordon clouted twenty-four. Rizzuto hit only three home runs but batted .307, second on the team to DiMaggio's .357, and, although he only played in 133 of the regular season's 154 games, combined with Gordon to lead the league with 109 double plays. With Lefty Gomez, Red Ruffing, Spud Chandler, and Marius Russo (the only other New Yorker on the team) all winning at least ten games, the Yankees also had a formidable pitching staff, which helped the team win the pennant by an astonishing seventeen games and then beat the Dodgers in the World Series.

DiMaggio's amazing fifty-six-game hitting streak was of course the team's most remarkable accomplishment and overshadowed Rizzuto's solid rookie performance. Sportswriters and fans particularly marveled at his play in the field. Small as Rizzuto was, he not only was sure-handed at balls hit his way but often made spectacular stops of balls hit towards the "hole" between second and third base or balls hit "up the middle" towards center field. And, despite his small size, he had a strong arm and perhaps the fastest release of any shortstop in the American League in the 1940s.

DiMaggio, whom Rizzuto idolized, once said of his team's shortstop, "The little guy in front of me made my job easy, since I didn't have to pick up many ground balls." Ted Williams was another admirer, who said, "Pound for pound, he was one of the best players I ever played against," while adding that he felt the Red Sox would have won a number of World Series if they had had Rizzuto at shortstop in the 1940s and early 1950s. In another accolade, Vic Raschi, a Yankee pitcher from 1946 through 1953 who won twenty-one games three times during that period, said, "My best pitch is anything the batter grounds, lines, or pops-up in the direction of Rizzuto."

Ironically, Rizzuto wound up playing under Casey Stengel from 1949 through Rizzuto's final season in 1956, a period during which the Yankees won nine World Series, including five in a row from 1949 to 1953. "I used to remind Casey of how he told me to get a shoe-shine stand when I went to the tryout when he was managing the Dodgers," Rizzuto said, "but he'd say he didn't remember it, although I think he did. By 1949 I didn't need a shoebox anyway. The clubhouse boy at Yankee Stadium shined my Yankee spikes every day." Stengel never acknowledged having ignored Rizzuto during his tryout with the Dodgers, if indeed he was even present, and his praise of Rizzuto could not have been more effusive. "He's the greatest shortstop I've ever seen in my entire baseball career," Stengel once said, "and I have seen some beauties." He certainly had, going back to 1912, when he broke into the major leagues as an outfielder with the Brooklyn Dodgers. Stengel was even more effusive following a play Rizzuto made in 1951 in a game against Cleveland. With Bob Lemon pitching for the Indians and with DiMaggio on third base in a tie game, a squeeze play was called. However, Lemon, apparently wise to the call, threw a pitch high and inside to Rizzuto, one of baseball's all-time great bunters. With DiMaggio breaking for home, Rizzuto knew he still had to bunt to protect him and, leaving his feet, he bunted from around his head and got the ball to roll towards first base, enabling DiMaggio to score the winning run. "If I didn't bunt, the pitch would have hit me in the head," said Rizzuto, always modest about his accomplishments. To Stengel, "It was the greatest play I ever saw."

In the field, Rizzuto amazed fans and players alike with his quickness and speed and his collaborative work with Joe Gordon. Following a game in 1942, one New York sportswriter wrote, "It is almost impossible to tell when one of these Yankee streaks, Rizzuto and Gordon, receives the ball, steps on the bag, and sends the pill on its way to first. In the case of little Philip, it all looks like a blur."

During a game against the Phillies in Philadelphia in August 1942, the Yankees set a major league record with seven double plays, three of them by Rizzuto and Gordon, who combined for the record-breaker in the last inning when Billy Knickerbocker of the Phillies hit a ground ball to Rizzuto. Describing the play, John Drebinger, the *New York Time*'s beat writer for the Yankees, wrote, "This time, Little Phil and Joe-the-Flash moved so fast that Knickerbocker was retired for the second out before he had come within ten feet of first base."

And Knickerbocker, a 170-pound second baseman, was a fast runner.

Rizzuto's best year was 1950, when he hit .324, had two hundred hits, set a major league record for shortstops when he handled 238 consecutive chances without an error, led the league in fielding percentage, and was named the Most Valuable Player in the American League after finishing second in the voting to Ted Williams the year before. Rizzuto himself was surprised, knowing that the award usually went to a slugger like DiMaggio or Ted Williams or even to his double-play teammate Joe Gordon, and not to the best bunter in the league, which Rizzuto was. "My stats don't shout," he once said. "They kind of whisper."

When Rizzuto was unceremoniously released midway through the 1956 season, by which time he had lost his starting role, his 1,217 career double plays ranked second in major league history to Luke Appling, while his .968 fielding percentage trailed only Lou Boudreau's .973. At the time of his forced retirement, he also had appeared in more World Series games (fifty-two) than any other player. Rizzuto had to wait a long time, but in 1984, the Scooter finally was voted into the National Baseball Hall of Fame. His reaction: He wasn't sure he belonged.

"I never thought I deserved to be in the Hall of Fame," said Rizzuto, whose number "10" had been retired by then by the Yankees. "The Hall of Fame is for the big guys, pitchers with 100-mile-per-hour fastball, and hitters who sock homers and drive in a lot of runs. That's the way it's always been, and the way it should be."

But most of those who had played with and against Rizzuto, including Joe DiMaggio and Ted Williams, disagreed, as did thousands of fans who had seen him play. They felt the Scooter belonged in the Hall of Fame with those big guys and those fastball pitchers.

13

A PINT OF BLOOD GETS YOU INTO THE BALLPARK

BY 1942, **TICKET** prices at Yankee Stadium and at most big
league ballparks ranged from 50¢ for a bleacher seat to around
$2 for box seats. But 1942 was not a normal year, and on some days,
you could get to see little Phil Rizzuto work his magic at shortstop
for a pint of blood, five pounds of kitchen grease, or maybe even five
or ten pounds of scrap metal. All those commodities were needed
for the U.S. war effort, and baseball club officials were more than
willing to accept these items for free admission to a ball game.

On a number of specially designated summer days at many big
league ballparks, fans lined up with toasters, kitchen irons, and
other forms of aluminum, which was in short supply in the country
and was badly needed by the government and defense plants and
therefore became an entry fee to a game. It was baseball's way of
trying to help the war effort, as was, to a lesser degree, granting free
admission to servicemen and servicewomen in uniform.

At the request of the Dodgers' popular broadcaster Red Barber, the entire Dodger team, including starting pitcher Kirby Higbe, along with manager Leo Durocher, went to a Red Cross center in Brooklyn the morning before an afternoon game in June and gave blood. As Barber said later, "And they won the game that day. Can you imagine the impact it had in Brooklyn?" It most certainly did, especially photos of such Dodger stars as Pete Reiser and Dolph Camilli and Durocher that made most of the New York papers and, of course, the old *Brooklyn Eagle*. Largely as a result of that mass blood donation by the Dodgers, several weeks later almost a thousand fans showed up at Ebbets Field to donate blood, which was their ticket to the game that afternoon.

Because of an aluminum shortage, the Dodgers announced in late August that anyone bringing at least ten pounds of scrap metal to Ebbets Field over the next five days would be admitted to the ballpark. Almost a thousand did, bringing in frying pans, cooking pots, coffee percolators, waffle irons, shovels, and other items, which added up to an eight-foot-high stack of metal in the back of the left-field grandstand. Then on September 24, 13,461 of the 19,062 spectators were admitted free to a game between the Dodgers and the Boston Braves after they had each brought the required share of scrap metal to Ebbets Field. One teenager had presented his mother's new toaster, while another brought the family meat grinder as his ticket of admission. Whether their parents were aware of the boys' contributions to the war effort was impossible to determine. By then, the total accumulation after four days of the scrap-metal drive was approximately 520 pounds. It turned out, however, that the aluminum in those items could not be converted into airplane parts, bullets, hand grenades, and other weaponry, and it eventually wound up being recycled and remanufactured into toasters, frying pans, and so on. But it did not diminish major league baseball's effort to help the country's war production and to let contributing spectators get to see a big league ball game for helping that cause in the process.

Other big league teams held similar scrap-metal drives, along with promotions to collect much-needed kitchen grease and paper. In one such "kitchen-fat" drive at Ebbets Field in September 1942, almost five thousand people, most of them women, showed up with cans and bottles filled with kitchen grease that totaled almost five thousand pounds. Hardly anyone knew how the grease was going to aid the war effort until, when anyone asked, they were told it could be converted into glycerin for use as gunpowder. The Brooklyn drive was so successful that it would be repeated over the next three years of the war. In addition to getting to see a big league game without having to pay for it, the fans contributing blood, scrap metal, grease, and paper could justifiably feel that they were contributing to the war effort against the Germans and Japanese.

If the government needed grease, aluminum, and blood, it also needed more dogs as sentries in the army, navy, and coast guard. An announcement to that effect was made in late August when dog owners were asked to donate their dogs, at least temporarily, for military use. To qualify, dogs had to be in good health, from one to five years old, and at least eighteen inches tall. The government pointed out that dogs were needed because their highly developed senses of hearing and smell could detect an enemy's approach much quicker than human sentries. How many dogs were recruited by the armed forces as a result of appeal was never disclosed.

As 1942 went on, shortages of certain food stuffs, including meat, coffee, tea, sugar, butter, and cheese, and certain clothes and shoes grew worse and led to increased rationing. Because the Japanese now occupied Malaya and most other rubber-producing countries, buying tires was almost impossible until the Goodyear Rubber Company began to make tires from artificial rubber that had been developed in 1941. Responding to appeals for rubber, some car owners donated the rubber mats from their automobiles, congressmen contributed the rubber mats from under their spittoons, and women sent in girdles and garters, because, as the government kept reminding civilians, every little bit helped. Even bicycles, typewriters, fountain pens, and ink were rationed under a system controlled by the Office of Price Administration (OPA), which dispensed rationing books to OPA offices throughout the country. Because of a shortage of silk and nylon, women found it almost impossible to buy silk stockings. Some people got around the rationing by trading coupons, which was perfectly legal. For example, someone who didn't drink coffee might exchange his or her coffee coupons for milk coupons from someone who didn't drink milk. There were even meatless days when stores were not supposed to sell any meat products, but no one got arrested if they failed to go along with the recommendation. And although you could still buy a 1942 model car, it most likely had been made in 1941, when more than four thousand cars were manufactured in the United States, and not in 1942, when only a few hundred were made, since automakers stopped producing cars and trucks for civilian use early in the year and shifted to the manufacture of planes, tanks, jeeps, and other war materials.

Some Americans could live without coffee, tea, sugar, or a new pair of shoes but didn't like having to get by with only three gallons of gasoline a week, which was the amount limited to so-called Sunday drivers in seventeen northeastern states in the spring of 1942. That amount was increased later in the year, when rationing was expanded throughout the country, to four gallons of week to people with "A" cards whose work was deemed unessential. Drivers who worked in defense plants or at other jobs considered essential got "B" cards, which entitled them to eight gallons a week. "C" cards, which enabled drivers to get ten gallons a week, went to doctors, clergymen, letter carriers, and railroad workers, among others who, the government felt, needed more gasoline than A- or B-card holders. Figuring the slower you drove, the more economical your gas usage would be, New York State reduced its speed limit to thirty-five miles an hour in May, and some other states followed suit shortly thereafter. Then in June, the federal government stepped in and decreed a nationwide forty-mile-an-hour speed limit. It must be remembered that, in the early 1940s, no one was driving sixty-five or seventy-five miles an hour on highways, as became commonplace by the 1950s, when better highways began to be built.

If a lot of things that Americans had been accustomed to buying were now difficult, or even impossible, to buy, as many people started to produce things on their own in Victory Gardens, which sprang up throughout the nation at homes, schools, and other locations. Growing their own vegetables proved so popular and, of course, economical, that many homeowners who had never cultivated gardens in the past continued to do so after the war ended, either as a hobby or as a money-saving endeavor. Even apartment dwellers in large cities began to plant vegetables on terraces, patios, and rooftops, both out of necessity and as a patriotic gesture.

Cigarettes were still plentiful, even though millions of cartons were being shipped to servicemen and women overseas. At a time when many, if perhaps even most, people smoked, it was perceived to be both sophisticated and somewhat debonair. Famous baseball players and actors, in particular, appeared in newspaper and magazine advertisements extolling smoking. Cigarette companies, which donated huge amounts of their product to the military, also featured smokers connected with the war effort. For instance, in June 1942, a newspaper advertisement by the R. J. Reynolds Company, the manufacturer of Camels, featured a photo of Betty Weaver, a pilot, who flew war planes from factories to "the Army's flying line," as the ad said, with a cigarette in her hand and saying, "Easy on my throat—That's one reason I smoke Camels. And they have such a grand flavor." That, of course, was two decades before the landmark U.S. Surgeon General's report that cigarettes could cause cancer, most notably lung and throat cancer, among other diseases.

Almost two thousand other women from among about twenty-five hundred who applied—all of whom were licensed pilots—would join Weaver in ferrying new bombers and other military aircraft from factories to air bases and other military installations in the United States (which included the WASPs). Before she died in 2009 at the age of ninety-four, one of the WASPs, Violet Cowden, recalled how she had flown several hundred thousand miles in all kinds of weather, landed on runways without lights in planes that had never been tested, and survived after a plane she was ferrying caught fire in flight. Thirty-eight WASPS died in accidents during training and on duty, while many others were injured, some seriously. Yet they were civil employees and not military personnel and had to pay for their own food and lodging. In 1977, twenty-two years after the war ended, President Jimmy Carter signed a bill granting the WASPS recognition as veterans with some limited benefits. Then in 2010, Mrs. Cowden and about two hundred WASP veterans were awarded the Congressional Gold Medal, one of the country's highest civilian awards.

After the war, at a time when there were very few women flying for commercial airlines, Mrs. Cowden found that despite her experience, the only airline job she could get was as a ticket agent for Trans World Airlines. Finding the job unrewarding, she soon left to marry, gave birth to a daughter, and started her own business, while continuing to fly into her early nineties. Her inability to get a job flying a commercial airliner was ironic, because during World War II, airlines had to displace passengers when WASPs, with their high priority, had to fly to an assignment. On one occasion, a crowd of women had gathered on the tarmac in Memphis to greet Frank Sinatra, who was supposed to have been on the flight. But "the Voice" wasn't aboard, having been displaced by Mrs. Cowden, who had a higher priority but had no idea she was getting Sinatra's seat.

One thing there was no shortage of was gossip regarding celebrities. The thirties, forties, and fifties were the heyday of such gossip columnists as Walter Winchell, Hedda Hopper, Louella Parsons, and Dorothy Kilgallen. In her syndicated column of August 1, Kilgallen, whose father, James, was a nationally known reporter, wrote of how Olympic skating champion and actress Sonya Henie was "wearing the best sun tan in town"; actress and comedian Martha Raye was "in pigtails, jitterbugging at Jack Dempsey's [restaurant] with her sweetie, Nick Condos"; Milton Berle was in Lindy's popular delicatessen "stag because Joyce [his wife] is in Hollywood;" and actress Betty Hutton, "full-fledged glamour girl," was seen "ring-siding at La Martinque in the best Hollywood tradition— with her hairdresser secretary." Another item that made it into the gossip columns in August was the news that eighteen-year-old Lois Andrews had filed for divorce from forty-four-year-old actor and comedian George Jessel, America's so-called toastmaster general, two years after they had been married and had a daughter. "He was too old for me, and I was too young for him," Andrews said, while adding that Jessel "was tired of married life." Apparently he was, since, after having been married three times, he never married again, although he frequently squired many famous Hollywood actresses. Like the items in Kilgallen's column, the divorce action was hardly significant news, but many readers loved reading about it, in part, perhaps, because it took their minds off the war.

As the year went on, more and more women were hired to do jobs vacated by men who were drafted or had enlisted in the military. By August, an estimated thirteen million women were working, including about two million in "war plants," with the government hoping to have another five million more at work by the end of 1943 as more men went off to war. Women could be seen where they had never been seen before, working as ticket agents at railroad stations and airports, driving taxicabs and trucks, and even working as bartenders. Much of the work was at manual labor, such as at the Brooklyn Navy Yard, where more than two hundred women, who had been hired from a pool of about twenty thousand applicants, worked as mechanics, welders, and at other heavy-duty jobs that men had handled before and during the early months of the war. Working an average of fifty-eight hours a week, the "Rosie the Riveters" at the 140-year-old Navy Yard helped build the battleships *North Carolina*, the *Iowa*, and the *Missouri*, on which the Japanese surrender would ultimately be signed, and the aircraft carrier *Franklin Delano Roosevelt*.

Many of those women, like other Americans, were desperate for entertainment, and by the summer of 1942, Hollywood had quickly turned out a number of war movies to help fill that need (including *Wake Island*, *Sands of Iwo Jima*, *Stand by for Action*, *Mrs. Miniver*, and *Saboteur*). Those films all did well at the box office, but by early in the year, Hollywood film moguls realized that moviegoers wanted more light-hearted, escapist-type motion pictures and by August had released such movies as *Tarzan's New York Adventure* with Johnny Weismuller and Maureen O'Sullivan, *Big Street* with Henry Fonda and Lucille Ball, *Top Hat* with Fred Astaire and Ginger Rogers, Army Lieutenant Jimmy Stewart in *Mr. Smith Goes to Washington*, *The Magnificent Ambersons* with Orson Welles, and *Bambi*, which opened at the Radio City Music Hall; Rita Hayworth in *My Gal Sal*, Charlie Chaplin in *The Gold Rush*, Bob Hope in *My Favorite Blonde*, Shirley Temple in *Miss Annie Rooney*, *To Be or Not to Be* with Carole Lombard and Jack Benny, *I Married an Angel* with Jeannette MacDonald, and *Take a Letter Darling* with Fred McMurray and Rosalind Russell opened at the Paramount Theater in Times Square with the Benny Goodman Orchestra on stage as an added attraction (something that was common in Times Square theaters during the pretelevision era). And the biggest hits of the year were *Casablanca* with Humphrey Bogart and Ingrid Bergman, *This Is the Army* with Irving Berlin, and *Holiday Inn* in which Bing Crosby introduced "White Christmas," which developed into a Christmas staple and became the biggest-selling Christmas song of all time. And of course there was *Yankee Doodle Dandy*, which had a glittering patriotic theme, such rousing and uplifting George M. Cohan songs as "You're a Grand Old Flag," colorful pageantry, and an outstanding singing, dancing, and acting performance by James Cagney.

Stan Musial, seated fourth from left, on the Donora, Pennsylvania, high school basketball team. Stan was such a good basketball player that he was offered a scholarship to the University of Pittsburgh. (Donora Historical Society)

Joe DiMaggio with young Yankees shortstop Phil Rizzuto. (National Baseball Hall of Fame)

Bob Feller being sworn into the Navy by former heavyweight champion Gene Tunney on Dec. 10, 1941. (Associated Press)

Two of baseball's best second baseman, Bobby Doerr of the Red Sox and Joe Gordon of the Yankees. (Boston Public Library)

Pepper Martin, the colorful leader of the Cardinals Mudcat Band and a terror on the bases. (National Baseball Hall of Fame)

Leo Durocher with Dodgers president and general manager Larry MacPhail. They rarely saw eye to eye.
(National Baseball Hall of Fame)

Ted Williams taking a few swings during batting practice. (Boston Public Library)

Philadelphia Athletics manager Connie Mack, with his trademark scorecard. (National Baseball Hall of Fame)

Stan Musial in his peek-a-boo batting stance. (National Baseball Hall of Fame)

Good thing Ernie Lombardi could hit, because he sure couldn't run. (Cincinnati Reds)

Bob Feller, who had gone off to war before the 1942 season. (Boston Public Library)

The Polo Grounds, where the baseball Giants played until they left for Los Angeles after the 1957 season. (Bill Goff, Inc./goodsportsart.com)

Hall of Fame first baseman Jimmie Foxx, whom the Red Sox traded to the Chicago Cubs during the 1942 season. (Boston Public Library)

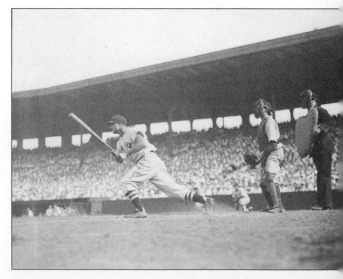

Ted Williams being sworn into the Navy in Boston on May 22, 1942. He would become a marine pilot in both WWII and the Korean War. (Boston Public Library)

Lou Boudreau, a shortstop, was the player-manager of the Cleveland Indians in 1942 and designed the eventual "Boudreau Shift" which almost every American League team used against Ted Williams. (Cleveland Indians)

Dodger outfielder Pete Reiser, who unfortunately had a penchant for crashing into outfield walls. (National Baseball Hall of Fame)

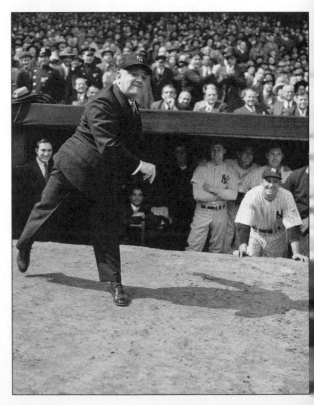

New York's flamboyant and popular Mayor Fiorello La Guardia throwing out the first pitch at Yankee Stadium on April 17, 1942, with Yankee players cheering him on. (Associated Press)

Joe and Dom DiMaggio with Ted Williams in the middle in 1942. (Associated Press)

John Cullen, the young Coast-guardsman who encountered four German saboteurs on a Long Island beach in 1942. (Cullen Family)

Ebbets Field, the longtime cozy home of the Brooklyn Dodgers, with its inviting right field fence. (Bill Goff, Inc./goodsportsart.com)

The Cardinals Cooper brothers, catcher Walker and pitcher Mort. (Boston Public Library)

The Cardinals outfield in 1942, and one of the best of all time, from left to right: Enos Slaughter, Terry Moore, and Stan Musial. (Associated Press)

Yankee Stadium as it looked before a massive renovation that made it more home-run friendly. (Bill Goff, Inc./goodsportsart.com)

Red Sox center fielder Dom DiMaggio, Joe's younger brother. (Boston Public Library)

Stan Musial with Cardinal teammate and first baseman Johnny Hopp. (Boston Public Library)

Monte Irvin, who along with Hank Thompson, was one of the first two black players from the Negro Leagues to be signed by the New York Giants in 1949. Monte previously had played for the Newark Eagles, perennially one of the best teams in the Negro Leagues. (Lawrence Hogan)

Lennie Merullo, the Chicago Cubs shortstop who committed four errors in one inning in 1942, with his son "Boots." (Lennie Merullo)

Cincinnati Reds pitcher Johnny Vander Meer, the only man to pitch consecutive no-hit games. (Cincinnati Reds)

Fenway Park with advertising signs that defaced the famed Green Monster in the 1940s. (Bill Goff, Inc./goodsportsart.com)

Fenway Park Gold © Andy Jurinko 1992

Cardinal third baseman Whitey Kurowski, like Stan Musial, a rookie in 1942.
(Boston Public Library)

Satchel Paige, who went from the Negro Leagues to the Cleveland Indians, with Indian manager Lou Boudreau. (Boston Public Library)

Ted Williams crosses the plate during a Red Sox victory in 1942. (Boston Public Library)

Joe DiMaggio and wife #2, Marilyn Monroe, on their wedding day, January 14, 1954. (Associated Press)

Sportsman's Park in St. Louis, home of both the Cardinals and Browns in the 1940s. (Bill Goff, Inc./goodsportsart.com)

Stan Musial home on leave in 1945. (Donora Historical Society)

Cardinal shortstop Marty Marion, who was called The Octopus because of his wing span and remarkable range. (National Baseball Hall of Fame)

Vince DiMaggio, the lesser known and older brother of Joe and Dominic DiMaggio and an outfielder for the Pittsburgh Pirates in 1942. (Pittsburgh Pirates)

A PINT OF BLOOD GETS YOU INTO THE BALLPARK

On the Broadway stage during the summer of '42, productions included *Porgy and Bess, Life with Father, Tobacco Road, My Sister Eileen, Sons o' Fun* with Olsen and Johnson, and Gypsy Rose Lee in *Star and Garter*. Meanwhile, in late summer, Harry James and his orchestra, one of the most popular bands in the country, was playing "I've Heard That Song Before," "You Made Me Love You," and many of their other hits at the Astor Roof, atop the Astor Hotel in Times Square, where a "deluxe dinner" cost $2.25, and the cover charge after 10:00 p.m. was 75¢ Sunday through Friday and $1 on Saturday.

In sports, Sugar Ray Robinson dominated boxing on his way to becoming possibly the greatest all-around boxer of all time, while Ben Hogan was on the cusp of stardom on the Professional Golfers Association. The great thoroughbred Whirlaway, now four years old, topped Seabiscuit as racing's leading money-winner when the colt won the Massachusetts Handicap for its twenty-fifth victory in forty-six starts. Little Pancho Segura of Ecuador, an incoming sophomore at the University of Miami, was the sensation of the summer tennis circuit with his two-handed forehands and backhands, beating such long-established stars like Gardner Mulloy and Billy Talbert and reaching the semifinals of the U.S. Nationals at Forest Hills, the forerunner of the U.S. Open, which was won by Frank Parker. Meanwhile, at a time when most male tennis players still wore long white pants, Don Budge, the first player to win tennis's "Grand Slam," which included the U.S., Australian, French, and Wimbledon championships in the same calendar year, captured the U.S. National Professional title by beating Bobby Riggs in the final and then joined the army air corps. In football, the Chicago Bears, the fabled "Monsters of the Midway" who had won the last two

National Football League titles, beat the College All-Stars, 21–0, before a crowd of 101,100 at Soldier Field in Chicago. Of the gate receipts of $306,250, $160,000 was donated to army and navy relief organizations. Almost half the players in the game, a traditional affair between the NFL champion and a team consisting of the best college players of the previous season, would be in the service by the time the next College All-Star game was played.

So, too, would many of the players still playing in baseball's major leagues, but not the extraordinarily unusual catcher who would wind up as the batting champion of the National League in 1942.

14

RUNNING DOUBLES
INTO SINGLES

ENTERING THE LAST two months of the 1942 season, four of the five leading hitters in the National League were either Dodgers (Pete Reiser, who had won the batting title in 1941, and Joe Medwick) or Cardinals (Enos Slaughter and rookie Stan Musial). Medwick, of course, was also a former Cardinal. The fifth player was catcher Ernie Lombardi, who, at thirty-four, was in his twelfth big league season, and who, unlike the other four, was a plodding runner, probably the slowest in major league history. Indeed, the six-foot two-inch 235-pound Lombardi was so slow that he once hit a line drive off the left-field wall at Crosley Field in Cincinnati, 330 feet from home plate, and was thrown out at first base by the left fielder. In later years, he would hit a tremendous shot that reached the clubhouse at the Polo Grounds in New York, almost five hundred feet from home plate, and yet he barely made it to third base for a rare triple. Several times he also hit liners off the right-field fence at Ebbets Field in Brooklyn, only to be thrown out at first base.

So far as is known, during his seventeen years in the big leagues, Lombardi, not surprisingly, never had an infield hit, and during a game at Ebbets Field in Brooklyn in 1942, he stole second base without drawing a throw, because neither shortstop Pee Wee Reese nor second baseman Billy Herman covered the bag, as they never expected Lombardi to try to steal, seeing as he almost never did. "We just froze and watched him steal second," Herman said later. To no one's surprise, Lombardi was always among the leaders in hitting into double plays, which he did 249 times during his career.

Despite his slowness afoot, Lombardi batted over .300 during seven of his previous ten seasons before being traded from the Cincinnati Reds to the Boston Braves in 1942 and had led the National League with a .342 average in 1938 when he was named the league's Most Valuable Player. That year, Lombardi was also behind the plate when Johnny Vander Meer threw back-to-back no-hitters in Cincinnati and Brooklyn, something no other pitcher has ever done going into the 2012 season. Attesting to Lombardi's skill and intelligence as a catcher, Vander Meer later said he never once shook Lombardi off on a sign during either of those games. "Ernie was a great catcher," Vander Meer said. So good, in fact, that Lombardi, who had huge hands, often threw runners out from his crouch. Those big hands also enabled him to prevent wild pitches when he caught them with his bare right hand. Vander Meer also said that Lombardi made a quick and intelligent decision during the last inning of his second no-hitter in the first night game ever played at Ebbets Field. With the bases loaded and one out, Dodger outfielder Ernie Koy hit a ground ball to third baseman Lew Riggs, who threw home for the force out. Lombardi was going to try for a double play at first base, but, as Vander Meer recalled, he saw Koy running inside the baseline and knew that his throw to first might hit Koy, who was a fast runner. "So Ernie held the ball instead of taking a chance of hitting Koy or throwing the ball into right field," Vander Meer said. "It was a smart decision, and Lom had to make it quickly." The next batter, Leo Durocher, flew out to end the game and put Vander Meer in the baseball record books for one of the most remarkable achievements in baseball history.

Lombardi's running was another story. Infielders almost always played back on the outfield grass when Lombardi was at bat, knowing they could still throw him out at first base. "I always played at least ten feet back on the grass for Lombardi," said Lenny Merullo, a former Chicago Cub shortstop in November 2012, "but I had no trouble throwing Ernie out from there because I had a very strong arm." That infielders played on the outfield grass for Lombardi was not surprising, because Lombardi, a right-handed hitter, was timed at seven seconds running from home plate to first base, about three seconds slower than the average big league position player. "You have to be awfully good to hit three hundred when you can't run," said Stan Musial, after watching Lombardi lumber around the bases one day during his rookie year in 1942. Mike Sandlock, who played briefly with Lombardi in Boston in September 1942 and against him when he was a shortstop and then a catcher with the Brooklyn Dodgers in 1945 and 1946, recalled Dodger manager Leo Durocher calling out to him, "'Get back, back, back,' even when I was way out of the outfield grass behind the infield when Lombardi was at bat." As a teammate, Sandlock remembered Lombardi as a "happy go-lucky guy who was always smiling."

Sandlock, who in 2012 at the age of ninety-six was the third-oldest living major leaguer and the oldest living catcher, recalled a game against the Dodgers when, with Dodger third baseman Cookie Lavagetto playing on the outfield grass, Lombardi lay down a bunt and beat it out. "Ernie and Lavagetto were good friends, and Lombardi was smiling while running to first base with the bat still in his hands," Sandlock said in November 2011.

What made Lombardi all the more remarkable was that he used an interlocking grip, much like that of most golfers, and rarely ever struck out. During his long career, Lombardi never fanned more than twenty-five times, as he did in 1944 when he was thirty-six years old, and struck out only six times in 1935, his fifth year in the league, when he finished fourth among the National League's leading hitters with a .343 average. In all, he averaged about fifteen strikeouts a season during his seventeen-year career, which was remarkable for someone his size who hit the ball as hard as any player in major league history.

Because of his slowness, Lombardi rarely hit a triple, although he often ran what would have been a triple for almost every other player into a double. For example, during a game in 1935, Lombardi hit four straight doubles. "Considering the fact that he always had to hit the equivalent of a triple to make a double, you can picture what sort of clouts some of them were," wrote Arthur Daley of the *New York Times*.

Big and strong as he was, Lombardi was not a home-run hitter, averaging about twelve homers a year and never hitting more than the twenty he hit in 1920. His tendency was to hit screaming line drives, some of which would ordinarily be singles, to the outfield, but in Lombardi's case often would be converted into outs at first base. Humble and self-effacing, Lombardi was extremely popular with teammates and fans, particularly in Cincinnati, where he spent ten seasons before being traded to the Braves. To many of his most ardent fans, he was something of an Everyman: heavy, slow, and unathletic looking, yet an outstanding ballplayer. Rather than being overly sensitive about his large nose, Lombardi was inclined to laugh or at least smile when he was kidded about it. That was true when famed comedian Jimmy Durante visited the Reds clubhouse at Ebbets Field in 1942, ostensibly to compare noses and to have a picture of them together that focused on their prominent proboscises.

To most Reds fans, his trade to the Braves in February 1942, for cash, no less, was inexplicable and unforgivable, because, although his batting average had slipped to an all-time low of .264 in 1941, he had hit over .300 in six of his previous nine years with the Reds. Cincinnati would regret the trade, since Lombardi would hit .330 in 1942 to lead the National League in batting for the second time and would wind up having hit over .300 ten times. Even Hall of Fame catchers Yogi Berra, Johnny Bench, and Gabby Hartnett had never done that. And it would be sixty-four years before another big league catcher, Joe Mauer of the Minnesota Twins, would lead either league in batting. Only one other National League catcher has won a batting title: Bubbles Hargrave, who hit .353 while also playing for the Reds in 1926. Joe Torre, after nine years as a catcher, also won a batting crown in 1971 when he hit .363 during his first season as a third baseman with the St. Louis Cardinals.

To add insult to injury in his trade to the Braves, Lombardi had to sign for only $10,000, $8,000 less than he had received from the Reds in 1941. Though he had an outstanding year playing for Casey Stengel in Boston, Lombardi was embittered at his cut in pay and let the Braves' management know about it. Aware of his disgruntlement, the Braves traded him in 1943 to the New York Giants, where his salary jumped by 50 percent to $15,000. After hitting .305 during his first year with the Giants, whose fans, many of them Italian-American, loved "Lom," as he was frequently called, he fell to an all-time low of .255 in 1944 but then rebounded with a .307 average the next year. Heavier than ever, perhaps as much as three hundred pounds, and even slower, Lombardi was relegated to being a backup catcher his next, and last, two years but still batted a respectable .292 and .282 in 1946 and 1947 and retired with a big league average of .306, one of the highest averages ever for a catcher, and the highest ever for a catcher who couldn't run.

Lombardi would close out his professional baseball career where it started in his native Oakland, playing one season, in 1948, when he was forty and batted .264, after he had been coaxed to play one more year by Casey Stengel, the then-manager of the Oakland Oaks. On a team loaded with future and former big leaguers, Lombardi helped the Oaks to a Pacific Coast League championship. Twenty years earlier, he had signed with the Oaks on graduating from high school and hit .377 during his first season and .366 and .370 the next two years. Those performances attracted the attention of the Brooklyn Robins in 1931, with which he would hit .297 in seventy-three games, but nevertheless he was traded to Cincinnati in 1932, where he would become a fixture for ten glorious years. Strangely, despite his outstanding career as one of the most feared hitters of his time, his popularity with fans and sportswriters, his likeability, and as an eight-time National League All-Star, Lombardi was passed over by Hall of Fame voters until 1986, when he was elected by the Veterans Committee, composed of Hall of Fame members, almost forty years after he retired and nine years after he died.

Some of Lombardi's fans, along with many others, felt that a play during the 1939 World Series might have kept him from being voted into the Hall of Fame earlier. With the score tied in the top of the tenth inning in the fourth game of the Series in Cincinnati after the New York Yankees had won the first three games, the Yankees got a run to go ahead, mainly on two Cincinnati errors. They then scored a third run when left fielder Ival Goodman bobbled a single by Joe DiMaggio, which scored Charley Keller, who barreled into Lombardi at home plate, dislodging the ball from Lombardi's glove. With the ball only a few feet away, a dazed Lombardi lay sprawled in the dirt, enabling DiMaggio to also score and give the Yankees a sweep of the Series. The run was not decisive, but some sportswriters and sportscasters criticized Lombardi for not reacting quickly and retrieving the ball before DiMaggio scored. Bucky Walters, the losing pitcher, said the criticism was "a silly rap, but the Yankees beat us four straight and they had to pick on something, I guess." Walters said that if anyone were to blame, it was him. "I was pitching, and I should have been behind the plate, backing up Lombardi," Walters said. "But the run didn't mean anything anyway." As for Lombardi, he said he had been knocked dizzy by Keller. Nevertheless, the play became known as "Lombardi's Snooze"—as if a proud intensely competitive player like Lombardi would have deliberately lain on the ground when a runner was approaching home plate during a World Series game.

Johnny Vander Meer also rose to his battery mate's defense. "The throw from the outfield came in on a hop and hit Lom in the cup," the Hall of Fame pitcher said. "You just don't get up too quick after that happens. The word got around that Lom took a snooze. Actually, he was paralyzed and couldn't move. With anybody but Lombardi, they would have had to carry him off the field."

The Reds came back to win the World Series in 1940 by beating the Detroit Tigers in seven games. Though Lombardi had been runner-up with a .319 batting average that season, he appeared in only two games in the Series, getting one hit in three times at bat while forty-year-old Jimmy Wilson, who had been Lombardi's backup and had appeared in only sixteen games during the regular season, inexplicably caught six of the seven Series games. That left Lombardi embittered at the Reds' general manager Warren Giles, who he believed was behind the slight. Far worse, though, was the memory of the tenth-inning play involving his collision with Charley Keller in the last game of the previous year's World Series, which tormented the sensitive Lombardi for the rest of his life, as did his failure to make it to the Hall of Fame while he was alive. After his retirement, he suffered from depression, brought on, some said, by not having been elected to the Hall of Fame, and, according to some accounts, attempted suicide about ten years before he died in Santa Cruz, California, at the age of sixty-nine.

When he was reminded that Lombardi eventually was elected to the Hall of Fame, albeit very belatedly, Vander Meer said, "Yeah, nine years after he died. That bothered me." It also bothered a lot of longtime Lombardi fans, who were fond of the lumbering catcher with the rifle arm and interlocking grip who couldn't run but could still hit .300 almost every one of his seventeen big league seasons and twice led the National League in hitting. His old team thought so much of Lombardi, though, that he was voted into the Reds Hall of Fame in 1958, and in 2004, had a statue of Lombardi, in his catcher's gear and poised to receive a throw, built outside the Reds' current home, Great American Ballpark.

For big, likeable Ernie Lombardi, all the honors were belated, but very much deserved. As a catcher and hitter, he had been one of a very special kind.

15

LAST OF THE .400 HITTERS

OR AN EVEN better hitter than Ernie Lombardi—Ted Williams—1942 had been a rough season at the start. Taunted by fans and some sports columnists for requesting, and getting, a draft deferment as the sole support of his mother, Williams frequently got booed and jeered when he failed to hit in crucial situations or appeared lackadaisical in the field, which he sometimes was. Such behavior was hardly wise, because even ardent Red Sox fans knew that the twenty-three-year-old slugger was fortunate to be playing big league baseball when young American men were getting killed and wounded in World War II. The boos and jeers abated somewhat when Williams, in a highly publicized photo op, joined the navy in May with the understanding that he would not have to report for active duty until after the season ended. But even then, he subjected himself to catcalls and sportswriters' criticism by some of his on-field behavior while leading the American League in batting through most of the season. Williams actually had said in March that he would enlist after the 1942 season. Regarding his criticized exemption, he said, "My conscience is clear. I have as much right to be exempted as anyone else, since I have a mother to support. When the season is over, I'll get into the navy as soon as I can." And he did.

By 1942, Williams, DiMaggio, and heavyweight champion Joe Louis were not only the best-known athletes in the United States but among the country's biggest celebrities. But where DiMaggio and Louis were soft-spoken and withdrawn, Williams was gregarious, boisterous, outspoken, often loud, and controversial. Where DiMaggio could outwardly ignore whatever booing and taunts he endured, particularly early in the season, Williams did not, as was the case during the second game of a doubleheader against the Washington Senators on July 1 in Boston. After he appeared to take his time running down a base hit in left field, a spectator in the left-field stands screamed out at him. As he was often prone to do, Williams, obviously annoyed, angrily answered back. When he came to bat again, Williams took two half-hearted swings at pitches before he flied out, which drew a chorus of boos from the Fenway Park crowd of about sixteen thousand. The booing intensified in the fifth inning when, with the Red Sox leading, 1–0, Williams took two strikes, and then, with a lazy swing, fouled off a pitch. On the next pitch, he swung nonchalantly again but managed to hit a double to left center field, scoring Lou Finney from first base. After he eventually scored, Williams was jeered again, whereupon the Red Sox playing manager, Joe Cronin, rushed out of the dugout and yelled, "If you don't want to play, get out of the game." Williams did exactly that, trotting into the dugout and continuing to the clubhouse beneath the first-base grandstand. Fortunately for Williams, the Red Sox won both games of the doubleheader to move to within four games of the first-place Yankees.

Still furious at his star player, as were most of the Red Sox, Cronin called a team meeting before the next day's scheduled game with the Senators and denounced Williams in front of his teammates while giving him an opportunity to apologize. "I felt it was necessary to dress him down in front of the entire ball club," said Cronin, who, like Williams, also would be voted into the National Baseball Hall of Fame. Cronin also told sportswriters that Williams had been fined $250 (around $3,550 by monetary standards in 2012), which even then was a slap on the wrist for a player making $35,000, big money in the 1940s. Williams, who usually avoided sportswriters, with whom he had a testy relationship, went out of his way to talk to them the afternoon after his misbehavior.

Demonstrating that he could be a good team player, a week later at Fenway Park, Williams not only lay down what was intended to be a sacrifice bunt but beat it out for a single to advance Pete Fox to second. Following a walk, Cronin flied out to drive in Fox with the winning run to keep the Red Sox within four games of the Yankees.

Despite that bunt, which drew a roar from the crowd, Williams never did stop letting Red Sox fans get under his skin, often spitting in their direction as he ran in from left field over the next twenty years, apart from the three seasons he spent in the service during World War II and most of the 1952 and 1953 seasons, when he served in the marine air corps during the Korean War. In late August 1942, Williams had to be replaced in left field after arguing with fans during the second game of a doubleheader in Philadelphia, which made him the target of a barrage of fruit and other items. While the nickname "the Splendid Splinter" was the most often associated with Williams, especially in his early years when he was leaner than later on, sportswriters also dubbed him "Tempestuous Ted" and "Terrible Ted," names that he did not particularly appreciate.

Carl Yastrzemski, a much milder personality, to say the least, also endured some booing during his rookie year of 1961. But that was mainly because Yastrzemski batted only .262, far less than Williams's rookie-year average of .327 and well under his career average of .344. What made it worse for Yastrzemski was that he was replacing a legend, and, as good as he would become during his own Hall of Fame career, he never could match Williams as a hitter. But then, no one could. What also helped "Yaz," as Yastrzemski was usually called by fans and teammates alike, was that he was a very good hitter, a far better outfielder than Williams, and later an excellent fielding first baseman. Then, too, the much more mellow Yaz had a very good relationship with fans at Fenway Park.

For all his clashes with fans and Boston sportswriters, Williams almost never questioned an umpire's call when he was at bat. He rarely ever swung at a pitch outside the strike zone, much to the chagrin of such Red Sox managers as Cronin, who felt that if he did on borderline pitches, he would get even more hits. "It was easy to call balls and strikes on Ted, because he almost never swung at a pitch that wasn't a strike," Hank Soar, a longtime American League umpire, once told me, "You almost knew instinctively that if he didn't go for a pitch, it was a ball. And he was almost always right. And if you might have made a mistake on a close one and called it a strike, the worse that he would do was turn and look at you for a second. Because he was so selective and had such great eyesight, when that happened, you sometimes wondered if you made the right call. But I don't ever remember him questioning a call." Jim Hegan, a catcher with the Cleveland Indians and a contemporary of Williams, once said, "I think the umpires felt that he knew the strike zone as well if not better than they did, and that if he didn't swing at a close one, they'd automatically call it a ball." Bobby Shantz, a very good left-handed pitcher who won an American League–leading twenty-four victories in 1952 also marveled at Williams' unerring eye at the plate. "I threw him some wicked curveballs that didn't miss by more than a fraction of an inch and he'd just stand there looking at them, knowing they were just outside," Shantz said.

Williams, of course, would always be best remembered as the last player to hit .400, or in his case, .406, and for the way he did it. Going into the last day of the season against the Philadelphia Athletics in Philadelphia, Williams was hitting .39955, which would have been rounded out to .400 if Williams did not play that day, and Joe Cronin gave him the option of sitting out the double-header. But Williams insisted on playing both games and wound up getting four hits in six times at bat to finish with a flourish at .406. That accomplishment grew in significance as years passed and no one could reach that exalted batting average. Indeed, the only one who came close was Williams, who at the age of thirty-nine led the American League again in hitting with a .388 batting average. When Williams hit over .400 during his third year in the American League, it was not as monumental, since it had been done only eleven years earlier by first baseman Bill Terry of the New York Giants, who hit .401 in 1930, Terry's sixth full year in the National League. Though he hit over .300 his last ten years in a row, and during eleven of his twelve full years in the league, including five as the Giants' playing manager, Terry, unlike Williams, never came close to .400 again. Williams also batted under .300 only once, in 1959, when, bedeviled by injuries, he hit .254 but then bounced back to bat .316 in his final season of 1960 when he was forty-two years old. As of 2011, Williams was still one of only two players—Rogers Hornsby was the other—to have won three "triple crowns," as he would do in 1942, 1947, and 1949, when he led the American League in batting average, home runs, and runs batted in. What was especially remarkable was how Williams returned to the Red Sox in 1946 after three years as a marine pilot and batted .342, only fourteen fewer points than when he led the American League with a .356 average in 1942. Many other stars also did well during their first season back from military service, but most of them spent their time in the army or navy playing baseball. Williams, by contrast, spent almost all his time flying jet planes and rarely picked up a bat during the three years he was in the service. Later, after spending almost all the 1952 and 1953 seasons as a marine pilot during the Korean War, Williams returned in 1954 to hit .345. One wonders what he might have hit the two years after he returned from service if he had spent all his service time playing baseball. But that's not how Tempestuous Ted wanted to serve his country. Williams loved a challenge, and the way he got it in the military was by flying a jet fighter. Baseball could, and did, wait.

Like the two other best hitters of his era, DiMaggio and Stan Musial, Williams rarely struck out, even though he was more of a power hitter than DiMaggio and Musial and hit 521 home runs during his vaunted career. In 1941, when he hit .406, Williams only struck out 27 times in 456 times at bat while hitting thirty-seven home runs. His highest strikeout total was sixty-four, in 1939, his rookie year, and, thereafter, he only struck out more than fifty times twice while averaging slightly less than thirty-nine strikeouts a year.

If Williams had a passion other than hitting, it was fishing, both fly-fishing and big-game fishing, which he pursued avidly during the off season. As in hitting, he was a superb fisherman, so good that he became the only athlete to be voted into both the baseball and fishing halls of fame. During the Korean War he flew as a "wing man" for John Glenn, who, as an early astronaut, became the first American to orbit the earth. "Ted was the best wing man I ever had," Glenn, who later became a U.S. Senator from Ohio, said years later.

Though he loved to talk hitting with younger ballplayers following his retirement, Williams was modest about his batting accomplishments and was never critical of latter-day players or changes in the game. In a conversation with this writer in 1991, fifty years after he'd hit .406, Williams did make it a point to note that players of his era might have undergone more difficult traveling and playing conditions. "During the forties and early fifties, we still traveled by train, and some of the trips, like the one from Boston to St. Louis, lasted almost a whole day," he said at Fenway Park when he and DiMaggio were honored for their epochal accomplishments in May 1941. "And when we played doubleheaders, in the days before every ballpark had lights, the second games sometimes lasted past twilight. It was pretty hard trying to get a hit off of a Bob Feller or a Hal Newhouser when it was after eight o'clock and starting to get dark." Making it downright scary, and even dangerous, Williams might have mentioned, players at the time did not wear protective batting helmets. But that's the way it was in 1942 when neither Fenway Park nor four other ballparks had lights at the time.

Asked once how he'd like to be remembered as a baseball player, Williams paused and then said, "All I want out of life is that when I walk down the street, folks will turn and say, 'There goes the greatest hitter who ever lived.'" The consensus seems to be that that's what Williams became during his glorious, albeit sometimes tumultuous, career.

16

GUADALCANAL AND A DRAMATIC PENNANT RACE BACK HOME

KNOWING THAT THE 1942 season would be his last until the war ended, and no one had any idea when that would be, Ted Williams was determined to make it one of his best before he began serving in the marine air corps. Considering how the Axis— the Germans, Italians, and Japanese—still held the upper hand in Europe, the Pacific, the Western Atlantic, and North Africa, it looked as if an end to the war was very distant, perhaps as many as five or six years away, if not longer.

By early August, despite staunch opposition, German tanks and infantry were advancing on Stalingrad, one of Russia's largest cities, in what would be the biggest battle of the war to date. By mid-September, German forces would be within Stalingrad's city limits in the hope of capturing the city before the harsh winter began in late fall. Casualties on both sides were huge, with as many as three thousand Nazi troops killed in two days during a Russian counterattack northwest of Stalingrad on September 22. Desperate for supplies, Russia continued to count on the United States to transport jeeps, tanks, planes, and other tools of war across the North Atlantic in cargo ships escorted by navy convoys as the German U-boat threat continued unabated. Even with convoys, the voyage from the East Coast to Murmansk in Russia was a perilous one, fraught with danger because of the German submarines lurking along that treacherous sea route.

For the United States, an even larger concern was the unopposed Japanese invasion of the Solomon Islands, a little-known British protectorate in the southwestern Pacific, from May through July. The intention was to cut off American and Indian supply routes to nearby Australia and New Zealand, both U.S. allies, by establishing air bases on the three islands—Tulagi, Guadalcanal, and Florida Island, which form the one-thousand-mile-long archipelago. To cope with that threat, a force of about seventeen thousand American Marines, aided by a naval task force and troops from Australia and New Zealand, invaded the islands in early August to launch a battle that would last seven months and cost almost thirty thousand lives.

The first attack on August 7, which took the Japanese by surprise, was the first major land offensive by U.S. forces in the Pacific. Australia, about a thousand miles to the southeast, feared a Japanese invasion because of their presence in the Solomon Islands and realized that its fate was in the hands of the Allied force, which was predominantly American but would also include Australian and New Zealand forces. The most fearsome fighting would occur in the jungles of Guadalcanal, a mountainous tropical island about ninety miles long and twenty-five miles wide, whose green jungles contained poisonous snakes, huge rats and scorpions, and malaria-carrying mosquitoes but also strikingly beautiful mynah birds, cockatoos, coconuts, and other tropical fruits. By February 1943 when the last of the depleted Japanese force left, almost seven thousand American, Australian, and New Zealand marines, soldiers, sailors, and airmen had been killed and more than ten thousand wounded, while more than twenty-five thousand Japanese had lost their lives and another one thousand had been captured. Most of the Americans killed were sailors, including two admirals killed on the same day, during a series of intensive naval battles in August and November, during which the U.S. Navy lost twenty-four ships, including the aircraft carriers *Hornet* and *WASP*, six heavy cruisers, and fourteen destroyers, along with an undetermined number of aircraft and supply vessels.

In the first engagement on the night of August 8, which became known as the Battle of Savo Island, the Allied fleet of twenty-three ships was overwhelmed by a Japanese fleet of only eight ships that sank four heavy cruisers without losing a ship, although three of its heavy cruisers were moderately damaged. Sent to the bottom were the Australian heavy cruiser *Canberra* and the American cruisers *Astoria*, *Quincy*, and *Vincenne*, while the badly damaged *Chicago* managed to make it to port in Australia. In all, 1,077 American sailors were killed while the Japanese lost only 54 men in a battle that lasted a mere thirty-five minutes. The engagement was the worst disaster the U.S. Navy had ever suffered in a sea battle and eventually prompted a naval inquiry, which absolved the admirals and other top-ranking naval officers who survived, including Admiral John S. McCain, Sr., the commander of Allied Air Forces in the South Pacific, whose son was also a four-star admiral (his grandson, John S. McCain III, was the Republican candidate for president in 2008). The battle demonstrated that the Japanese Navy was far better prepared for night fighting than its American counterpart and also clearly outmaneuvered and out-fought the much-larger American fleet. News of the battle was not disclosed to the American public for more than two months, and even then the severity of the U.S. losses was toned down.

The *Hornet* was sunk during the three equally intensive sea battles that occurred over a period of three days in November. The seventh ship to carry the name, the *Hornet* had launched the sixteen bombers that took part in the April 18 raid on Tokyo, led by Colonel Jimmy Doolittle, and had also taken part in the Battle of Midway. Launched only a year and six days earlier, the Essex-class carrier went down with 140 men. One of the other ships sunk was the cruiser *Juneau*, which went down on November 13 after it was hit twice by torpedoes off Guadalcanal. It managed to stay afloat and limped away after being hit by the first torpedo but was sunk when it was struck on the same port side by one of three torpedoes aimed at the cruiser *San Francisco*, which was not hit. About one hundred men survived their ship's sinking, but only ten were still alive when they were picked up by a rescue ship that, unaccountably, did not reach the scene until eight days later. The others either drowned or were attacked by sharks, which were prevalent in the area, bringing the death toll to 647. Among the dead were five brothers named Sullivan from Waterloo, Iowa. The brothers, who ranged in age from twenty to twenty-eight, had joined the navy at the same time with the understanding that they would serve together. To its eternal regret, the navy agreed, realizing later it had made a terrible blunder in the case of the Sullivan brothers, for whom a destroyer was later named, and would not again let brothers serve together aboard the same ship.

Allowing multiple members of one family to enter the service, let alone to serve together on a ship in harm's way, was not unusual for the American armed forces during World War II. In my hometown of Stamford, Connecticut, seven members of the DePreta family served in four different branches of the military—the army, navy, marines, and coast guard. All of them served overseas during the war, and five saw action, including Jimmy, a marine, who was killed on November 21, 1943, during the fighting on Tarawa in the central Pacific four days before what would have been his twenty-first birthday. Jimmy DePreta was killed during the second day of an invasion by ten thousand marines who stormed the island in landing craft and amphibious tractors, some of which got beached on reefs several hundred yards from shore, making them easy targets for Japanese gunners. More than 1,000 marines were killed and about 2,300 wounded during the three days it took the marines to secure Tarawa during some of the most intensive fighting of the war. All but about twenty of the nearly five thousand Japanese forces on Tarawa were killed during the fighting.

"We heard of one other family that had seven brothers in the service, but they weren't all overseas together," Tony DePreta, one of the DePreta brothers, who served in the navy, told me in January 2012. That family and the DePretas are believed to have sent more sons to war than any other family in the United States during World War II.

The overall U.S. loss during the Solomon Islands campaign was the worst in terms of personnel and ships that the navy had endured yet in what would be a prelude to later invasions in the Pacific of Tarawa, Okinawa, Kwajalein, and Iwo Jima. But it also dealt a devastating blow to Japan's hopes of cutting off supply and communications routes between the United States, Australia, and New Zealand in establishing a perimeter across the Pacific, stretching from the Aleutian Islands to Australia. Despite the severe losses, the campaign was one of the most notable successes of the war for the U.S. Navy, which had lost so much of its fleet at Pearl Harbor, in the Coral Sea in early May, and during the Battle of Midway in June. Indeed, the loss of so many ships, both by the U.S. Navy and the Japanese, during the naval battles around the Solomon Islands led many sailors to refer to the body of water from Guadalcanal to Savo Island and to Florida Island in the Solomons as "Ironbottom Sound" because of the number of ships that had gone to the bottom of the South Pacific in that area.

❧ ❧

Back in the United States, both naval vessels and merchant ships were being built and launched at a remarkable rate and quicker than had been anticipated. On September 23, a record was set when the Liberty ship *Joseph N. Teal* was launched at the Kaiser Oregon Shipbuilding Company in Portland ten days after its keel had been laid. The swift launching of the 10,500-ton cargo ship broke the previous record of twenty-four days set by workers at the Richmond, California, shipyard twenty-six days earlier. The record did not last long. On November 12, the Richmond shipyard, which was also owned by Henry Kaiser, regained the record when the Liberty ship *Robert Peary*, named for the admiral who was the first explorer to reach the North Pole, was launched four days after its keel had been laid. The ship had a glorious history, serving off Guadalcanal in early 1943 and later off Omaha Beach following the Allied D-Day invasion of occupied France in June 1944. Liberty ships were cargo vessels that the government started having built for England as part of President Franklin Roosevelt's Lend-Lease Act in early 1941 and were named for prominent, if not always famous, Americans. (Two of the best-known sports figures of the previous twenty-five years, Knute Rockne and George Gipp, the famed Notre Dame coach and his greatest player, had Liberty ships named in their honor during the war.) Between 1941 and September 1945, 2,751 of the ships had been built, with those built starting in 1942 made exclusively for American use. To say the least, they were a major factor in the American war effort. Scores of them were sunk by German and Japanese submarines and planes, while hundreds of others had to elude U-boat and air attacks.

Although ships were being built at an incredible rate, it took much longer to build a large carrier or a battleship. On July 31, fifteen months after its keel had been laid, the twenty-five-thousand-ton carrier *Essex* slid into the James River in Newport News, Virginia. Eleven other Essex-class carriers were under construction and expected to be launched in late 1942 and during 1943. Less than a month later, on August 24, the largest battleship ever built, the forty-five-thousand-ton *Iowa*, was launched at the Brooklyn Navy Yard. Five others of the same class were being built and expected to be in service by 1943. Overall, ships were being built at an astonishing rate in the United States. On Labor Day, September 7—no holiday for shipyard workers during wartime—174 ships of varying types were launched, and keels were laid for 49 more at shipyards across the country, believed to be a record for a single day.

❧❧

By August 1942, what criticisms there had been of seemingly healthy and robust young men playing baseball during the war had abated. Although draft boards seemed to continue to be lenient toward big league ballplayers, a few of them were called up during the season. The most prominent was Yankees' right fielder Tommy Henrich, who was called to active duty in late August, while batting .264 and with thirteen home runs and sixty-six runs batted in. Why Henrich was called up is surprising, because he was married and the father of an infant daughter and had three brothers in the service. What made that choice particularly strange is that a large number of single players without dependents would play through the entire 1942 season. Surprising, too, was that Ted Lyons, a star pitcher for the Chicago White Sox and an eventual Hall of Famer, was notified in late August that he was about to be called up at the age of forty-one—the fact that Lyons was a bachelor no doubt was a factor—but was allowed to finish the season and then enlist in the marines in 1943, where he became a captain before returning to the White Sox in 1946 when he was forty-five. The same situation applied to Birdie Tebbetts, a twenty-nine-year-old catcher for the Detroit Tigers, who enlisted in the army air corps on August 20 but did not have to report for active duty until after the season had ended. However, Tebbetts's teammate, rookie shortstop Billy Hitchcock, got no such reprieve. The twenty-six-year-old Hitchcock, a lieutenant in the army reserve, was suddenly called to active duty on August 10 after showing flashes of brilliance at shortstop. The twenty-nine-year-old Henrich received a huge ovation when the public-address announcer at Yankee Stadium told a crowd of 50,398 on Sunday, August 30, during the second game of a doubleheader against Detroit, that it was his last one before putting on a coast guard uniform. The popular Yankee outfielder, known as "Old Reliable" for his consistency, went out in style with four hits in seven times at bat during a sweep of the Tigers, including going three for three in his times at bat in the second game.

Most major league teams played a few exhibition games during the 1942 season, mainly against military base teams, some of which, such as the ones at the Great Lakes Naval Training Center in Chicago and the Norfolk Naval Station in Virginia, were good enough to beat the big leaguers and were even better in 1943 when they had such players as Joe and Dominic DiMaggio, Johnny Pesky, Johnny Mize, Red Ruffing, and Enos Slaughter. In one such game on August 24, an enthusiastic overflow crowd of about fifteen-thousand soldiers watched the Yankees post a 4–2 victory over the Fort Dix Army Base team in New Jersey, which included Jack Wallaesa, a shortstop for the Philadelphia Athletics who had been drafted earlier in the season. The Yankee regulars played most of the game and even started veteran star pitcher Lefty Gomez. That same day, the Cincinnati Reds were beaten by the Great Lakes Naval Station team, 8–0, as Russ Meers, who had pitched in one game for the Chicago Cubs in 1941 before being drafted, limited the Reds to five hits, while the sailors got fifteen hits off veteran Clyde Shoun. It was the forty-ninth victory for Great Lakes and the team's fourth over a big league team, which indicated that the sailors were not spending too much time learning how to tie knots, steer a ship, or signal with semaphore flags. The defeat was hardly embarrassing, because the navy team included several major league players. It had become evident as the season went on that major league baseball apparently had a morale and entertainment value to many GIs and defense workers who were able to relax while watching a ball game.

Demonstrating how popular major league baseball remained during the first full year of America's involvement in World War II, a capacity crowd of 68,136 watched the Yankees and Washington Senators split a doubleheader at Yankee Stadium on Sunday, August

23, while in Brooklyn, a full house of 34,000 saw the Dodgers sweep two game from the Giants. An even bigger crowd of 50,756 looked on in Detroit as the Tigers won both games of a doubleheader from the St. Louis Browns that raised $68,172 for army and navy relief. In Philadelphia, the Red Sox shut out the Athletics twice, 2–0, 7–0, in a doubleheader that lasted only three hours and forty-six minutes, even less time than some single major league games took by the start of the 21st century. Even quicker was a doubleheader between the White Sox and the Athletics on August 30, which lasted three and a half hours—one hour and forty-four minutes for the first game and an hour and forty-six minutes for the second game—even though fourteen runs were scored in the two games. Again, hardly anyone stepped out of the batter's box to adjust batting gloves, which no one wore at the time. Nor did pitchers repeatedly take more than a minute between pitches, either reaching for a rosin bag or staring down hitters for what in later years would seem like eternities.

Two days later, the Swedish liner *Gripsholm* arrived in New York with fifteen hundred evacuees from Japanese-held islands in the Orient, who had been exchanged for a like number of Japanese held by U.S. forces in the Pacific. Also on board was Joseph Grew, who was the American ambassador to Japan when the Japanese attacked Pearl Harbor. Sailing with a Swedish crew under the auspices of the International Red Cross, the *Gripsholm* would make about another dozen repatriation voyages in the Pacific. Newspapers that same week in August also reported that Marine Major General James Roosevelt, the oldest of the president's three sons, was second in command of a raid on Makin in the Japanese-occupied Gilbert Islands and would be awarded the Navy Cross for his service during the successful attack. Earlier, on February 9, the French luxury liner *Normandie* caught fire, capsized, and sank at a Hudson River pier in Manhattan while it was being converted to an American troop ship that could have carried as many as ten thousand GIs. Sabotage was suspected at first, but it was determined that sparks from a welder's torch had ignited bales of burlap, setting off the fast-spreading fire. Ironically, the French government had sent the *Normandie* to New York in 1939 so that the ship would be kept out of German hands.

Shortly after the *Normandie* fire, fears of sabotage on New York docks led to perhaps the most unusual alliance of the war. At the suggestion of Manhattan District Attorney Frank Hogan, a high ranking naval intelligence officer met with top-echelon Mafia leaders, such as Frank Costello and Meyer Lansky, to work out an arrangement wherein the Mob, which controlled the New York waterfront, would instruct dock workers to look out for possible sabotage and to report any other suspicious activities or conversations along the waterfront. Moreover, the Mob leaders would see to it that no strikes were called during the duration of the war and had fishing boat crews keep their eyes open for German submarines off the East Coast. In exchange for the Mob's cooperation and intelligence gathering, Hogan agreed to have Mob leader Charles "Lucky" Luciano, then serving time in maximum-security Dannemora Prison in upstate New York, be sentenced to a less-harsh prison in downstate New York with a guarantee that he would be released and deported to Italy after the war. Ironically, Luciano's long sentence for organizing and running prostitution rings in New York was commuted by New York Governor Thomas E. Dewey, who had prosecuted Luciano when he was a famed racket-busting prosecutor in Manhattan and had him sent "up the river." The alliance seemed to have worked, because no acts of sabotage were known to have occurred along New York or New Jersey docks during the rest of the war, U-boat attacks decreased, and labor peace prevailed. Neither the navy nor any New York State agency ever revealed details of the arrangement, but Dewey, in commuting Luciano's sentence, intimated that the Mafia boss had aided the American war effort. In 1942, the United States would take any help it could get, even from the Mafia, which did its part for the U.S. war effort.

In July 1942, the FBI announced that it had arrested four hundred German aliens in the New York City area and in Altoona, Pennsylvania, and its vicinity. In the Pennsylvania raids on July 1, FBI agents seized 250 aliens in connection with an alleged plot to blow up the Horseshoe Curve of the Pennsylvania Railroad near Altoona. Then on July 11, the FBI announced in New York that its agents had rounded up 158 "spies, saboteurs, and enemy aliens" in the New York metropolitan area on charges that they were dangerous to the security of the United States. Those arrested ranged in age from eighteen to sixty and included thirty-eight women. The raids were said to be the largest yet of enemy aliens of one nationality. An even larger group of approximately 110,000 Japanese Americans and Japanese nationals had been rounded up on the West Coast in February and placed in ten so-called relocation camps in the West, where they would be kept for the duration of the war, apart from those who, somewhat ironically, joined the military and served in the war, many of them with distinction.

Facing a manpower shortage, the Selective Service System announced in August that it would probably soon start drafting eighteen-and nineteen-year-old college students who had received deferments while in school. Army Secretary Henry Stimson also said that the age limit for men with desirable skills had been raised to fifty. Up until then, enlistment had been restricted to men between eighteen and forty-five. Also in August, Major General Lewis Hershey, the director of the national Selective Service System, announced that many married men would probably lose their draft deferments before the end of the year. "If I were a man with a wife only and were not engaged in important war work, I would begin now to make arrangements to enter the army," Hershey said. His announcement also gave married men an opportunity to enlist in another branch of service than the army if they so desired. Men who were drafted were almost certain to go into the army without the option of serving in another military branch, although it sometimes happened. The shortage of army personnel had grown so severe, Hershey said, that the army was being urged to accept illiterates and men with "curable diseases and correctable defects." Hershey never did say what curable diseases and correctable defects he was referring to, but his statement indicated how desperate the army was for men.

∞ ∞

With major league baseball playoffs still twenty-seven years away, there was virtually no interest in the American League standings late in the baseball season, since the Yankees again were running away with the division. After finishing seventeen games ahead of the Red Sox in 1941, the Bronx Bombers, in first place since early April and ahead by as many as thirteen games in late July, finished nine games in front of Boston in 1942. Cries, usually in jest, of "break up the Yankees" would be answered involuntarily by 1943, when three regulars from the '42 team—Joe DiMaggio, Phil Rizzuto, and Buddy Hassett, along with pitcher Red Ruffing—would join Tommy Henrich in the service, while third baseman Red Rolfe would have retired to become the baseball and basketball coach at his alma mater of Dartmouth. The only interest over the last two months of the '42 season would be in the race for the batting championship between Ted Williams and the Yankees power-hitting second baseman Joe Gordon. Williams had taken the early lead in his quest for his second straight batting title, but by July 1, Gordon had overtaken him with a .357 batting average, followed by Red Sox second baseman Bobby Doerr, who was at .347, with Williams at .336. But by the end of July, Williams had added fifteen points and, at .351, had taken the lead for good, with Gordon in second with a .339 batting average. Williams would eventually finish first at .356, fifty points below the .406 he hit in 1941, and would also lead the American League with thirty-six home runs and 137 runs batted in to capture the Triple Crown. Williams's rookie teammate, Johnny Pesky, would finish second in batting at .331, while leading the league in hits, and Gordon fourth at .322. It would be the only time during his eleven big league seasons that Gordon would ever hit over .300, let alone challenge for a battle title.

If the American League pennant was decided early, the National League's was not, as for the second year in a row, the Dodgers and Cardinals would go right down to the wire, with the race undecided until the last day of the season, something that hadn't happened since the Cardinals won the pennant and World Series in 1934. The Dodgers, who had edged out the Cardinals by two and a half games to win the 1941 National League pennant, got off to a fast start, leading throughout the first five months of the season. At the end of May, Brooklyn was six games ahead of the Cardinals, and by August 4, that lead had been extended to ten games. With Pete Reiser and Joe Medwick leading the way at bat, and with an excellent defense that included the league's best double-play combination in Harold "Pee Wee" Reese and Billy Herman, along with a veteran pitching staff that included four pitchers who would wind up with at least fifteen victories and two who would have ten, the Dodgers were a very well-balanced team, and it showed. They also felt that they had strengthened their pitching staff on August 30 by obtaining thirty-five-year-old Bobo Newsom from Washington for $25,000. It was the sixth time that Newsom had been traded, the second time by Washington, and eleven months later he would be traded for the seventh of what eventually would be ten times, from the Dodgers to the St. Louis Browns, with whom he already had been traded twice. Loud, flamboyant, blustery, and hefty at six feet three inches and around 230 pounds, Newsom had begun his major league career with Brooklyn in 1929 (when the team was still known as the Robins) and had also pitched for the Chicago Cubs in addition to the Robins, Senators, and Browns, winning twenty games twice and leading the American League in losses three times. When he rejoined the Dodgers, Newsom strutted into the Dodgers' clubhouse and said, with typical braggadocio, to his new teammates, "You got nothing to worry about; old Bobo's here." Well, as it turned out, that's not exactly what happened. Newsom would start out with a flourish for the Dodgers, pitching a four-hit shut-out against Cincinnati on September 2, but the best he could do was win two games and lose two in six starts for the Dodgers while leading the league in strikeouts for the second time, with 134. By the time Newsom arrived, the young Cardinal team had gone on a run, winning nineteen of twenty-two games to pull within three of Brooklyn, heading into the last month of the season.

Along with a pennant race in the National League plus scrap metal, kitchen fat, paper, bedding, and other promotional drives at big league ballparks, the summer of 1942 had its share of other diversions. One of the most heralded was the appearance of Babe Ruth and Walter Johnson, two of baseball's greatest players, between games of a doubleheader at Yankee Stadium on Sunday, August 23, before a standing room-only crowd of almost seventy-thousand (the original Yankee Stadium had a capacity of about sixty-eight thousand until it was gradually reduced from a wholesale refurbishing to fifty-sixty thousand in the 1970s). With the fifty-eight-year-old Johnson, who led the National League in strikeouts twelve times and won 416 games, second only to Cy Young's 511, still sharp and throwing surprisingly fast, the pot-bellied forty-eight-year-old Ruth had trouble getting into a groove. But once he did, he hit a home run into the lower right field stands, clouted a drive of more than four hundred feet to deep center field, lined several singles into the outfield, and drove one of Johnson's pitches into the upper deck in right field, but just foul, whereupon Ruth jogged around the bases in his pigeon-toed fashion, tipping his cap as he did, while the crowd roared its approval. It was Ruth's first appearance at bat at the stadium since his last home game with the Yankees in 1934—and would also be his last—and the crowd reveled in his surprisingly good prowess at the plate. In large measure because of the appearance of Ruth and Johnson, the double-header between the Yankees and Johnson's old team, the Washington Senators, produced $68,172 (almost $1 million in 2012's monetary standards) for army and navy relief.

Negro League games, still at the height of their popularity five years before Jackie Robinson joined the Brooklyn Dodgers, continued to draw well during 1942. The league's annual All-Star Game on Sunday, August 16, drew a crowd of around forty-five thousand, the largest of the season at Comiskey Park, where the Eastern All-Stars beat the Western All-Stars, 5–2. Satchel Paige, not known for punctuality, may have been partially to blame for the defeat. Scheduled to be the starting pitcher for the West, Paige got caught up in heavy traffic on the way to the stadium and did not make it to the mound until the seventh inning, when he gave up what turned out to be the winning, albeit unearned, run.

Big crowds also attended the league's World Series in September, when the Kansas City Monarchs swept the Homestead Grays in four games. The third game drew a crowd of more than twenty-five thousand to Yankee Stadium, where the Monarchs beat the Pittsburgh-based Grays, 9–3, with the legendary Paige allowing three hits while pitching the first three innings. As had been the case since the late 1930s, Yankee Stadium in 1942 was again home for the Black Yankees of the Negro League when the New York Yankees were on the road. Josh Gibson, who caught for the Grays in the game at the stadium, hit what is believed to have been the longest home run ever hit at the stadium a few years earlier, with the ball reportedly having cleared the center-field bleachers, 461 feet from home plate, and landed on the elevated tracks behind the bleachers. The mammoth clout would have covered almost six hundred feet, entirely possible for Gibson, many of whose home runs had become things of legend, and would have been the only ball ever hit out of the original Yankee Stadium. At least one former Negro League player claimed that he remembered Gibson hitting a ball out of Yankee Stadium, but at a different spot, during a Negro League doubleheader in 1934. "They say a ball has never been hit out of Yankee Stadium. Well, that's a lie," said Jack Marshall, who played for the Chicago American Giants. "Josh hit the ball over that triple deck next to the bullpen in left field. Over and out. I'll never forget it."

Though they in effect were barred from playing in baseball's major leagues, some Negro League players played with service teams. Among them were pitcher Herb Bracken and third baseman Andy "Big Six" Watts of the Cleveland Buckeyes, who in 1944 played for the powerful Great Lakes Naval Training Station team, which included a number of big leaguers, before serving in the Pacific Theater of Operations. A number of other Negro League players served in Europe and in the Pacific during the war, including Hall of Fame outfielder Monte Irvin and third baseman Hank Thompson, who in 1949 became the first black players for the New York Giants; and pitcher Leon Day, who like Irvin played for the perennial powerhouse Newark Eagles and was one of the first Negro League players elected to the National Baseball Hall of Fame. Irvin, who had endured bigotry while growing up in Alabama and later barnstorming in the off season with all black teams against major league players in the South, said he also faced discrimination while serving at army bases in Virginia and Louisiana. "We actually were treated better in France, England, and Germany than we were in the states," said Irvin, who served in Europe with an all-black engineering unit. "But even in Europe we faced discrimination and name-calling from American GIs. So you couldn't help wondering, 'What are we fighting for?'"

❧ ❧

Though the Cardinals had battled the Dodgers down to the wire in 1941, they gave no indication of that happening again during the first three months of the 1942 season. They split their fourteen games in April, went 18–11 in May, and only 13–9 in June. But over the last three months of the season, they looked like an entirely different team. The Dodgers, by contrast, got off to a fast start and were in first place through the first three months of the season. Even though they had improved to 22–9 in July, they still trailed the Dodgers by ten games on August 4. However, they then won fifteen of their next nineteen games before taking on the Dodgers in a four-game series in brutally hot St. Louis. In four previous series, the teams had split sixteen games. In the first game of the series, on August 24, left-hander Max Lanier, pitching on two days rest, went all the way as the Cardinals beat the Dodgers, 7–1. In his fifth season with the Cardinals, the twenty-five-year-old Lanier, whose son, Hal, would spend ten years as a major league infielder with the San Francisco Giants and the New York Yankees and then three years as a manager, had been born right-handed but began throwing left-handed after breaking his right arm twice as a boy. The following night, Mort Cooper went all fourteen innings (not entirely unusual in the 1940s), giving up the game's first run in the thirteenth inning, after which the Cardinals tied the score in their half and then won it in the fourteenth inning. After the Cardinals had also won the third game, 2–1, the Dodgers salvaged a victory in the final game of the series by the score of 7–4. Indicative of the excellence of the Cardinal pitching staff, the home team had held the Dodgers, one of the best-hitting teams in the league, to three runs over the first three games and seven during the four-game series, and had cut the Dodgers' lead to five and a half games. Strangely, Medwick, a former Cardinal star, was booed throughout the series. That made no sense, because he had let it be known that he was upset when Branch Rickey traded him to Brooklyn in 1940. Apparently, just seeing Medwick in a Dodger uniform at a time when the Dodgers had become the

Cardinals' biggest rival made him anathema to Cardinal fans, always among baseball's most fervent.

It was in one of the early Cardinal–Dodger games that Stan Musial did something he would never do again—make a move towards a pitcher. In the fourth inning of the first game of a doubleheader at Sportsman's Park in St. Louis on July 19, with the Cardinals leading, 7–0, rookie Dodger pitcher Les Webber, most likely on orders from Leo Durocher, threw two pitches very close to Musial, who managed to avoid them. After the second of what appeared to be "dust-off" pitches, Musial headed toward the mound with his bat in his hands— but was restrained by Dodger catcher Mickey Owen and umpires Al Barlick and Babe Pinelli. Musial then trotted to first base, never to make a move on a pitcher again, no matter how provoked, nor was he ever ejected from a game during his twenty-three year career with the Cardinals. Actually, Webber, who came on to pitch in the third inning, may just have been very wild. He unleashed one wild pitch and also hit Walker Cooper with a pitch during the game, which the Cardinals won, along with the second game, leaving them only six games behind the Dodgers.

If anything, Durocher's occasional attempts to unnerve Musial only served to inspire him against the Dodgers, against whom he hit better than any other team in the National League. Far more consequential than Musial's rare display of anger was the head injury that defending batting champion Pete Reiser, who was leading the National League with a .350 batting average, suffered late in the same game when he crashed into the concrete center-field wall while pursuing what turned out to be a game-winning inside-the-park home run by Enos Slaughter in the eleventh inning. Reiser was helped off the field by Durocher, roommate Pee Wee Reese, and right fielder Frenchy Bordagaray and then taken to a hospital, where it was determined he had suffered a concussion. Even though Reiser admitted that he was still having double vision and suffering sporadic headaches, he returned to action six days later in a move that might have hurt the Dodgers more than helped during the remainder of the season.

⚜⚜

Continuing to win at a remarkable late-season pace, by the end of August, the Cardinals had drawn within three games of the Dodgers after winning five straight, including two doubleheaders, and won nineteen of their last twenty-two. With Cooper winning his nineteenth game on Sunday, September 6, Johnny Mize did his old Cardinal teammates a giant favor when he hit a three-run homer to enable the New York Giants to earn a split with the Dodgers before a season-high crowd of 59,453 at the Polo Grounds. This whittled down the Dodgers lead to two and a half games, their shortest lead since early May, which would be reduced to two on September 10 when the Cardinals edged the Giants, 2–1, at the Polo Grounds, while across the East River, another former Cardinal, Lon Warneke, was limiting the Dodgers to eight hits in a 10–2 victory by the Cubs at Ebbets Field.

In the biggest series of the season, the Cardinals invaded Ebbets Field the following day, Friday, September 11, prepared to throw their ace, Mort Cooper, and one of the team's very good left-handed pitchers, Max Lanier, against the Dodgers in a crucial two-game series. And once again, the home team would have the enthusiastic support of superfan Hilda Chester with her shrill and loud voice and clanging cowbell in the center-field bleachers, the Brooklyn

Symphony sextet, and the most raucous fans in baseball. On both days, crowds of nearly thirty thousand, many of whom gained admission after bringing at least five pounds of metal to Ebbets Field, would crowd into the cozy and quirky ballpark, which had one of the smallest capacities of any major league team—thirty-four thousand. Yankee Stadium, by comparison, had double that capacity and arguably the best team in baseball, but yet for the second season in a row, the Dodgers would be the only team to draw more than a million fans. In the opener, Cooper struck out eight and walked only one while winning his twentieth game of the year and his eighth shutout, which brought the Cardinals to within a game of the Dodgers. It was also Cooper's seventh victory and fifth shutout over the Dodgers in a game that lasted an hour and fifty-seven minutes. The following day, Lanier, who had already beaten the Dodgers four times in a row, limited the suddenly silent Dodger bats to five hits as the Cardinals downed Brooklyn, 2–1, on a two-run homer by third baseman George (Whitey) Kurowski into the left-field stands to tie the Redbirds with the Dodgers for first place.

Like Musial, Kurowski, one of ten children, was of Polish descent and from Pennsylvania; and, like Musial, he had been brought up from Rochester in the International League in late September 1941 and had hit .333 in six games. By the spring of 1942, Kurowski had won the third-base position from veteran Jimmy Brown, who was shifted to second base, where he shared time with Frank "Creepy" Crespi. Kurowski remained the Cardinals regular third baseman for six full seasons, during which he played in four World Series, and sparingly in two more. Like Lanier, Kurowski also had injured an arm as a boy, in his case his right one, when at the age of seven he fell off a fence and landed on some shards of glass, severely cutting his throwing arm, in his hometown of Reading, Pennsylvania, sixty miles northwest of Philadelphia. Blood poisoning developed and led to a bone infection. At first doctors thought they might have to amputate the arm, as doctors were often quick to do in the 1920s. In fact, they did just that to six-year-old Pete Gray, another Pennsylvanian, after he fell off a farmer's wagon in his hometown of Nanticoke and his right arm became tangled in a wheel as the wagon continued moving. Even though doctors amputated Gray's right arm (which was his throwing arm), he managed to make it to the major leagues in 1945 as an outfielder with the St. Louis Browns. In Kurowski's case, doctors managed to save his arm by removing four inches of bone, which left the arm both crooked and shorter than his left one. However, it did not deter Kurowski from developing into an outstanding infielder and hitter as a teenager, who, despite his disability, became a very good third baseman in a very good Cardinal lineup. In large measure, that motivation stemmed from Kurowski's determination not to wind up working in the mines as his father and brother did, especially after his older brother was killed in a mining accident. Because of the shorter right arm, Kurowski, a right-handed hitter, had trouble hitting outside pitches and thus had to crowd the plate, which led to him being hit often. It also meant that when he swung a bat, he had to turn his right wrist over, which tended to make him a pull hitter. A muscular five feet eleven inches and weighing 190 pounds, Kurowski hit for both average and power, slugging more than twenty home runs three times and driving in more than a hundred runs twice. A good contact hitter, Kurowski, like Musial, rarely struck out, never fanning more than sixty times in a season.

The lead in the *New York Times* story the day after the Cardinals had tied the Dodgers said it all: "Flatbush fandom's worst fears today are a woeful reality. Those irrepressible St. Louis Cardinals tied Brooklyn's Dodgers for the National League lead."

It only got worse the next day, a Sunday, when the Dodgers lost a doubleheader to the Cincinnati Reds before another big crowd of about thirty-two thousand at Ebbets Field for their fourth and fifth consecutive losses, while the Cardinals split a doubleheader with the Phillies in Philadelphia to take over first place by a half game.

That same day, Lenny Merullo of the Chicago Cubs had what was probably the most memorable day of his life. In the second game of a doubleheader against the Braves in Boston, Merullo set an unenviable record for a shortstop by committing four errors in the second inning. If he was nervous in the field, it was understandable, because he had been informed before the doubleheader that his wife, Jean, had given birth to their first child, a son, in a Boston hospital. The Merullos named their infant boy Leonard, Jr., but, after seeing headlines in Boston newspapers the following day referring to Merullo's errors as "boots," nicknamed their infant son Boots, a baseball term for an error. "The nickname stuck, and everyone, including my parents, still call me Boots," said Leonard Merullo, Jr., who spent three years in the Pittsburgh Pirates organization. Asked in 2012 for his recollection of how he felt when he took the field on that memorable day, the ninety-four-year-old former Cub shortstop said, "I was very excited and wanted to play perfectly, but I didn't, I guess, because I was very anxious to see my son." His first of four sons, Leonard "Boots" Merullo, Jr., had a better explanation: "Knowing my dad, he was probably a basket case out there."

Meanwhile, the following day, September 14, the Cardinals scored four runs in the ninth inning to beat the Phillies, 6–3, on three Phillies' errors and a game-winning single by Stan Musial. That same day, the Yankees clinched their sixth pennant in the last seven years with an 8–3 victory over the Indians in Cleveland as Ernie Bonham won his twentieth game, Joe DiMaggio hit his nineteenth home run, and Phil Rizzuto had three hits.

As they had the day before, the Cardinals came from behind to edge the Phillies, 3–2, in the fourteenth inning, when Jimmy Brown drove in pitcher Murray Dickson with a single to increase the St. Louis lead two games over the idle Dodgers. After ending a five-game losing streak with a win over Pittsburgh, Brooklyn fell to the Pirates, while the resilient Cardinals again came from behind by scoring five runs in the ninth inning to defeat the Boston Braves, 6–4, on a game-winning single by Coaker Triplett, who was batting for Musial, even though Stan the Man was among the five top hitters in the National League. Some might have criticized letting Triplett, a .280 hitter, bat for Musial in a crucial situation, but as he had done so often all season long, Cardinal manager Bill Southworth once again went with his instincts and prevailed as the Redbirds opened up a three-game lead over the Dodgers.

By then, the football season was in full swing, although the Cardinal–Dodger stretch drive was still the biggest sports story of the month. Army football teams, like a number of navy baseball teams, included former professional players and more than held their own with National Football League teams. For example, on Wednesday, September 16, the Army All-Stars, consisting primarily of former All-American players, beat the Baltimore Colts after having beaten the New York Giants and the Brooklyn Dodgers in their two previous games. Both for morale and entertainment purposes, military officials felt that large army bases and naval installations should field teams capable of beating major league baseball and football teams, and they were, especially teams representing the Great Lakes Naval Training Center, which continued to field the strongest baseball and football teams through the war. Football, both college and pro, though, could not match the spurt by a young Cardinal team, which by then was being cheered on not only in Missouri but in most of the Southwest and whose ability to overcome the veteran Dodgers had also drawn the interest of sports fans throughout much of the rest of the country. They may not have been the Gas House Gang of the thirties, but they certainly were exciting, aggressive, and fast, running the bases with abandon and repeatedly coming from behind to win. By mid-September, it was clear that they had the best defensive outfield in baseball, and in the tall, slender Marty Marion, in his second year with the Cardinals, a far-ranging and spectacular shortstop. They also had two of the game's best hitters in the forever hustling Slaughter and young Musial, an outstanding young pitching staff, and, in Southworth, a father-figure manager perfectly suited for this young team and who seemingly always made the right moves, even when pinch-hitting for Musial.

Though there was still a week to go, on September 19, the Cardinal management announced that all the reserved seats at Sportsman's Park had been sold out, which indicated that the Cardinals felt that the Dodger swoon would continue—and it did. So, too, would the Cardinals remarkable late-season run in which they won twelve of their last thirteen games and forty-five of their final fifty-six. Moreover, they would do it the hard way, playing and winning their last six games on the road, with the clincher coming on September 24, when

Mort Cooper won his league-leading twenty-second victory and tenth shutout by limiting Cincinnati to two hits, while Musial, having his second great September, went three-for-four and made a spectacular catch in left field. Still, the pennant race went down to the last day, Sunday, September 27. To force a one-game playoff the next day, the Dodgers had to win their eighth straight game by beating the Phillies in Philadelphia, while the Cardinals would need to lose both games of a doubleheader to the Cubs in St. Louis. The Dodgers won, 4–3, but so did the Cardinals, twice, defeating the Cubs, 9–2 and 4–1.

By finishing with 106 victories, they had won more games than any team since 1909, when the Pittsburgh Pirates won 110. With 104 victories, the Dodgers, as the second-place finisher, had recorded more victories than the hundred they scored in 1941 when they captured the National League pennant. That was little consolation for the Dodgers, who had been in first place from April 19 until September 5, by which time the bottom had already fallen out. Over their first 104 games, the Dodgers had posted a 74–30 record, far better than the Cardinals' 64–40. But during their last sixty games, the Dodgers had a 30–20 record, while St. Louis had finished at 42–8. For the Dodgers, it had been an epic collapse, and for the Cardinals a remarkable finish. Now, to complete their remarkable late-season surge, all the Cardinals had to do was beat the Yankees in the World Series, which would start on Wednesday, September 30, in St. Louis, where the Redbirds had won sixty of seventy-seven games, more than any other major league team. Once again, the Yankees had won the American League championship easily, winning 103 games and finishing 9 games ahead of the Red Sox. No one would give the flying Redbirds much of a chance in the first-ever World Series between the two teams.

Reflecting their dominance in the second half of the 1942 season, the Cardinals led the league in most offensive categories—batting average, hits, runs, doubles, triples, on-base percentage, and slugging percentage. In pitching, they led in earned-run average, fewest hits allowed, most shutouts, and strikeouts. Individually, Mort Cooper led the league with twenty-two victories, a 1.78 earned-run average, and ten shutouts, while also pitching twenty-two complete games, second to the twenty-eight completed by knuckleballer Jim Tobin, who also led the league with twenty-two losses and most home runs by a pitcher, with five. At bat, Slaughter led the National League with 188 hits and seventeen triples, and in total bases with 292, while Marty Marion's thirty-eight doubles were also a league-high. The Dodgers, by contrast, led in only two offensive team categories: bases on balls and stolen bases; in one offensive category: the twenty stolen bases by Pete Reiser; and in pitching saves with thirteen by Hugh Casey.

Years later, Kirby Higbe recalled how Larry MacPhail called a team meeting in mid-August after the Dodgers had edged the Phillies, 1–0, in Brooklyn, when the Dodgers were ten games ahead of the Cardinals. "He called us over after the game, and he said, 'I'm telling you boys, the Cardinals are going to beat you out if you're not careful.'" Higbe, who finished with a 16–11 record and a 3.50 earned-run average, quoted MacPhail as saying, "'You guys are getting lackadaisical. You think you have it clinched, and before you know it, they're going to beat you.' And in '42, damn if they didn't."

As it was, the Dodgers went 18–11 in August and 16–10 in September, which wasn't bad. What did the Dodgers in was the three-game sweep by the Cardinals in St. Louis in late August and a five-game losing streak in mid-September, which included two more losses to the Redbirds, and to the fact that the Cardinals were a blistering 25–9 in August and 21–4 in September. Perhaps as significant a factor was Pete Reiser's head injury on July 18, when he crashed into the center-field fence at Ebbets Field and which affected his play for the rest of the season. After leading the league in batting through the first four months of the season, and with his average as high as .383 in early July, Reiser, still plagued by double vision and headaches, hit below .200 over the last two months of the season and ended up at .310. Reiser would never be the same after his injury but refused to blame Durocher for playing him so soon after he was hurt.

"I have never blamed Leo for keeping me in there," Reiser told author Peter Golenbock. "I blame myself. He wanted to win so badly it hurt, and I wanted to win so bad it hurt."

Still, the decision to let Reiser keep playing in 1942 proved costly to the Dodgers during the final two months of the season, when they no doubt would have fared better with another player in center field, even if it had to be one of the two reserve outfielders, Augie Galan or Johnny Rizzo, or perhaps a player obtained in a late-season trade. After serving in the army for three years, Reiser returned to the Dodgers in 1946 and hit .277 while again leading the National League in stolen bases with a career-high thirty-four. But after hitting .309 in 1947, when the Dodgers won the National League pennant but lost to the Yankees in the World Series, and .236 in 1948, Reiser was traded to the Boston Braves in 1940, where he batted .271 and .205 during limited playing time. Traded again in 1951, this time to Pittsburgh, he hit .271 in seventy-four games and then a career-low of .136 in thirty-four games during a final season with the Cleveland Indians in 1953 when he was thirty-three years old.

After having hit over .300 in three of his first five big league seasons, Reiser never hit higher than .271 over his last five years and finished with a career batting average of .295. Most managers, coaches, players, and sportswriters who had watched Reiser play often during the start of his career were convinced that had it not been for his propensity to play with a reckless abandon and to crash into outfield walls several times, and also come back too soon after his serious head injury in July 1942, Reiser could possibly have enjoyed a career similar to that of such stars as Stan Musial and Willie Mays, players who could do it all—hit consistently, field brilliantly, and dazzle fans with their speed on the bases. Sadly, everyone had to be left to wonder whether Pete Reiser never really had the chance to reach his potential because of his tendency to crash into outfield fences and then to return to play much too soon.

17

A MISMATCHED WORLD SERIES?

BY THE TIME the major league season ended on September 27, scores of players knew that it had been their last one until the war was over, and the end seemed far away, even though the United States had made considerable progress against Japan and, with its allies, against Germany and Italy, but with a great loss of life. Indeed, by September, there were thousands of gold stars on house windows, signifying that a member of the family had been killed in action. Most of the American military deaths in August and September were during the fierce fighting against the Japanese—much of it hand-to-hand—in the Solomon Islands in the southwestern Pacific, where U.S., Australian, and New Zealand troops were trying to dislodge Japanese Marines and soldiers who had invaded the British protectorate in May. The worse fighting was on the island of Guadalcanal—the "Canal," as the marines and soldiers who fought there called it—while nearby, American and Japanese ships would later fight one of the most ferocious naval battles in history over a three-day period in November that resulted in the loss of about five thousand American lives and twenty ships. On the first day alone, thirteen hundred American sailors, including two admirals, would be killed, and the American cruisers *Atlanta* and *Juneau* as well as four destroyers would be sunk in a battle in which American and Japanese warships were at times blasting away at one another with deadly salvos while fewer than a thousand feet apart. The greatest American naval loss was that of the carrier *Hornet*, which sank on October 26 after being hit by about a half dozen bombs and nine torpedoes in the battle of the Santa Cruz Islands, but not before almost all its planes had been flown off the ship.

In Europe, house to house fighting raged between Russian and German forces in and around Stalingrad as the Russians sought to drive back tens of thousands of Nazi troops bent on occupying Russia's second-largest city. In North Africa, the famed Panzer divisions of the brilliant German General Erwin Rommel, the so-called "Desert Fox," had captured the British stronghold of Tobruk in Libya, capturing twenty-five thousand Allied troops, and had driven the British into Egypt while threatening to take over most of the Middle East. Overall, the wartime picture was considerably brighter for the United States and its Allies by late September 1942 than it had been on baseball's opening day five and a half months earlier. Thanks to increased navy and coast guard patrols and escorts, far fewer tankers and cargo ships were being sunk in the western Atlantic near the East Coast. The most encouraging development was the awesome production capacity of America's industrial might, which was turning out bombers in a single day, along with warships and cargo vessels, fighters, transport and cargo planes, tanks, jeeps, trucks, weaponry, and other materials for the U.S. military at an astonishing rate. Also encouraging were the sacrifices being made on the home front, as most people willingly accepted the rationing of gasoline, meat, coffee, tea, sugar, and even shoes and clothing. Encouraging, too, was the increasing participation of millions of Americans as air-raid wardens, aircraft spotters, and volunteer pilots in the country's civil air patrol along the U.S. coast lines.

By September, it seemed clear that what opposition had existed to major league baseball during wartime had faded and that the games had provided a form of entertainment and relaxation that was beneficial on the home front, especially to defense workers and military personnel, and even to GIs abroad. Because of baseball's wartime popularity, and in light of the intriguing pairing in the 1942 World Series between the young underdog St. Louis Cardinals and the veteran defending champion New York Yankees, Armed Forces Radio, a major provider of entertainment for American troops stationed abroad and on ships at sea, announced it would broadcast the so-called "Fall Classic" to American GIs in war zones throughout the world.

Because the Series shaped up as a mismatch to most baseball writers and columnists, the Yankees were established as a prohibitive favorite at one-to-four odds, meaning a Yankee bettor had to wager $4 to win $1, while a $1 wager on the Cardinals could earn $4 should they win. That was not surprising, since the Yanks had breezed through their American League opposition to win the pennant by nine games, while the Cardinals had to go through the crucible of an intense pennant race before clinching the National League pennant. Also, in Joe DiMaggio, Bill Dickey, and Joe Gordon, the Yankees had three of baseball's best players, along with young Phil Rizzuto, a future Hall of Famer like DiMaggio; Dickey, Red Ruffing; and Lefty Gomez, all of whom had been on a Yankee team that had beaten the Brooklyn Dodgers in five games the year before in winning their fifth World Series in six years. And the team had a wealth of World Series experience. Dickey, Ruffing, and Gomez had been in six World Series, DiMaggio and third baseman Red Rolfe in five, and Gordon in three. The so-called Bronx Bombers also had a veteran pitching staff, with four pitchers who had won at least fourteen games, led by Ernie Bonham, who had twenty-one victories, second only to the Red Sox's Tex Hughson's twenty-two, while leading the league with twenty-two complete games and an .808 winning percentage, losing only five games. By contrast, none of the current Cardinals had ever played in a World Series, and the team hadn't played in one since 1934, during the Gas House Gang era.

Of the four Yankee starters, two, Ruffing and Spud Chandler, were thirty-seven and thirty-five years old, while none of the Cardinal pitchers were older than twenty-nine-year-old Mort Cooper. Of the position players, three Yankees were over thirty—Dickey, Rolfe, and Buddy Hassett—while only one Cardinal, second baseman Jimmy Brown, at thirty-two, was over thirty. With DiMaggio, Keller, Gordon, and Dickey all home-run threats, the Yankees had more power, while the Cardinals had greater speed, with Musial, Slaughter, and Brown, in particular, being very fast on the bases. Keller, DiMaggio, and Gordon, with twenty-six, twenty-one, and eighteen home runs each, had more than anyone on the Cardinals, who were led by Slaughter and Musial, who had hit thirteen and ten homers, respectively. Only two players on each team had hit over .300—DiMaggio and Gordon for the Yankees, and Slaughter and Musial for the Cardinals. Again, if experience was to count, the Yankees had the advantage, particularly in pitching and catching.

And historically, in the World Series, pitching was usually the most important factor in determining the winner.

⁂

The opening game was played in Sportsman's Park in St. Louis, whose field was well-worn and hardened by the summer sun and having endured the cumulative 154 games played on it by the Cardinals and the Browns, who shared the stadium. "It was a rock pile," Marty Marion said years later. Along with the condition of the field, the Sportsman's Park included a covered "pavilion" in right field that had a twenty-foot-high wire screen in front of the stands. The screen had been installed in 1929 after the Detroit Tigers hit eight home runs into the pavilion during a game against the Browns, the original tenant of the stadium, which was built in 1909. The screen, and the roof on top of it, were favorite targets of such players as Musial and Slaughter, because it was only 310 feet down the line, although the pavilion extended as far as 354 feet to right center field. Like Ebbets Field, it was a left-handed hitters ballpark, because it was 351 feet to the left-field corner, where the open bleachers began and extended to 422 feet in dead center. Unlike Yankee Stadium, which had no outfield signage in 1942, there were ample signs at Sportsman's Park, including no fewer than three signs for local beers. Sportsman's Park was also the home field for some games played by the Kansas City Monarchs, a team whose roster in 1941 included Satchel Paige and Jackie Robinson. Compared to Yankee Stadium, which in the 1940s had a capacity of almost seventy thousand, Sportsman's Park held slightly more than thirty thousand spectators in 1942. The cities also could hardly be more different. New York, perhaps the most cosmopolitan city in the world, had eight million people, most of whom rode to work and almost everywhere else, including Yankee Stadium, by subway. New York also had three major league baseball teams, two teams in the National Football League, and a team in the National Hockey League. It also had the country's best-known sports arena, Madison Square Garden, a Mecca for boxing, hockey, and college basketball (professional basketball would not come to New York until the 1946–47 season). It also had the Metropolitan Opera House and several world-class museums, and it was the country's theatrical center, with more than a dozen legitimate theaters in the Times Square area. St. Louis, by contrast, was an industrial Mississippi River city of about a half million people known as the Gateway to the West. One of the most cosmopolitan western cities, it had several universities and an opera house, where touring Broadway productions often appeared. It also had a number of breweries, the best known of which was Anheuser-Busch, whose owner, August Busch, Jr., the grandson of the brewery's founder, would buy the Cardinals in 1953.

Like many other manufacturing cities, St. Louis was booming during World War II, with many of its factories having become "defense plants," employing thousands of people, many of whom had moved up from the deep South. Historically, it was remembered as the site of the 1904 World's Fair, which later served as the backdrop of the 1944 movie *Meet Me in St. Louis*, starring Judy Garland and Margaret O'Brien. For most of its residents in 1942, the city's streetcars were the most popular mode of travel, and that's how most baseball fans got to Sportsman's Park, which was situated at Grand and Dodier streets in a run-down section of town. At that, it wasn't until the Cardinals began their spectacular late-season run that St. Louisians turned out to see them in relatively large numbers. But despite those late turnouts, the Cardinals drew only 553,552 fans to finish seventh of the sixteen major league clubs in attendance. And it wasn't because the Browns were competing for spectators, because they attracted only 255,617, the second-lowest home attendance in the major leagues, while finishing third in the American League, nineteen and a half games behind the Yankees, under first-year manager Luke Sewell, who also caught in six games in what was his last year as a player after twenty years in the major leagues.

With box and reserved seats sold out before the Cardinals clinched the National League pennant, about fifteen thousand fans bought all the general admission and bleacher tickets within two hours of them going on sale. To accommodate additional spectators, seats had been placed in the outfield from the left-field to the right-field corners and sold at box-seat prices, something that was frequently done during the World Series at smaller ballparks, such as Sportsman's Park. (To the chagrin of outfielders, balls hit into those temporary seats became automatic ground-rule doubles.) By game time, a more-than-capacity crowd of almost thirty-five thousand was jammed into the cozy ballpark. Earlier, scalpers, a rarity outside Sportsman's Park, fetched more than double the face value of box and reserved seats, while nearby parking lots quadruped their fees from 25¢ to $1 (about $15 by 2012's monetary standards). What few blacks were in attendance were restricted to the bleachers in left and left-center fields, as they would be until the early 1960s, by which time the Cardinals had a number of black players, including Hall of Fame pitcher Bob Gibson, first baseman Bill White, and outfielder Curt Flood, the team's first black player, whose suit in Federal Court after he refused to report to the Phillies in a trade in 1969 led to free agency in 1975.

Surprisingly, rather than start twenty-one-game winner Ernie "Tiny" Bonham, who had led the American League in complete games (twenty-two), most shutouts (six), fewest walks (twenty-four), and winning percentage (.808), manager Joe McCarthy went with thirty-eight-year-old Red Ruffing. A Yankee since 1930, Ruffing was obtained from the Red Sox in a trade for outfielder Cedric Durst. It was not quite as bad a trade as when the Red Sox traded Babe Ruth to the Yankees in 1920 for $125,000 and a $300,000 loan to Red Sox owner Harry Frazee, but it was still a very bad one, because Ruffing wound up winning 273 games, 234 of them during his fifteen years with the Yankees, while Durst batted .245 in 102 games for the Red Sox and never appeared in another big league game. Actually, the Red Sox could be forgiven for trading Ruffing, who had led the league in losses during his last two years with the team and had lost more games than he had won in his five years and two months with the Red Sox.

McCarthy's decision turned out to be a prescient one, as Ruffing failed to allow a hit until Terry Moore singled to right with two outs in the eighth inning, by which time the Yankees had taken a 7–0 lead and chased Cardinal starter Mort Cooper in the top of the eighth. No other pitcher had ever gone that far in a World Series game without giving up a hit. "I lost all my stuff in the ninth," said Ruffing, who came within four outs of going the distance. "Didn't have a thing at the end. I was using speed all the time, pitching to spots. But I got my seventh victory in my seventh World Series." Ruffing got help from another World Series veteran, Joe DiMaggio, playing in his sixth World Series, who led the Yankees with three hits, while Bill Dickey, first baseman Buddy Hassett, and third baseman Red Rolfe, who was also playing in his sixth, and in his case final, World Series, each had two. What made it worse, and potentially a bad omen, was that the Cardinals looked bad both in the field and at bat. Besides going hitless for eight and two-thirds innings, they had committed four errors, two of them by Max Lanier, normally a starter, who had replaced Cooper, which allowed two Yankees to score. The most costly miscue came in the eighth inning when Slaughter, normally a flawless outfielder, dropped a fly ball hit by Ruffing to right center, which enabled Dickey and Hassett to score to make it 7–0. But then to the delight of what had been a very quiet crowd, the Cardinals responded during their last time at bat, in the last half of the ninth inning, with four runs and six hits, with three of the runs scoring on a triple by shortstop Marty Marion, the number-eight hitter in the St. Louis lineup. With Spud Chandler, like Lanier, usually a starter and a player who had won sixteen games during the regular season, now pitching for the Yankees, the home team had a chance to tie the score, with the bases loaded and Musial at bat. However, Musial hit a sharp grounder to first baseman Hassett, who flipped the ball to Chandler to end the game, with the Yankees winning 7–4.

That the Yankees would hit Cooper so hard, collecting eleven hits, after the Cardinal ace had won his last nine games as the National League's most dominant pitcher throughout the regular season, appeared to presage a one-sided World Series. On the other hand, the Cardinals and their fans were heartened by the Redbirds' late rally, which they hoped was a favorable portent for the home team. As for the game's significance during a war that wasn't going very well for the United States and its allies, an unbylined writer for the *New York Times* wrote, "The grim shadow of war was in eclipse for the time being." This would be the case for at least a few more days.

Many Cardinal fans left Sportsman's Park distressed over the loss and the Cardinals poor performance but somewhat heartened by the Redbirds' late rally. Given the team's sloppy play and ineptness at bat over the first seven and a half innings, some Cardinals fans— and there were tens of thousands of them in the Midwest, the South, and the Southwest—wondered whether the young Cardinal team was intimidated by the Bronx Bombers, who had won five of the last six World Series and whose 1942 team included five future Hall of Famers in Ruffing, DiMaggio, Dickey, and Gomez, who had been members of all those teams, along with Rizzuto, in his second year as the Yankee shortstop and playing in what would become almost an annual ritual in late September and early October.

For the Cardinals, the second game of the series the following day shaped up as a "must win," because, if the Redbirds lost, they would have to win at least two of the three games scheduled to be played at Yankee Stadium. Both manager Billy Southworth and Joe McCarthy sent twenty-one-game winners, rookie Johnny Beazley and Ernie Bonham, to the mound before another capacity crowd at Sportsman's Park. This time, the Cardinals struck first, scoring twice in the opening inning when catcher Walker Cooper doubled to drive in second baseman Jimmy Brown and Terry Moore, who had reached on a walk and a fielder's choice. The Cardinals added a third run in the seventh on first baseman Johnny Hopp's single and a triple by third baseman Whitey Kurowski to give Beazley a 3–0 lead. But then in the eighth inning, the Yankees tied the score when, with two outs, switch-hitting journeyman Roy Cullenbine, who had been obtained from Detroit for cash on August 31 to replace coast guard–bound Tommy Henrich in right field, beat out an infield hit, stole second base, and scored on a single by

DiMaggio, his fourth hit of the series. Left fielder Keller, always a home-run threat, then drove a Beazley fastball over the right-field pavilion to get all the Yankees up on their feet in what had been a very subdued dugout while silencing the clapping and cheering Cardinal crowd.

The Yankees threatened to take the lead in the ninth when Dickey and Hassett singled before Beazley set down Rizzuto, Rolfe, and Cullenbine to end the threat. Then in the last half of the ninth, Slaughter doubled, took third on an error by Rizzuto, and raced home with the winning run on Musial's first hit of the series, a line single to center, which gave the Cardinals a 4–3 victory, tied the series, and touched off pandemonium at Sportsman's Park.

The twenty-one-year-old Beazley was brilliant, especially in the clutch, and though he yielded ten hits and walked only two batters, he had struck out four. Bonham also pitched extremely well, giving up only six hits, walking only one batter, and striking out three. In his front-page story in the next day's *New York Times,* John Drebinger, who had covered the Yankees all season, waxed somewhat hyperbolically about the Cardinals' win, writing that the "astonishing infants had put another of their electrifying finishes." With thirty-two-year-old Brown, and Mort Cooper and Moore, both twenty-nine, in their lineup, the Redbirds were hardly "infants" in a milieu of men in their twenties and thirties, but as a team they were collectively much younger than the Yankees, and, indeed, the youngest team in the big leagues.

As both teams left on the same train that night for the twenty-six-hour trip to New York, a rarity resulting from shortage of train space due to the war, most Cardinal fans expected them to return for a sixth game at Sportsman's Park. Certainly, after the first two nail-biters, neither team seemed poised to win three straight games, which, if it happened in New York, would end the series.

❧ ❧

About two thousand people, almost all of them Yankee fans, were on hand at Grand Central Terminal to greet the teams when they arrived on Friday, an off day. However, many of the fans were disappointed to learn that most of the Yankees had gotten off the train at 125th Street, much closer to Yankee Stadium than Grand Central, and where some of the players had left their cars before going to St. Louis. Cardinal fans aboard the train, along with others who had arrived in New York to see the series at Yankee Stadium but hadn't been in New York since before Pearl Harbor, were to find a drastically different Manhattan. In Times Square, a few blocks from Grand Central, they found the onetime "Great White Way" mostly in darkness. The famed glittering white lights throughout the Times Square area, along with theater marquee lights, had been doused, as were the signs for the Wrigley Aquarium, Coca-Cola, Bond clothes, Four Roses whiskey, and Bromo-Seltzer. So were the lights on the Empire State Building and in the Rockefeller Center building complex. Even many streetlights were turned off, while traffic lights were partially covered with dark-slitted hoods, subway stairways were darkened, and the famed news scroll around the Times Tower in Times Square had gone dark for the duration, as the time frame for the war became known. World Series visitors also saw hundreds of servicemen and servicewomen in uniform, especially in Times Square and at Grand Central Terminal and Penn Station, either on leave or on liberty from warships tied up at Hudson River and East River docks or at anchor in New York

Harbor. If baseball fans ventured to the Battery at night to look out on the harbor, they would see a blacked-out Statue of Liberty, with only her torch lit so that low-flying pilots going in and out of New York Municipal Airport (currently known as LaGuardia Airport) could see France's famous 1886 gift to the United States.

Yankee Stadium, however, had not changed. With its nearly seventy thousand–seat capacity, it was second in size only to Municipal Stadium in Cleveland, which held seventy-five thousand spectators and, like Yankee Stadium in later years, was also the home field for a National Football League team. By 1942, it had become America's version of the Roman Coliseum, hosting major boxing bouts in addition to being the home of the New York Yankees since it opened in 1923, where, on opening day, Babe Ruth, appropriately enough, hit the first home run in what became known as "the House That Ruth Built." The most distinctive features of the triple-decked stadium were the 461-foot distance to dead center field and the monuments to Lou Gehrig, Babe Ruth, and former Yankee manager Miller Huggins, which were on the field in front of the center field bleachers. Fielders, including DiMaggio, who patrolled the vast space in center field at the stadium with such brilliance and seemingly effortless grace, often had to retrieve balls in play from behind the monuments. That was no longer necessary when the stadium was refurbished in 1975 and the bleacher walls moved in considerably—into center field by almost forty-five feet—so that more home runs could be hit. Another feature of the stadium in its original configuration was the low four-foot barriers in front of the grandstand in left and right field, where outfielders would literally lean into the stands to rob hitters of home runs. That feature also was done away with and higher walls erected during the renovation, which radically changed the contours and, many thought, the charm and distinctiveness of the country's best-known stadium, as did advertising signs displayed above the bleachers from left-center field to right field. Even the traditional green-painted fences and grandstand seats and railings were repainted a light blue on orders from the team's new owner, George Steinbrenner. Home runs became even easier to hit, especially to right field, when in 2009, the Yankees moved to a new Yankee Stadium, which, unlike the original one, had no advertising from 1923, when it opened, until 1975, when it was in the eyes of many spectators despoiled by a plethora of advertising signs both on and beyond the outfield stands.

If many of the Cardinal fans had traveled to Sportsman's Park by streetcar, most of the spectators attending the Series at Yankee Stadium arrived by subway trains that were elevated by the time they discharged passengers on a platform beyond the centerfield bleachers and were elevated the entire route from the Woodlawn station in the northern Bronx. Most Yankee fans at the time were New Yorkers, few of whom had cars, compared with latter-day crowds in the 21st century, which consists primarily of fans from the New York suburbs of Westchester County, New Jersey, Connecticut, and Long Island.

Almost thirty thousand people were lined up by nine o'clock on Saturday morning, hoping to buy the fourteen thousand grandstand seats for $3.30 and a like number of bleacher-seat tickets for $1.10, all of which were gone by noon, as were several thousand standing-room tickets, also for $1.10. (Fans did not have to buy blocks of at least three tickets for World Series games as they did by the latter part of the 20th century, by which time, sadly, most ticket prices were outside the reach of most baseball fans.) Not surprisingly, with the game being in New York, there were far more notables in attendance than for the first two games in St. Louis. Among them were Republican gubernatorial nominee Thomas E. Dewey, who in 1944 and 1948 would be the Republican presidential nominee; New York Governor Herbert Lehman; former Postmaster General and Democratic power James J. Farley; New York's flamboyant former mayor Jimmy Walker; Baseball Commissioner Kenesaw Mountain Landis; Will Harridge and Ford Frick, the presidents of the American and National leagues, respectively; former Dodger general manager Larry MacPhail, resplendent in his army lieutenant colonel's uniform; the greatest Yankee of them all, Babe Ruth; and New York's diminutive mayor Fiorello La Guardia, who, feisty as ever and beloved by most New Yorkers, had recently told a graduating class of 150 police cadets to crack down on "tinhorn gamblers" and if they resisted arrest to "sock them in the jaw" and, in difficult situations, to "be quick on the trigger." Such advice would hardly be condoned in a more politically correct later era, but it was perfectly acceptable in the 1940s, when there was far worse violence going on abroad and in the Atlantic, the Pacific, and the Mediterranean.

Again in the third game, Southworth sent a young pitcher, twenty-six-year-old left-hander Ernie White to the mound, while McCarthy used another World Series veteran, Spud Chandler, who, in a surprise move by McCarthy, had relieved Ruffing in the ninth inning of the first game. Again the Cardinals got a brilliant pitching performance, aided by outstanding catches by Terry Moore and Slaughter, with White shutting down the Yankees with six hits, striking out six, and issuing nary a base on ball. Chandler was almost as good, giving up five hits, fanning three, and walking only one batter. The difference was that the Cardinals managed to push across two runs in the third and ninth innings. In the third inning, after Chandler had struck out five of the first six Cardinal batters, Whitey Kurowski walked, moved to second on an infield hit by Marty Marion, advanced to third on a sacrifice bunt by White, and scored when Jimmy Brown grounded out to first baseman Jerry Priddy. Priddy was a utility infielder after failing to make it as a second baseman as a rookie in 1941, when Joe Gordon had been moved to first base. In the third game, Priddy had been moved to first base from third base after regular Yankee first baseman Buddy Hassett broke his right thumb while trying to sacrifice Phil Rizzuto, who had singled, to second base in the first inning. While White was holding the big Yankee bats hitless, the Redbirds scored their second run in the ninth inning when Brown singled and was safe at second when pitcher Marvin Breuer fielded a bunt by Moore and threw late to second. Slaughter, who had driven in the winning run in the second game, then singled to center to score Brown.

The first of two scintillating catches by the Cardinals came in the sixth inning, when, with Roy Cullenbine on first, DiMaggio hit a long drive to left center, which both Musial, playing left field, and Moore, in center, raced after. At the last split second, Musial ducked out of the way, and Moore made a spectacular backhanded catch. Much had been written in advance of the series about DiMaggio as one of baseball's all-time great defensive center fielders, and perhaps even *the* greatest, but little about Moore, arguably as good as DiMaggio and most definitely the best defensive center fielder in the National League, who was being given a chance to show what he could do while playing against the famed Yankee Clipper on the drive by DiMaggio and as he would do throughout the Series. Then in the seventh inning, the other two Cardinal outfielders demonstrated their fielding prowess. First, the left-handed Musial snared a drive by second baseman Joe Gordon that appeared bound for the left-field stands, after which Charley Keller, who had driven in two of the Yankees' three runs in their second-game loss, hit a clout that seemed destined for the right-field stands, which Slaughter, who batted left-but threw right-handed, leaped high and caught the ball with his gloved hand against the right-field barrier. It was the third outstanding catch, each one by a different Cardinal outfielder, and in effect sealed the Redbirds' victory. As it developed, the Yankees put two more runners on base in the last two innings, when Rizzuto singled in the eighth and DiMaggio did the same in the ninth, but to no avail.

The defeat stunned the huge crowd, which filed out of the stadium in silence, except for scattered cheers for the victorious Cardinals, who had now limited the Yankees to three runs in two games. It marked the first time the Yankees had lost two World Series games in a row since the 1926 Series, when the Cardinals won the last two games of a seven-game series in the first World Series between the two teams. Besides losing the game, the Yankees lost their tempers on several occasions while arguing close calls. At one point, a protest turned physical when veteran Frank Crosetti, who had replaced Priddy at third base and was, like Red Ruffing, playing in his seventh World Series, pushed umpire Bill Summers in the chest while arguing a call and still, amazingly, wasn't thrown out of the game. The Yankees' frustration reached a somewhat ludicrous level later when McCarthy protested that the Cardinal batboy had taken a position in the team's batter's circle and was biased towards the Yankees, which, of course, he no doubt was, as might be expected. Even John Kieran, the sports columnist for the *New York Times*, the first and only one at the time, who in the past had usually written favorably about the Yankees, was annoyed at the team's constant bickering with the umpires during the third game. "Maybe the Yankees should show up today with their mouths taped shut to keep them from talking themselves into a hole again," he wrote in the next day's paper. Some avid Yankees fans probably agreed.

The barrage of complaints in the third game was delightful fodder for anti-Yankee fans throughout the country, and they were legion, mainly because of the Yankees unparalleled success, and, to a considerable degree, because they played in New York. Joe DiMaggio may have had millions of baseball fans throughout the country rooting for him and even had a song about him and his hitting streak the year before recorded and played by disc jockeys from coast to coast, but in 1942, that was old news, and the Yankee haters were back in full force. By contrast, many fans outside New York, and even some in the city, including Brooklyn, found themselves pulling for the Cardinal team, which had no big-name stars, against the entrenched Yankees, who seemed to win the World Series every year. Many wondered how someone could not like this team of primarily young players in those colorful Cardinal uniforms and how they ran the bases with such abandon. Rooting for the Yankees by comparison was like, as the saying went, cheering for U.S. Steel, the quintessential, and highly profitable, American corporation at the time.

So what? many Yankee fans felt. The Cardinals had beaten the Yankees twice in a row, but there was no way in the world that this young, relatively inexperienced team could beat them again on Monday; and even if they did, not again on Tuesday, the last of the three games at Yankee Stadium. If they did, heaven forbid, the Series would be over, and the Yankees would have lost it at home by losing four games in a row, and the last three at Yankee Stadium.

❧ ❧

Aware that the Yankees were in trouble, 779 more fans turned out for the fourth game of the series on Monday, October 5, for a total attendance of 69,902, which broke the previous day's record for a World Series game. Again, the game went down to the wire, this time after the Cardinals had taken a 6–1 lead after four innings. The Yankees took a 1–0 lead in the first inning when third baseman Red Rolfe doubled across Roy Cullenbine, who had singled. But then in the fourth inning, the Cardinals erupted for six innings, driving rookie pitcher Hank Borowy from the mound. In that at bat, Stan Musial tied a Series record with two hits, a bunt single and a double; while Walker Cooper, Whitey Kurowski, Mort Cooper, and Terry Moore all singled, and Borowy gave up two walks as the Cardinals batted around. Atley Donald relieved Borowy following Mort Cooper's hit. But then after Cooper had limited the Yankees to one run in the first inning, the Bronx Bombers exploded for five runs in the sixth inning to tie the score and knock out Cooper, with the biggest blow being a three-run home run by Charley Keller, which evoked a tremendous roar from the crowd, followed by a run-scoring double by Priddy off reliever Harry Gumbert.

But the Cardinals responded with two more runs off Donald in the top of the seventh inning on walks to the Cardinals' best hitters, Musial and Slaughter, another single by Walker Cooper, and a long fly ball to center by shortstop Marty Marion off reliever Ernie Bonham that scored Musial to make it 8–6. The Cardinals would add another run in the ninth off Ernie Bonham, the Yankees twenty-two-game winner during the regular season, on a single by first baseman Johnny Hopp, a sacrifice bunt, and a single by Max Lanier. The left-handed Lanier, a thirteen-game winner for the Cardinals, had relieved another lefty, rookie Howie Pollet, in the seventh and kept the Yankees scoreless and with only two hits during the last three innings—Phil Rizzuto's third single in the seventh and a single by pinch hitter and backup catcher Buddy Rosar in the ninth—as the surging Redbirds won their third straight, 9–6. And they did so despite committing an uncharacteristic four errors.

The Yankees had thrown their best pitchers against the flying Redbirds from St. Louis, even in relief, but now trailed three games to one, with the fifth game of the series the following day, again at Yankee Stadium. With the Yankees' clubhouse solemn and quiet, and many of the players sitting on stools in front of their lockers, their heads down, they needed a pep talk, and they got it from the most famous Yankee of all time, Babe Ruth. Poking his head into the clubhouse, Ruth called out, "Keep your chins up, boys. You're not licked. We'll get 'em yet. There's always tomorrow." Earle Combs, the Yankee Hall of Fame center fielder during Ruth's playing days with the team, also had some motivational words for the team with which he had spent eleven years. "You said it, Babe," Combs said, loud enough for the players to hear. "Remember 1926? We came in here leading, three games to two against the Cardinals, and they beat us. We can still beat them, too."

Not ready to give up yet, either, was Mayor La Guardia. Leaving the stadium with a police escort, the "Little Flower," as the half Italian and half Jewish La Guardia was often called in New York newspapers (his first name, Fiorello, means small flower in Italian), turned to reporters and said, "The Yankees aren't beaten yet. Not by a darned sight." Yankee fans could only hope that Ruth, Combs, and La Guardia were right and not just whistling past what could become a baseball graveyard for the Yankees in 1942.

If the Yankees had never before lost two World Series games in a row, then they most certainly had never lost three in a row, but there was that distinct possibility when rookie Johnny Beazley, who won the first of three Cardinal victories, was the obvious starter in the fifth game, as was Red Ruffing, the winning pitcher in the opening game, for the defending world champions. It was a classic matchup that typified this Series: a twenty-four-year-old pitcher who had won twenty-one games during his rookie season and was seven years old when the thirty-eight-year-old Ruffing joined the Yankees in 1935.

Once again, Yankee Stadium was packed with around seventy thousand spectators as Ruffing took the mound on a sunny Monday at a time when all World Series games were played in the afternoon. (The first World Series game to be played entirely at night was between the Baltimore Orioles and the Pittsburgh Pirates at Three Rivers Stadium in Pittsburgh in 1971.) After Ruffing had set down the Cardinals in order in the first inning, Phil Rizzuto, the five-foot six-inch shortstop from Brooklyn, drilled a home run into the lower left-field stands. Rizzuto's blast prompted a collective roar from the huge crowd, all the more so because it was hit by the immensely popular young Rizzuto, the only native New Yorker in the Yankee lineup. But in the fourth inning, Enos Slaughter, a thorn in the Yankees' side both at bat and in the field throughout the series, hit a home run into the right-field stands to tie the game. Once again, the Cardinals were sloppy in the field, making four errors, one of which by Beazley led to another run by the Yankees in the fourth inning, when Joe DiMaggio singled home Red Rolfe, who had reached base on a bunt single. Charley Keller also singled, sending DiMaggio to third with one out. But then Beazley, whose poise and unflappability belied both his age and relative inexperience, struck out Joe Gordon, who fanned for the seventh time in the series, and got Bill Dickey to ground to Marion at shortstop for a force out at second base.

The Yankees had another opportunity to add to their slim lead in the fifth inning, when they loaded the bases with one out. First, Ruffing reached first when he beat out a slow roller down the third-base line, and, on the next two plays, Hopp and Brown, the right side of the Cardinals infield, made errors on a bad throw and a mis-handled ground ball. But again, Beazley stiffened, unfazed by the errors and the loaded bases, got Cullenbine to pop out to Marion at shortstop, and, with the crowd in a frenzy, induced DiMaggio to hit a ground ball to Kurowski, who stepped on third base for a force out to end the inning. The Yankees had taken the lead, but, in two consecutive at bats, they had left five men on base and had failed to capitalize on four Cardinal errors. Taking advantage of those squandered opportunities, the Cardinals evened matters when they scored a run in the sixth inning on singles by Moore and Slaughter and a fly to right field by Walker Cooper, which sent Moore home.

Then, in the top of the ninth came the biggest hit of the Series. After Walker Cooper had singled, Whitey Kurowski, the third base-man with the short right arm who, like Musial, was playing his first full major league season, jumped on a Ruffing fast ball and belted it into the lower left-field stands for a two-run homer to give the Redbirds a 4–2 lead. Watching the ball in flight, Ruffing appeared dazed, as did most of the huge throng in the stadium, and then stared dejectedly as Kurowski was greeted at home plate by Moore and Marion, who was on deck to bat next. The tableau seemed surreal,

with Yankee fans watching another player doing what Yankee sluggers like DiMaggio, Ruth, and Gehrig had done so often over the
last nineteen years. Still, the Yankees had another time at bat, need-
ing at least two runs to tie the score and three to require a sixth, and
perhaps a seventh, game in St. Louis.

But it was not to be.

Yankee fans took heart when Joe Gordon singled to start the
last half of the ninth inning. Dickey then hit what appeared to be
a double-play ground ball to second baseman Brown, but Brown
bobbled the ball for his second error of the game and third of the
Series, and both Dickey and Gordon were safe with no outs. By
now, Yankee fans in the crowd were on their feet, many of them
screaming, while trying to exhort the home team on, as outfielder
Tuck Stainback went in to run for Dickey, who represented the
tying run. A near-disaster then came for the Yankees. Apparently
assuming that Priddy, the batter, would bunt, Gordon took a big
lead off second base. But Priddy apparently had no intention of
bunting and took the first pitch, whereupon Cooper, an outstanding catcher, fired the ball on a line to Brown at second base, and
Brown easily tagged out Gordon as he dived back towards the base.
That left only Stainback on base with one out. Beazley, still as sharp
as he was at the start, then got Priddy to hit a pop fly to Brown. With
two outs, it was now up to the thirty-four-year-old George Selkirk,
who had replaced Babe Ruth in right field in 1935. Following Ruth
was a daunting task, but Selkirk did very well, averaging over .300
during his first three years as the Yankees full-time right fielder and
five times during his first six seasons while hitting .290 during his
nine-year career. Selkirk, a left-handed batter who had been born
in Hamilton, Ontario, also hit with power, belting 108 home runs

during his first eight years with the Yankees but none in seventy-eight at bats during the 1942 season—which would be his last—when he was relegated to pinch-hitting and occasionally filling in for Tommy Henrich in right field. Making it all the more difficult in succeeding Ruth, Selkirk also wore the same number, 3, which wasn't retired until June 1948, shortly before Ruth died of cancer, at a time when players' numbers were not regularly retired. Indeed, the first number retired was Lou Gehrig's number, 4, which was retired the day of Gehrig's farewell speech at Yankee Stadium on July 4, 1939, shortly after he had retired that season and two years before he died. One Yankee number became retired twice, on the same day in 1972, when the number 8, worn first by Bill Dickey and then by Dickey's successor as the Yankees' catcher, Yogi Berra, was retired in a ceremony at Yankee Stadium while Dickey was a coach with the Yankees.

Perhaps Selkirk's greatest legacy was his suggestion, in 1935, that a six-foot swath of cinders be placed in front of the outfield walls at Yankee Stadium so that outfielders would be alerted that they were approaching those walls while pursuing deeply hit balls. Other teams eventually did the same, installing what became known as the "warning track."

With two runners on and the Yankees down to the last out in the '42 Series, the pressure was on Selkirk, whose entire nine-year career had been spent with the Yankees, and who was one of the team's best clutch hitters. Beazley had already given up nine hits but had twice before come through with multiple players on base and knew the game was on the line with the still dangerous Selkirk at bat. On what appeared to be a sharp curveball, Selkirk hit a hit ground ball to Brown, who had already made two errors in the game; but this time, the veteran second baseman scooped up the ball and tossed it to Hopp at first to end the game and the series.

Within seconds, Beazley, the winner of two of the four games the Cardinals had won, was engulfed by his teammates, while most of the spectators stood and looked down incredulously at the celebrating Cardinals around the pitcher's mound. Despite four errors, including one by himself, Beazley had stared down such veteran players as DiMaggio, Keller, and Selkirk in clutch situations and had gotten the best of them. The outcome was a stunning one and the biggest upset in a World Series since 1914, when the so-called Miracle Braves swept the heavily favored Philadelphia Athletics in four games. Ironically, the last time the Yankees had lost a World Series was in 1926, to the Cardinals, who had edged the Yankees in seven games. Since the arrival of the so-called Bronx Bombers, who had hit only three home runs in the series—two by Keller and one by Rizzuto, who had hit only four homers during the regular season—they had won seven series while winning twenty-eight games and losing only four. And here, against the Cardinals, they had lost four games in one series, and all of them in a row. Another irony was that the Cardinals manager Billy Southworth, as a Cardinal outfielder, had been one of the Cardinal stars in the 1926 series, with ten hits in twenty-nine times at bat for a .345 batting average.

After being hoisted aloft by some of his young players, Southworth, not prone to braggadocio, said amid the din in the Cardinals' clubhouse, "We beat them, and we beat them decisively, in clean, honest, sportsmanship fashion. We won the pennant with a dash, and we won the series the same way. If ever a bunch of fellows was typical of American youth, this bunch of mine is." Though the Cardinals were ecstatic about their surprise World Series victory, the celebration was relatively muted, consisting mainly of the players hugging one another as well as coaches Southworth, Mike Gonzales, and Buzzy Wares. There was no champagne or even beer, apparently because owner Sam Breadon and Branch Rickey felt that going too far in celebrating the World Series victory would be poor taste when other young men were fighting and dying for a far greater cause than winning a World Series. Winning the World Series was important for the Cardinals, but it was not a "must win," to use a term often employed in sports as a rallying cry. Winning World War II, on the other hand, was definitely a "must win," and Southworth, Rickey, Breadon, and the team's coaches and players knew it all too well.

Next door, the atmosphere in the Yankees' clubhouse was solemn but hardly funereal. The Yankees, like the Cardinals, knew that losing the World Series wasn't a matter of life or death; fighting in World War II could be, but not baseball. Still, the Yankees obviously were downcast over losing. Those who had played on at least five Yankee World Series championship teams—DiMaggio, Dickey, Ruffing, Gomez, and Keller—sat silently in front of their lockers, looking downward or off into space. Despite his outstanding play, Rizzuto, who had played in his second straight Series, was also obviously upset. Rizzuto had eight hits, which was more than anyone else, and a .381 batting average, a high for both teams, and also had fielded brilliantly with fourteen assists and a series record fifteen put outs for a shortstop, including seven in the final game. The only other players to reach .300 were DiMaggio, at .333; Rolfe, who in his final World Series batted .353; and Jimmy Brown, who hit .300. DiMaggio, the Yankees' foremost slugger, had seven hits, but all of them were singles. Slaughter and Musial, who finished second and third among the leading hitters in the National League, hit .263

and .222, respectively, but both came through in crucial situations at bat and in the field, as did Terry Moore, who batted .294 and demonstrated to Yankee fans that he was good, and faster an outfielder than DiMaggio, who by playing in New York had received far more media attention than the Cardinal captain. On the debit side, the Cardinals made ten errors in the Series, five more than the Yankees, but their young pitching staff was superior to that of the Yankees over the last four games, demonstrating anew that good pitching is more important than good hitting in a World Series.

Except for Musial, the jubilant Cardinals' party departed for home from Grand Central Terminal several hours after the final game had ended and was greeted by a crowd of around twenty-five thousand the following evening at Union Station in downtown St. Louis. Musial had opted to go directly to his hometown of Donora, Pennsylvania, after tearfully seeing the Cardinals off at Penn Station. In keeping with a federal order banning groups from traveling in separate cars, as was the case during normal baseball seasons, Southworth, his coaches, his players, and other members of the Cardinal party had to take whatever seats they could find on the train, although most of them managed to find space in the same car.

At Union Station, where the greeters included Missouri Governor Forrest Donnell and Mayor William Becker, Southworth introduced each player as "one of my boys." Acting as a master of ceremonies, the manager went on to say, "They were all stars in my book, and we beat the Yankees without making a single complaint during the series." That, of course, was an allusion to a number of heated complaints to umpires by Yankee players and manager Joe McCarthy during the series. "Our team was a great ball club, and we showed the world that St. Louis has something else besides the zoo and the

[Mississippi] river." Speaking on behalf of the players, the team's captain, Terry Moore, hailed his teammates as "the grandest bunch of players in the world, who have the best manager in the world." Southworth reciprocated by hailing Moore as "the greatest center fielder in baseball today, and the same goes for Marty Marion at shortstop." Each comment drew cheers from the lively crowd, many of whom had come to be especially fond of the young group of players who had come from ten games back in early August to overtake the defending National League Champion Dodgers and then shock the baseball world by defeating the world-champion Yankees in five games.

Some New York sports columnists had odd rationalizations for the Yankees' defeat. Joe Williams of the *New York World-Telegram* wrote that the "aristocratic and well-fed Yankees were forced to bend to the Oakies of baseball, the under-privileged St. Louis Cardinals." As if that weren't condescending enough, Williams, whose column was syndicated by the Scripps-Howard chain, added that "the poor man's team from the Missouri metropolis, little fellows who relied on little hits and their great speed, knocked the Bombers out cold with home runs." That was hardly the case, since the Cardinals had hit only two home runs in the series, one fewer than the Bronx Bombers. Moreover, the Cardinals actually had fewer "little hits," with thirty-nine singles, compared with forty-four singles by the Yankees. At that, Williams's analysis was not as bad as that of another well-known New York sportswriter, Dan Daniel. Writing in the *Sporting News*, Daniel suggested that the Yankees, which Daniel covered on a regular basis for the *World-Telegram*, may have been distracted in the series by the war, while "the Cardinals conceivably were not as yet bothered by wartime considerations." Daniel never did elaborate on that rationale, which to say the least was a dubious one. John Kieran, the erudite sports columnist for the *New York Times*, seemed to have had a better perspective on the outcome when he wrote, "The Cardinals, younger all along the line, fired by the fresher enthusiasm that the Yankees couldn't possibly have, fast enough to take advantage of every turn, pressed ahead to win a thoroughly merited victory."

❧ ❧

Thanks in large part to the third and fourth games of the Series being played in Yankee Stadium, the Cardinals' winning shares came out to $6,192.50, a record for a World Series in which the players did not share in the broadcast rights. By preagreement, all the broadcast rights money went to the United Service Organizations (USOs), where GIs often gathered during the war while on leave or liberty in major cities. Under a formula that still exists, the Cardinals' individual shares were based, as were the Yankees individual shares of $3,351, on receipts from the first four games of the series. The Cardinals' shares were more than Musial, Kurowski, and Beazley made during their rookie season, meaning they had made more money in five games than they had during the 154-game regular season, when all three received less than $4,500.

Just how good was that 1942 Cardinal team? "That '42 team was the best team I ever played on, even better than the all the Yankee teams I played on," said Enos Slaughter, years after he retired. "It was a young team, but we had a lot of desire." That was high praise indeed, because three of the Yankee teams Slaughter played with included Hall of Famers Mickey Mantle, Yogi Berra, and Whitey Ford and won three straight American League pennants and two World Series. Stan Musial agreed with his former outfield teammate, saying after his retirement in 1963 that the 1942 Redbirds were the best of the twenty-two Cardinal teams he had played on. Of the '42 team, he said, "We thought we could beat anybody, and we did."

The Cardinals upset victory was far and away the biggest sports story of the year, and it was a bracing one for not only Yankee-haters, but for sports fans who reveled in seeing underdogs win, whatever the sport. Nothing in football came close. In the National Football League, which still hadn't overtaken the college game in popularity as it would by the 1960s, the Washington Redskins would beat the Chicago Bears, 14–6, in the title game. That was a remarkable turnabout from the championship game two years earlier, when the Bears had trounced the Redskins, 73–0, in the most one-sided title game in NFL history. Ohio State would eventually win the college national championship, succeeding defending champion Minnesota, which, after twenty consecutive victories, was beaten by Iowa Pre-Flight, a team loaded with former all-Americans and some former professional players that was based at the University of Iowa, where the players were training to be army air corps pilots. As the war went on, more and more military teams would be formed and more than hold their own against leading college squads. In thoroughbred racing, then America's fourth-favorite sport after baseball, football, and boxing, Whirlaway, one of the greatest racehorses of all time and winner of the Triple Crown in 1941 (there was no Triple Crown winner in 1942), continued to dominate, while in boxing, the biggest story of the year was the continued success of a young welterweight boxer from Detroit named Walker Smith, who, fighting under the name of Sugar Ray Robinson, had won his thirty-sixth consecutive fight without a loss at Madison Square Garden in

New York the night before the World Series began and was being heralded as a future champion. (Robinson would win forty fights in a row before losing to Jake LaMotta in a rematch in Detroit the following February 5. Two weeks later, Robinson would outpoint LaMotta, also in Detroit—as world-class boxers fighting within such a short span was not uncommon at the time—and would beat him twice more in 1945, the year before Robinson won the world welterweight championship.) As for basketball, the National Basketball Association was still five years in the future, but in college basketball, which was continuing to grow in popularity, Stanford won the men's championship, beating Dartmouth in the final in Kansas City in a battle between two of the country's best academic institutions, something that would be very unlikely to happen in the early part of the 21st century.

In a way, it was only fitting that the 1942 baseball season would end with a dramatic come-from-behind pennant victory and then a stunning upset in the World Series, because baseball would not be the same in the next three wartime seasons. Though it had been a wartime season, most of the players on rosters in 1941 were still playing in 1942, which meant the level of play was still high. But then more than a hundred of those players would be in a different kind of uniform by the time the 1943 season began, including such stars as Joe DiMaggio; his brother, Dom; Ted Williams; Pete Reiser; Slaughter; Johnny Mize; Pee Wee Reese; Warren Spahn; Luke Appling; and Johnny Pesky, who during his rookie year in 1942 led the league in hits and finished second to teammate Williams in batting average. Of the World Series–winning Cardinals, Beazley, Brown, Moore, and Slaughter would be in service during the 1943 season, while the Yankees would be without the previously stated DiMaggio, Rizzuto,

Hassett, Ruffing, and Selkirk, all of whom would also enter the military to join Tommy Henrich, who had entered the coast guard in August, while Rolfe would have retired. All of them would return at the war's end except for Rolfe and Selkirk, who would manage in the Yankee and Milwaukee Braves' farm systems and serve as an executive with the Kansas City Athletics, Baltimore Orioles, and Texas Rangers, where he became the team's first general manager. Many others, including Musial, Walker Cooper, Harry Walker, and Ernie White also would enter the service during the war, with most of them not returning to the major leagues until 1946, the year after the war ended. Ruffing's drafting was particularly hard to explain. "I was thirty-eight years old, had four toes missing from my left foot from a mining accident when I was young, had a wife and kids, and a mother-in-law who was my responsibility," Ruffing later said, "but there it was, 'Greetings from the President.' At the induction center, several doctors rejected me as a 4-F, but the last doctor I saw said that [what] I could do on the outside, I could do on the inside, and that's how I went in." As it developed, Ruffing did just that, pitching for several air force base teams in California and Hawaii during his three years in the army and also managing one of the teams. Ruffing returned to the Yankees in 1945, and after pitching two more seasons for the Yanks, finished up with the Chicago White Sox in 1947 when he was forty-three years old. In addition to winning 273 games, the protean Ruffing is remembered as one of the best hitting pitchers in baseball history, with a lifetime batting average of .269 that included thirty-six home runs, and seven seasons in which he hit over .300. Indicative of how good a hitter Ruffing was, on one of the best hitting teams ever, he often was used as a pinch hitter.

A MISMATCHED WORLD SERIES?

For the Cardinals who entered the service after the 1942 season, no other season would ever compare with that first wartime season when they electrified the sports world with their late charge that enabled them to overtake a veteran Dodger team and then record one of the biggest upsets in baseball history by beating the Yankees decisively in the World Series. It had truly been a season for the ages. It was also the crowning glory of Branch Rickey's twenty-three years with the Cardinal organization. It was Rickey who in the early 1930s began to organize what would become baseball's first and largest "farm" system, which at one point included thirty-two teams, and where all the Cardinals on the victorious 1942 World Series team had been developed, with the exception of pitcher Harry Gumbert, who had been obtained in a trade with the Giants. That all the Cardinal regulars and, apart from Gumbert, the predominantly young pitching staff had been nurtured in the farm system was unusual even in the pre–free agency era, because trades were frequent, particularly among the better teams. Practically all the Yankees had also come up through the team's farm system, with the exceptions of first baseman Buddy Hassett, who had previously played for the Dodgers and Boston Braves, and right fielder Roy Cullenbine, who was obtained in a trade with the Detroit Tigers in August after Tommy Henrich was called up for service in the coast guard. Though players were bound to their teams before free agency took effect in 1976, the old system, which prevented players from leaving teams on their own, gave big league teams far greater stability, usually enabling them to field the same starting lineups for years, as was the case with the Cardinals and Yankees, even during the first wartime year of 1942. That, of course, meant that fans knew from year to year, and even from game to game, that, apart from occasional trades, teams would almost assuredly have virtually the same lineups, along with a few rookies from the teams' farm systems every spring. That was the case with the Cardinals, whose starting lineup in 1942 was the same as in 1941, with the exception of rookies Musial and Kurowski and first basemen Johnny Hopp and Ray Sanders, who had replaced future Hall of Famer Johnny Mize at first base.

Rickey, who had spent twenty-three years with the Cardinals as a manager, scout, and executive, had an extraordinary eye for talent and was responsible for the signing and development of most of the players on the 1942 team. As it were, it was the third Cardinal team under Rickey's stewardship that had won a World Series, and the one that he often said was his favorite, since it had overcome almost insuperable odds to win the National League pennant and the World Series. Though he now was leaving, the Cardinals would still be very much aware of Rickey in the years to come.

EPILOGUE

AMERICANS WHO HAD been caught up in a fascinating and
surprising World Series matchup that had dominated water-
cooler conversations in offices and factories across the country, even
overshadowing war news from abroad, woke up to the real world
again on Tuesday, October 6. The thrilling exploits of a young baseball team made up largely of unsophisticated Southerners against
an older, more experienced, and dynastic team consisting primarily
of players from the North and California, had managed to take the
attention of many people away from the war; but now it was over,
and big league baseball would not be the same again for four years.
Both the National League pennant race and the World Series had
been pleasant diversions during a stressful time, but now it was time
to shift attention back to the war.

For those who did, including, presumably, most of the players,
not much had changed since early August, when the pennant race
between the Cardinals and Dodgers had begun with the Redbirds

ten games behind. German forces were on Stalingrad's doorstep but were being repulsed by Soviet troops in furious fighting that had claimed thousands of lives, most of them German. Despite aerial attacks by the British Royal Air Force, German troops under the command of General Erwin Rommel continued their sweep across North Africa, which had taken them into Egypt. In the Aleutians, American bombers hammered away at a decreasing number of Japanese troops, who had invaded in June but had now been relegated to the island of Kiska after having withdrawn from the islands of Attu and Agattu. Meanwhile, the worst fighting of the war to date in the Pacific went on unabated in the Solomon Islands, with the War Department claiming that Allied forces from the United States, Australia, and New Zealand now had the upper hand against the Japanese on the ground, in the air, and at sea.

On the home front, FBI agents continued to round up aliens, most of them German nationals, and, in some cases, citizens suspected of trying to aid the enemy; but no actual acts of sabotage had been reported, so far as was known. Despite rationing, shortages of some food supplies, such as sugar and coffee, grew worse. As a coffee substitute, some Americans switched to Postum (a drink made from okra or acorns), which did not come close to resembling coffee. Perhaps the most unpopular form of rationing was gasoline, even though millions of Americans in the 1940s did not own cars. Siphoning of gas, a serious crime, grew as the year and the war went on. So did the hoarding of or trading for gas.

More and more accounts of heroism by American GIs were being written by reporters in war zones, such as Ernie Pyle, who became the country's best-known war correspondent before he himself became a casualty of the war. Cartoons drawn in battle areas by Bill Mauldin about conversations between two fictitious, battle-hardened, grizzled, and cynical soldiers, usually drawn while in foxholes, became hugely popular among both GIs and Americans back home. So did commentaries from London by CBS correspondent Edward R. Murrow, best known for his graphic rooftop radio reports during air attacks on London by the German Luftwaffe, and Gabriel Heatter, whose broadcasts on the Mutual Radio Network were consistently optimistic and uplifting, if at times hyperbolic, and whose catchword phrase at the beginning of his nightly newscasts was "There's good news tonight," even when there actually was very little good news during 1942. But then, Heatter's tendency to find traces of blue skies among the dark clouds of the war gave his millions of listeners a feeling that things were not that bad after all.

❧ ❧

Draft boards, which had seemed overly generous towards big league baseball players before and during the 1942 season, realized by that fall that deferments would not be dispensed as readily as they had been during the past baseball season because of a critical manpower shortage. Where only three stars were in the service when the '42 season began, scores of them had been drafted or enlisted before the 1943 season started, by which time slightly more than two hundred players who had been on big league teams in 1942 would be in uniform. Among them would be forty-two-year-old pitcher Ted Lyons of the White Sox, who would return to manage the team in 1946, when he would appear in five games at the age of forty-six, until 1948, when he would retire from baseball. Others included pitcher Sid Hudson of the Senators, first baseman Eddie Waitkus and second baseman Lou Stringer of the Cubs, outfielder

Walt Judnich of the Browns, and outfielder Ernie Koy of the Phillies. Apart from Lyons, almost all of them would return as full-time players. Most of the players who became GIs spent their service time playing baseball, but some, such as Cardinal utility outfielder Harry Walker and his teammate, pitcher Murry Dickson, Dodger pitchers Larry French and Kirby Higbe, and pitcher Phil Marchildon of the Philadelphia Athletics saw considerable action. Walker received the Bronze Star after he was wounded in battle when he killed two German soldiers in Germany shortly before the war ended; Dickson, an army sergeant, took part in the Battle of the Bulge, while French participated in the Normandy invasion in June 1944 and rose to lieutenant commander in the navy, and Marchildon, a tail gunner in the Royal Canadian Air Force, spent nine months in a German prisoner-of-war camp after his bomber was shot down over the North Sea in Europe. A number of other future big leaguers who saw action included Yogi Berra, who was a nineteen-year-old sailor aboard a navy rocket boat that lobbed rockets at German machine-gun nests and land mines and also provided cover for troops landing on Utah and Omaha beaches during the D-Day invasion. "I thought it was like the Fourth of July, to tell you the truth," Berra said years later. "I said, 'Boy, it looks pretty, all the planes coming over.' I never saw so many planes in my life. At one point, I was looking out, and my officer said, 'You better get your head down.'" Fortunately, Berra emerged from his D-Day adventure unscathed. Others who saw action were Berra's eventual Yankee teammate and manager, Ralph Houk, who received a battlefield commission as a major, and Bert Shepard, who as a bomber pilot had his right foot shot off on a bombing mission in Germany in 1944, received the Distinguished Flying Cross, and made it to the big leagues for one game with the Washington Senators in 1945, allowing three hits in five and a third innings while striking out three batters. Shepard then became a playing manager in the minor leagues for the next nine years. Another eventual major league pitcher, Lou Brissie, was a corporal and an infantryman in Italy in November 1944 and was so badly wounded in the leg by a German shell that he had to beg doctors not to amputate. Determined to pitch again, Brissie, who had already signed with the Philadelphia Athletics, subsequently underwent twenty-three major operations and forty blood transfusions. After months in army hospitals and with a plate in his leg and having to walk with a cane for a year, Brissie made it to the As in 1947 when manager Connie Mack called him up in September, as he had promised he would do after Brissie had spent most of the season pitching for Savannah in the Class-A Sally League, where he won twenty-three games with a 1.19 earned-run average. The left-handed Brissie, who had difficulty fielding bunts at the start, spent four years with the Athletics and three with the Cleveland Indians, making the American League All-Star team in 1949, while continuing to undergo treatments for his leg all the while. Once left for dead in a creek bed in Italy, Brissie became a profile in courage and proof of what even an infantryman who had to persuade doctors to save a badly wounded leg could do.

Not surprisingly, more than a few players who returned to the majors after the war were never as good as they had been before going into the service. For instance, in his first season back in 1946, Johnny Beazley, who as a rookie was one of the stars of the 1942 World Series at the age of twenty-one, won seven games and lost five with an earned-run average of 4.46, more than double what it was in 1942. And Cecil Travis, the outstanding shortstop who hit over .300

in eight of his nine seasons with the Washington Senators, missed almost four full seasons; when he returned, he never batted higher than .252 in his last three years, almost assuredly because of the frozen feet he had endured while fighting in the Battle of the Bulge in Belgium. In 1941, his last season before entering the army, Travis had hit .359, second in the American League to Ted Williams, and led the league with 218 hits.

As the war went on, teams became so desperate for players that such former stars as Babe Herman and Pepper Martin were lured back to their old teams, the Dodgers and Cardinals, respectively. Like many former major leaguers, Herman, who had broken in with the Brooklyn Robins in 1926, played in the Pacific Coast League after "retiring" from the major leagues in 1937. When he returned in 1945 to Brooklyn, he received a royal welcome, as he had been one of the team's most popular and eccentric players. The forty-year-old Herman was twenty-three years older than seventeen-year-old infielder Tommy Brown, a Brooklyn native who had been born a year after Herman broke in with the Robins. Against inferior pitching during that last wartime season, Herman batted a respectable .265 in thirty-five games. Martin, a leader of the famed Cardinals' Gas House Gang, who had last played for the Cardinals in 1940, returned at the age of forty for the 1944 season and hit .279 in forty games. With pitchers particularly in demand, a number of pitching careers were revived. In 1945, the Reds had three pitchers in their forties, while the Yankees put forty-two-year-old batting-practice pitcher Paul Schreiber on the roster; he appeared in two games in 1945, more than twenty years after he had pitched briefly during two seasons with the Brooklyn Robins. On June 10, 1944, fifteen-year-old left-handed pitcher Joe Nuxhall became the youngest player ever to appear in a big league game when he pitched two-thirds of an inning for the Reds against the St. Louis Cardinals at Crosley Field in Cincinnati. Called on in the ninth inning with the Reds trailing the Cardinals, 13–0, Nuxhall got the first batter out but then gave up two runs, two hits, and walked five before being relieved. "There I was playing against thirteen- and fourteen-year-old kids back in Hamilton, Ohio, and all of a sudden I look up and there's Stan Musial," Nuxhall said. "It was very scary."

After going back to Hamilton, Ohio, and back to high school to star in football, basketball, and baseball and to graduate, Nuxhall spent five years in the minor leagues before returning to the Reds in 1952. Nuxhall then spent fourteen years with the Reds that were interrupted by one year with the Kansas City Athletics and part of a season with the Los Angeles Angels. A two-time All-Star, Nuxhall finished with 135 victories and 117 defeats while becoming the Reds' all-time leader in completed games by a left-handed pitcher. Following his retirement in 1966, he spent thirty-seven years broadcasting Reds' games.

❧ ❧

Perhaps the biggest surprise of the 1942 postseason was Branch Rickey's move from the Cardinals to the team that had in the last two seasons become their biggest rival, the Dodgers, where he replaced Lee MacPhail as the team's president and general manager and also became a part owner of the team. The primary reason Rickey left the Cardinals was because he and owner Sam Breadon, who, like most owners, knew very little about baseball, did not get along, and Rickey had tired of Breadon's meddling in team affairs. Rickey later would became internationally known, and justifiably praised, for signing Jackie Robinson to a Dodger contract in 1946, making him the first black athlete to play in the major leagues in modern times.

At a time when the average major league salary was around $10,000, most of the players who had not been drafted or had not enlisted following the 1942 season took off-season jobs, many of them in defense plants. Stan Musial, still deferred from being drafted because he was married and had a child, went back to work at the Donora Zinc Works, where he had worked between seasons in the past, and which by then had a defense contract. Musial also continued to work part-time in his father-in-law's grocery store while going to football and basketball games and playing pick-up basketball games at his alma mater, Donora High School, where he had also been a basketball star good enough to have received several scholarship offers, including one from the University of Pittsburgh. By now a huge local celebrity, Musial was honored in his hometown at a testimonial dinner after returning from the World Series. The Cardinals' other rookie Polish American from Pennsylvania, Whitey Kurowski, who had hit the game-winning home run in the final game of the World Series, also was honored at a testimonial dinner and then during a parade in his hometown of Reading, where the City Council passed a resolution naming Kurowski "the outstanding player in baseball for 1942." That was something of a stretch, because although Kurowski had had a very good season and World Series, he was far from having been "the most outstanding player in baseball" in 1942. Like many other players, Kurowski, who had a 4-F deferment because of his shortened right arm, would spend the off-season working in a defense plant, where he made more money each month than he did with the Cardinals during his first full year in the big leagues. So did Bobby Doerr, the Red Sox Hall of Fame second baseman, who spent several winters working at a defense plant in Los Angeles that produced supplies for the army.

Surprisingly, not many Americans seemed to complain about how most big league baseball players who were drafted or enlisted spent their time in the military playing baseball. The rationale of top military officials seemed to have been that fielding baseball teams comprising major and minor leaguers was good for morale in that it provided entertainment for regular GIs, most of whom probably would wind up in war zones. Technically, the players were physical instructors who, for at least part of a day, would lead either soldiers, sailors, marines, airmen, or coast guardsmen in calisthenics—that is, when they were available, which, in many cases with star players, was hardly ever, because service base teams tended to travel extensively to play other military teams. Because of the more accommodating weather conditions, most service teams were in the South, in California, and Hawaii. That, of course, sounded like good duty, and it was, all the more so since the big leaguers, especially, tended to be a special elite group on a military base. They may have eaten and slept with the other GIs, but that was about all they had in common. And, unless they asked to serve aboard a ship or join a battle-bound army or navy unit, as did Bob Feller, Hank Greenberg, and some others, few players would ever find themselves in harm's way during the war. Indeed, most big league players, and especially such stars as Joe DiMaggio, received the red-carpet treatment from generals, admirals, and other high-ranking officers who liked being with them and often felt that their teams' success somehow improved the morale of the regular GIs and made the camp or base look good, at least to other generals and admirals. In addition, ballplayers stationed at the air base in Santa Ana in southern California had their own training table, and a menu that usually included steaks and other hard-to-get food, which was not available to other enlisted men at the air base. Moreover, officers often tried to ingratiate themselves with such stars as DiMaggio and Red Ruffing by inviting them to parties otherwise restricted to officers, where, again, there was food and drink unavailable to rank-and-file GIs.

Despite that good and safe duty, there were some complainers in the ballplayer ranks of the military, and one of the biggest, apparently, was DiMaggio, who spent his three years in the army air force playing baseball as a sergeant in his native California and in Hawaii. Always a loner who treasured his privacy, DiMaggio was suddenly thrust into a milieu where, unlike during his life as a ballplayer, he was forced to spend virtually all his time with other soldiers. Sent to an air base in Santa Ana shortly after he enlisted in January 1943, DiMaggio's assignment was as a drill instructor, but in reality he was a full-time baseball player, most of whose time was spent practicing and playing an average of two games a week. The team primarily consisted of minor leaguers and college players, but fortunately for DiMaggio, it also included a few big leaguers, such as Walt Judnich of the St. Louis Browns and Dario Lodigiani, who had played for the Philadelphia Athletics and the Chicago White Sox and whom DiMaggio had known since boyhood. Having Judnich and Lodigiani around made DiMaggio comfortable, as did Ruffing, who also played for the Santa Ana base team for a while and then later with DiMaggio in Hawaii. Though their marriage was on the rocks, Joe and his wife, movie actress Dorothy Arnold, whom he had married in 1939, and his two-year-old son, Joseph, Jr., rented a house in the San Fernando Valley, not far from the base and where

DiMaggio spent most of his weekends when he wasn't playing ball. But the marriage continued to deteriorate, and in July 1942, Dorothy Arnold filed for divorce in Los Angeles. That the marriage had lasted that long surprised many of DiMaggio's friends, given his temperament and his unsociable nature, which contrasted with Arnold's gregarious personality.

Phil Rizzuto, whom DiMaggio had taken under his wing when Rizzuto was a rookie in 1941, looked up to DiMaggio as an older brother for whom he had tremendous respect. Rizzuto once told sportswriter and author Maury Allen that DiMaggio could get moody, especially when women were around. The Yankee shortstop, recalling a dinner get-together with his wife, DiMaggio, and Arnold the night of the final game of the 1942 World Series, said, "Joe and Dorothy had invited Cora and me over to their penthouse apartment in Manhattan. Dorothy cooked dinner, and we stayed up all night talking and drinking. It was my farewell party before joining the navy the next day. Cora and Dorothy got along real well, but Joe would get a little moody and leave for a few minutes every so often. He didn't like the idea of sitting and talking all night with the women. Dorothy was a beautiful woman and a very solid person. But I guess Joe was tough to live with. When you marry a beautiful woman, she wants to be seen. I think Joe never really understood that. His whole life was baseball."

Somehow, DiMaggio managed to keep his wife from going through with her divorce until the spring of 1944, when she got a court date and testified that Joe had ruined the marriage by what she eventually testified was his "cruel indifference." DiMaggio declined to attend the hearing, and the next day the judge, after describing himself as a rabid baseball fan, said the evidence was overwhelming and granted Dorothy an interlocutory degree that would be effective for one year, during which she and Joe would still be legally married. Under the judge's order, Joe had to give Dorothy a lump sum of $14,000 along with $150 a month for the care of Joe, Jr., and to pay for a $10,000 life insurance policy for his son. Upset as he was by the judge's decision, Joe felt that he at least had an entire year in which to try to win Dorothy back.

A stomach ulcer, which DiMaggio had developed during the 1942 season, flared up occasionally, and apparently worsened when Arnold went ahead with her divorce action. By July 1944, Joltin' Joe, as he was often referred to by some sportswriters, had begun to vomit frequently and was in and out of the Santa Ana base hospital three times between July and September, and once at Letterman General Hospital in San Francisco, complaining of stomach distress and headaches, which doctors believed had been brought on by stress and tension. At one point, in late July and early August 1944, he remained in a hospital for eleven days. By September, army doctors felt that DiMaggio's distress might have been psychosomatic and that he showed symptoms that could lead to a mental breakdown. "His comments showed contradictions and a defective attitude towards the service, which were rationalized by his allegations of handling by the service," Major Emile Stolof, an army doctor, wrote in a report on DiMaggio. "His personal problems appeared to be of more consequence to him than his obligation to adjust to the demands of the service."

That summer, DiMaggio and the other big leaguers on the Santa Ana team shipped out to Hawaii, where they became part of an Army All-Star team that played a series against a Navy All-Star squad and Hawaiian amateur teams while spending most of their time on the beach, playing cards, and partying. Again, though, DiMaggio's ulcer acted up, and he was admitted to Triplett Hospital for observation. In his book about DiMaggio, author Richard Ben Cramer quoted Dario Lodigiani as recalling how Joe once said to him, "Somebody's going to pay me for all this time I lost." Lodigiani, apparently trying to console DiMaggio, told him that he was certainly guaranteed to get his job back with the Yankees. But DiMaggio was not about to be consoled. "Cost me three years," he responded. "They're gonna pay for it."

According to army medical accounts, DiMaggio frequently asked to be discharged and several times said he felt that he might have been if it weren't for his status as a well-known baseball player. "The patient feels that his prominence in the world of sports has interfered with his Army, and that the Army has exploited him," Major William Barret, an army doctor, said in his report. "He wanted to be a soldier, but he has had to be 'an exhibitionist.'" Here, Major Barret appeared to have been quoting DiMaggio. "The continuations of these tensions with no prospect of relief has caused him to be reclusive, irritable, easily depressed, and resentful." The reports by Major Barret and Major Stoloff concluded that DiMaggio's contention that he had developed an ulcer was valid and that if he had not been a well-known sports figure, he would probably have been discharged well before September 1945. The medical report also conceded that DiMaggio's "national prominence" had been capitalized on by the air force's "public relation department." Still, the overall report did not paint a good picture of DiMaggio's attitude while in the air force, saying at one point that he had "experienced no combat conditions or marked military stress, and who developed temporary aggravation of his chronic symptoms, manifested by tension state, irritability, mild depression, preoccupation with financial and domestic problems, and a defective attitude towards military service."

In other words, as a GI Joe, DiMaggio was hardly an exemplary solider, even though all he had to do during his three years in the army was play baseball, at least when he wasn't in a hospital, which was often. As for someone having to pay for Joe D having to spend all that time in the service, the Yankees did, paying him $43,750 when he returned in 1946, the same amount he had been paid in 1942. That grated on DiMaggio, because Williams, also back from service in the marine air corps, received $50,000 from the Red Sox that year and also was paid more than Joe D in 1947 and 1948 before they both received the same $100,000, more than any other player had ever been paid, in 1949.

By the time DiMaggio was discharged from the air force, Arnold's interlocutory decree had become final, meaning they were divorced. Joe would still stay in touch with her and Joe, Jr., who were living in Manhattan, hoping for a reconciliation. On several occasions in late August and in September, the three of them even went to Yankee Stadium together to see the Yankees play, but there would be no reconciliation. Thereafter, Joe and Dorothy would rarely see each other, and DiMaggio would not have a serious relationship until he met a blonde starlet named Marilyn Monroe in 1952, the year after he retired from the Yankees.

❧ ❧

If baseball was a nonessential business, which just about everyone conceded, the movie business, at least in the eyes of the person who mattered, General Lewis Hershey, the director of the Selective Service

System; in the fall of 1942, Hersey said the movie industry was "an activity essential to the national health, safety, interest, and in other instances to war production." Hershey no doubt was referring both to the entertainment value of motion pictures and films made for military training and other purposes related to the war effort. No one could say that about major league baseball games, which, overall, attracted far less interest and far fewer people than movies, and, apart from their entertainment value, the employment opportunities they provided, the money they raised for army and navy relief, and the scrap metal and other drives teams held, the games still could not compare with the impact films had, both on the home front and on the military. That fall, because of a shortage of men, Congress, at the recommendation of President Franklin Roosevelt, approved the drafting of young men eighteen and nineteen years of age. At the time, there were slightly more than four million men in service, and Secretary of the Army Henry Stimson said, the goal was to have at least seven million in the military by the end of 1943.

If the Cardinals upset victory over the Yankees in the World Series was a great sports story, it paled in comparison to the increasing Allied successes in the war against Japan and Germany. American Marines continued to make advances against Japanese troops in the Solomon Islands in the Southwest Pacific, with the most intensive fighting occurring on the island of Guadalcanal, where almost two thousand marines would die before the fighting ended in February 1943 with an American victory. But that was a small number compared with the approximately twenty-five thousand Japanese Marines and soldiers killed during the often hand-to-hand fighting on what American Marines called "the Canal." Meanwhile, by the fall of 1942, American troops had hooked up with British forces in North Africa, where the British General Bernard Montgomery—"Monty" to his troops and his countrymen at home—had blunted the advances of General Erwin Rommel's Panzer divisions from sweeping into Egypt with the intention of taking over oil fields in the Middle East and by November prepared to attack Tunisia. The news would get even better in 1943, although some of the worst fighting of the war was still to be fought in far off remote places in the Pacific that most Americans had never heard of, such as Tarawa, Kwajalein, Saipan, and Iwo Jima, where the United States would lose thousands of men in taking control of those island chains while tens of thousands of Japanese troops were killed after fighting to the end, as they almost always did.

By early 1942, the war had gone badly for the United States and its Allies. The American fleet at Pearl Harbor had been decimated; the Japanese had successfully invaded Singapore, Hong Kong, Indochina, Malaya, and the Philippines; the German Luftwaffe was continuing its unrelenting bombing of London; German forces were pushing ahead in Europe and in North Africa; and hundreds of merchants ships had been sunk by German submarines off the East Coast of the United States and in the North Atlantic. But by the fall of 1942, there was good reason to be optimistic at last, because it appeared that the tide might have been turned.

❧❧ ❧❧

In the grand scheme of the war, big league baseball was insignificant, to say the least, but apparently good for morale and of considerable recreational value. Despite the still-high quality of play, though, attendance in 1942 fell slightly more than a million from the last peacetime season of 1941, a drop of around 8 percent. It dropped just under a million in 1943, when the Dodgers again led the major leagues by drawing 661,739 after attracting more than a million fans in each of the previous two seasons. The Yankees finished second with 618,330, but that was only a third of what they had drawn in 1942. The hardest hit were the Red Sox, who, in falling from second place in 1942 to seventh in 1943, attracted 358,275 fans, about half of what they had drawn the previous season. Though the talent level had diminished even more, attendance in 1944 surprisingly increased to 8.7 million, an increase of 1.3 million over 1943. That year, the Cardinals beat the Browns in the one and only city World Series in St. Louis, after which Musial joined the navy. Though he was in his early twenties and in good health, Musial, who was married with a young son, was never called up for service by his draft board in St. Louis, which struck some people as odd, since the board was calling up other men of Musial's age who were also married. But there never was any indication that Musial had ever asked for a deferment or for special treatment. He most certainly did not seem like the type of young man who would have done so.

The year Musial entered the navy was the last wartime season. By then, the caliber of play was at an all-time low, and the Browns wound up using one-armed Pete Gray in the outfield, who during the previous year had batted over .300, hit five home runs, led the league in stolen bases, and been named the Most Valuable Player in the Double-A Southern Association. Still, attendance inexplicably soared to a record level of 10.9 million, with four teams, the Cubs and Tigers, who met in the World Series, and the Giants and Dodgers all drawing more than a million fans. The increases during the last two wartime years, which amounted to 22 percent from 1942 to 1945, indicated that by 1944, baseball fans who had been distracted by the war and its impact on the home front were anxious to return to one of their favorite diversions, even though a lot of play, relatively speaking, was well below par. What also helped in 1945 was that a number of star players, including Bob Feller, had rejoined their teams by late in the season after the war ended on August 15, by which time Hank Greenberg already had returned at mid season. By the following peacetime year of 1946, when baseball was pretty much back to normal, and with such stars as Feller, Greenberg, Williams, DiMaggio, and Musial having returned, attendance reached what was then an all-time high of 18.5 million.

Major league baseball, like all its stars who had gone off to service, if not necessarily to war, had survived World War II and had provided entertainment to millions of defense-plant workers, GIs, and other Americans, despite some early criticism. Many of the players who saw action during the war returned with a different perspective and better appreciation of being able to play baseball for a living. "Playing baseball for a living? What a great way to do it," said Warren Spahn on returning to the Braves, with whom he would win more than twenty games thirteen times while on his way to the National Baseball Hall of Fame. "If I screw up, there's going to be a relief pitcher coming in, and nobody's going to shoot me. I also think serving in the army gave me a fortitude that maybe I lacked before I went in." Johnny Sain, who teamed up with Spahn as the aces of the Braves' pitching staff from 1946 until 1951, when they won an astonishing 215 games between them, said that serving as a navy pilot during the war definitely helped him as a pitcher. "I think learning to fly an airplane helped me as much as anything," said Sain, who won at least twenty games during four of the five full seasons he spent with the Braves before being traded to the Yankees in

1951. "Learning to fly helped me to concentrate better as a pitcher." Not that serving in the war had helped all the players. "I could tell that some guys were not the same when they came back," Williams said in reference to players who had seen action. "Being away from the game for a long time definitely affected some of them."

Was baseball an essential activity during the war? Of course not. So was it right for baseball to have continued as it did with relatively healthy young men playing ball for far more money than American GIs were receiving while in harm's way? That would seem to be a judgment call or a matter of opinion. But for four somewhat unusual seasons, playing baseball during a war that took the lives of more than four hundred thousand American servicemen and about six thousand American merchant seamen seems to have been acceptable and tolerated, even though at times some of the players out on the big league fields didn't always look like big leaguers. But like most of the sixteen million Americans who went off to war, they did the best that they could, and for that, baseball fans, including many GIs, apparently were grateful for the fun and recreation the sport had provided during some of America's darkest days.

ACKNOWLEDGMENTS

ONE OF THE most pleasant aspects of being a nonfiction writer is that quite often one gets to learn so much surprising material about the subject matter, often in serendipitous fashion. That was certainly the case in researching the first major league baseball season during World War II, the war itself, and how well most Americans on the "home front" comported themselves despite shortages and sacrifices that they were asked to make.

Talking to some of the people who were "there," either playing baseball in 1942, serving in the U.S. military or in the Merchant Marines during the war, or working long hours in "defense" plants, was a particularly rewarding experience. In baseball, they included such players as Bobby Doerr and his Boston Red Sox teammates Ted Williams and Dom DiMaggio; former St. Louis Cardinals Enos Slaughter, Terry Moore, Marty Marion, and Don Gutteridge; Yankee stars Joe DiMaggio and Phil Rizzuto; Hall of Famer Monte Irvin, one of the first blacks to play for the New York Giants and who, sadly, endured more discrimination when he was in the U.S. Army during World War II than he did while playing in the National League after the war; Lennie Merullo, who once made four errors in one inning in 1942 while playing shortstop for the Chicago Cubs but could be excused for those miscues because they occurred only a few hours after he learned that his first son had been born; and Mike Sandlock, who couldn't make his high school baseball team in Connecticut but was good enough to play both shortstop and catcher for five seasons under such legendary managers as Casey Stengel and Leo Durocher. I talked with Doerr, Merullo, Irvin, and Sandlock in 2011 while they were in their nineties, and they seemed to revel in talking about their big league days, while most of the other players quoted in the book were interviewed in earlier years in connection with various sportswriting assignments, but whose comments were still relevant to this book.

Others who helped included a number of former Brooklynites, such as Dave Anderson, the Pulitzer Prize–winning sports columnist for the *New York Times*, who grew up watching—and later covering—the Brooklyn Dodgers as an avowed Stan Musial fan; and Stanley Englebardt of Westport, Connecticut, a longtime roving editor for *Reader's Digest*, whose recollections indicate how close the Dodgers of that era were to their devoted fans, both on and off Ebbets Field.

In addition to World War II veterans I interviewed, such as Tony DePreta of my hometown of Stamford, Connecticut, who was one of seven brothers to serve overseas during the war, I am indebted to Tony Pavia, the principal at Trinity Catholic High School in Stamford, largely because of his fascination with the war, during which his father served in the U.S. Navy. Pavia, a former history teacher, spent hundreds of hours doing research and interviews for his poignant book, *An American Town Goes to War*, which relates the wartime exploits of about fifty young men and women from Stamford who served in World War II, many of them heroically. Another fellow Stamford native who was of immeasurable help was the former Stamford mayor and later commissioner of the National Basketball Association, J. Walter Kennedy, who provided me some years ago with material on the two exhibition games the Cardinals played in Stamford, which he covered for the *Stamford Advocate*, along with serving as the official scorer and public-address announcer. Remarkably, Terry Moore, the great Cardinal center fielder, remembered those games more than a half century later, even though the Redbirds had played scores of such exhibitions during the regular National League season in the late 1930s and the 1940s, as I recount in the book.

Covering an entire baseball season, and parts of several others, requires poring through the microfilm of old newspapers, many of them long defunct. In that connection I was once again aided tremendously by Susan Madeo, the interlibrary loan staff member at the Westport Public Library in Connecticut, who managed to obtain microfilm of such long-ago newspapers as the *New York Journal-American,* the *New York Sun,* and the *New York World Telegram & Sun*, along with a number of hard-to-find books relating to both baseball and the war. Librarians at the Norwalk and Wilton public libraries in Connecticut also were generous with their help on this project, as were Pat Kelly of the National Baseball Hall of Fame and Jane Winton of the Boston Public Library. So, too, was Larry Hogan, a professor at Union County College in New Jersey and one of the leading historians on baseball's old Negro Leagues, who through his exhibits and other efforts is determined that that era not be forgotten.

Helpful, too, was Pam Ganley, the public-relations director of the Boston Red Sox, who helped arrange interviews with such Red Sox stars as Doerr. A tip of the cap also goes to Leonard "Boots" Merullo of Ridgefield, Connecticut, who led me to his father, Lennie Merullo, in his native Massachusetts, whose four errors during one inning of a game—in his hometown of Boston, no less—prompted a Boston sportswriter to label Len, Jr., with a nickname that has lasted for seven decades. It also was a delight to interview Alice Cullen, the widow of John Cullen, the young coast guardsman whose quick thinking during a late-night patrol on a Long Island beach in 1942 ultimately led to the apprehension of four German saboteurs who had been put ashore from a Nazi submarine.

Once again, I want to thank my agent, Andrew Blauner, for his diligence in seeing to it that this book, like my previous three books, got into print. Thanks also go out to Mark Weinstein for his belief in this project from the start and for his good advice and wise counsel in editing *Season of '42*. Mark, who also edited my previous book, *The Gipper,* is one of the most knowledgeable sports experts in publishing and also a joy to work with. I'm also grateful to Jason Katzman, who stepped in and went over the manuscript with a skilled hand at the end of the editing process.

Again, too, I must express my thanks to Paul McLaughlin, my computer guru from Norwalk, Connecticut, without whose help this book probably would never have seen the light of day. As was the case with my last three books, I frequently asked Paul to interrupt his busy schedule to help me out in technical emergencies that had reached the crisis stage.

To all the above, along with more than a few others, I am deeply indebted for the assistance I received in putting together a book that I hope will remind some readers and inform many others of a unique year in American history.

ABOUT THE AUTHOR

JACK CAVANAUGH IS a veteran sportswriter whose work has appeared most notably on the sports pages of the *New York Times*, for which he has covered hundreds of assignments. He is the author of *Damn the Disabilities: Full Speed Ahead!* (1995), *Tunney* (2006), *Giants Among Men* (2008), and *The Gipper* (2010). In addition, Cavanaugh has been a frequent contributor to *Sports Illustrated* and has written for *Reader's Digest,* the *Sporting News,* and *Tennis* and *Golf* magazines, as well as other national publications. He is also a former reporter for ABC News and CBS News. Cavanaugh is currently an adjunct professor at the Columbia University Graduate School of Journalism and at Quinnipiac University in Connecticut. A native of Stamford, Connecticut, Cavanaugh is also a columnist for his hometown newspaper, the *Stamford Advocate*. He lives with his wife, Marge, in Connecticut.

BIBLIOGRAPHY

BOOKS

Allen, Maury. *Where Have Your Gone. Joe DiMaggio.* New York. E.P. Dutton & Co., Inc. 1975

Alter, Jonathan. *The Defining Moment* New York: Simon & Schuster, 2006.

Anderson, Dave. *Sports of Our Times.* New York: Random House, 1979.

Berlace, Gai Ingham. *Women in Baseball.* Westport, Connecticut: Praeger Publishers, 199

Cramer, Richard Ben. *Joe DiMaggio: The Hero's Life.* New York: Simon &Schuster, 2000.

Diehl, Lorraine. *Over Here: New York City During World War II.* New York; Smithsonian, 2010.

Dobbs, Michael. Saboteurs: *The Nazi Raid on America.* New York: Alfred A. Knopf, 2004.

Durso, Joseph. *Baseball and the American Dream.* St. Louis: The Sporting News, 1986.

Gershman, Michael. *The1988 Baseball Card Engagement Book.* Boston: Houghton Mifflin Company, 1987.

Goldstein, Richard. *Spartan Seasons.* New York: Macmillan Publishing Company, 1980.

Goldstein, Richard. *Helluva Town:New York City During World War II*. New York: Free Press, 2010.

Golenbock, Peter. *Bums: The Oral History of the Brooklyn Dodgers*. New York: G.P. Putnam's Sons, 1984.

Goodwin, Doris Kearns. *No Ordinary Time*. New York: Touchstone, 1984.

Groom, Winston. *1942: The Year That Tried Men's Souls*. New York: Atlantic Monthly Press, 2005.

Heidenry, John. *The Gashouse Gang*. New York: Public Affairs, 2007.

Irvin, Monte with Pepe, Phil. *Few and Chosen: Defining Negro Leagues Greatness*. Chicago: Triumph Books, 2007

Kennedy, Kostya. *56; Joe DiMaggio and the Last Magic Number in Sports*. New York: Sports Illustrated Books, 2011.

Lieb, Frederick G. *The St. Louis Cardinals*. New York: G.P. Putnam's Sons, 1944

Lowry, Philip J. *Green Cathedrals*. New York: Walker Publishing Company, Inc., 2006.

Mead, William B. *Even the Browns*. Chicago: Contemporary Books, Inc., 1978.

McCullough, Davis. *Truman*. New York: Simon & Schuster, 1992.

Motte, James. *Everything Baseball*. New York: Prentice Hall Press, 1989.

Reidenbaugh, Lowell. *The Sporting News First Hundred Years*. St. Louis: The Sporting News, 1985.

Ritter, Lawrence. *The Story of Baseball*. New York: William Morrow Company, 1983.

Schlossberg, Dan. *The Baseball Catologue*. Middle Village, New York: Jonathan David Publishers, Inc., 1980.

Schoor, Gene. *The Scooter: The Phil Rizzuto Story*. New York: Charles Scribner's Sons, 1982.

Stewart, Wayne. *Stan The Man*. Chicago: Triumph Books, 2010

Stockton, J. Roy. *The Gashouse Gang*. New York: A.S. Barnes & Company, Inc., 1945.

Sugar, Bert Randolph. *The 50 Greatest Games*. New York: Wieser & Wieser, 1986.

Sugar, Bert Randolph. *The 100 Greatest Athletes of All Time*. New York: Citadel Press, 1995

Thorn, John. *A Century of Baseball Lore*. New York: Hart Publishing Company, 1974.

Vecsey, George. *Baseball: A History of America's Greatest Game*. New York: The Modern Library, 2006.

Vecsey, George. *Stan Musial: An American Life.* New York: Ballantine Books, 2011.

Ward, Geoffrey C. and Ken Burns. *The War:An Intimate History, 1941 to 1945.* New York: Alfred A. Knopf, 2007.

NEWSPAPERS

The Boston Globe
The Chicago Tribune
The New York Daily News
The New York Herald Tribune
The New York Journal-American
The New York Daily Mirror
The Sporting News
The St. Louis Post-Dispatch

MAGAZINES

Collier's
Life
Saturday Evening Post
Sport
Sports Illustrated
The Sporting News
Time

INTERNET
Baseball Almanac
Elias Sports Bureau
Wikipedia

INDEX